HONKY-TONKERS & WESTERN SWINGERS

Stories of Country Music in Wichita, Kansas

Orin Friesen

WICHITA, KANSAS
2021
ISBN: 978-1-929731-44-2

Library of Congress Control Number: 2021005988

ISBN: 978-1-929731-44-2

Copyright © 2021 Orin Friesen

All rights reserved, including the right to reproduce this book or portions thereof in any form.

Printed in the USA by Mennonite Press, Inc., Newton, Kansas.

In memory of my dear friends, Robbi Heck and Andy Oatman, who loved and supported live music throughout their entire lives.

Cover Illustrations

Wichita's Official City Flag, Designed by Cecil McAlister, 1937

Guitar on front cover: Ro-Pat-In Eletro-Spanish Guitar, Circa 1932

Guitar on back cover: Johnny Western's 1954 "Paladin" Fender Telecaster

CONTENTS

Foreword 1
Introduction 3
1. Everybody Knew Your Name. 7
2. Headin' Out for Wichita. 21
3. She Sang a Song 47
4. A Road Is Just a Road 65
5. Wichita Jail 69
6. Guitar Men. 75
7. Gonna Find Me a Bluebird. 83
8. Growing Up in Wichita 87
9. The Wichita Way. 91
10. Wichita Linemen 103
11. Fiddlin' Man 111
12. Pleasant Valley Sunday 115
13. Sam's Place 119
14. Gonna Get a Life 129
15. One Night. 133
16. Wichita Skyline 143
17. Urban Cowboys 149
18. Where the Grass Grows Tall 159
19. Men with Big Hats 177
20. Hillbilly Rock 195
21. The Gospel of Wichita 203
Epilogue. 211
Acknowledgements 213
Selected List of Wichita Clubs. 219
Bibliography 225
Interviews 227
Index 229

FOREWORD

In Kansas' largest city – Wichita - "Country & Western Music" has prevailed in all its various forms and commanded audiences just as various. As a legendary "Cow-town" in the 1870s, Wichita was considered the nation's "Wild West" and provided what would become the mythical setting and archetypal character which served to launch the genre. County music is free spirited, genuine and open to the full range of human experience, and as songwriter Harlan Howard described it, is simply "three chords and the truth."

Wichita, located in Sedgwick County Kansas, was first a place of infinite possibility. Its people gathered here just after the Civil War and looked to the future while sentimentally tied to an inescapable past including removal of the area's native people to Indian Territory 60 miles south. It is astonishing to consider that within a lifetime, the frontier town on the edge of an expanding nation, would usher in the electric guitar with a world debut and be known as the "Air Capital of the World" for its dynamic aircraft industry.

As time progressed and this music took shape, the population embraced it through recently acquired media players such as radios and phonographs, and at the theater watching movies. There was also live music featuring local talent with a flair for performance. They blazed trails, seeding the music's national culture by prevailing locally. The world in those days seemed smaller and regional celebrity was the pinnacle of success for most. Performers were typically propelled to popularity over the radio, work they often did for little or no pay. Their livelihood might come through a "regular job" and occasional live appearances. The wide appeal of the music was not lost on radio advertisers who hoped to catch the ear of the radio audience tuning-in.

The Second World War gave pause to Country Music's development and was a period where the Music's popularity gained patriotic status as Americans celebrated their identity through Country songs. This was especially true in Wichita as it ran 24 hours a day, 7 days a week producing aircraft for the war effort. The City was transformed during these years, increasing in size and strategic importance to the

Nation. After the War, Country Music became a cultural mainstay with traditions that defined lifestyle. That lifestyle went on to flourish through post-war prosperity giving rise to dedicated Country Music radio stations and the community they generated. Being a country music fan in Wichita in this period became a distinct identity. As the century wore on, the music's fandom expanded with increasing diversity including many outside of the mainstream demographic, drawn by the openness of the times and the universal appeal of the music's familiar themes.

A tip of the hat to Orin Friesen who embodies Country Music as a performer, an on-air proponent, and as a historian. He grew up on a farm just one state north (Nebraska), where at a young age built his own tiny radio station. After moving to Wichita to continue his education, he became immersed in the area's music culture. Friesen participated by making music of his own as well as making the music of others available over the airwaves through his broadcasts. Intrigued by stories of the past, he also witnessed history in the making and took care to preserve it here.

Eric Cale
Director
Wichita-Sedgwick County Historical Museum

INTRODUCTION

No one fooled with the Marshal of Wichita
And today it's a very nice town
Back in Wichita law and order prevailed
Take me back to Wichita
Let me ride that Wichita trail

From "Wichita" by Tex Ritter

Wichita is a sprawling city in South Central, Kansas, located at the confluence of the Big and Little Arkansas Rivers. Those of us who live here pronounce the name of the river the way we think it was intended, "Ar-Kansas." Wichita is defined by many things, but especially the aircraft industry. Airplane pioneers like Clyde Cessna, Lloyd Stearman, Walter Beech, Bill Lear, and many others helped Wichita become known as the "Air Capital of the World." But it did not start out that way. Indian traders were the first non-native settlers to make their homes in what is now Wichita. Men like Jesse Chisholm, James R. Mead, and William "Buffalo Bill" Mathewson were among the first to put down roots in the area. The village received a shot in the arm with the arrival of the cattle trade. Following the Civil War, Texas Longhorn cattle had begun to be driven to the railheads in Kansas, most notably the town of Abilene. As Wichita grew and the railroad reached the town, the cattle industry became highly important. Though there were quite a few "cowtowns" in Kansas, including Dodge City, Ellsworth, Newton, Caldwell, and others, Wichita set the record for the number of cattle shipped from one terminal in a single year.

Along with the growth of Wichita as a cattle trade destination came the need for entertainment. Saloons and dance halls prospered, and music was a big part of that. Sometimes the music was provided by a piano player. It is likely that the partying cowboys would sing along. The cowboys on the cattle trails from Texas were known to do a lot of singing, both to entertain themselves around the chuckwagon and to calm the cattle. They would sing the hymns from their childhood and the popular songs of the day. Before long, they were writing songs about their own experiences and cowboy songs came into existence. Songs like "The Old Chisholm Trail" and "Whoopee Ti-Yi-Yo, Git Along Little Dogies" soon became part of the cowboy legacy.

Refined citizens of Wichita had their music and dancing as well, but theirs was considered more "sophisticated" than that heard in the rowdy saloons. An indication of a town's cultural growth was the formation of a brass band. Most towns in the latter part of the 19th century had them. Wichita was no exception. Among the popular Wichita bands in the late 1890s was the Fehleisen Wichita Band and Orchestra, a ten-piece, uniformed group that featured both brass and stringed instruments. Around the same time, the Director of Music for Wichita schools, Jessica Clark, organized a "String Club." Students, both male and female, performed on mostly mandolins, guitars, and banjos.

Orchestras featuring stringed instruments brought even more culture to cities. Wichita's symphony orchestra was formed in 1906. Four years later, Wichita had its own 5,500 seat auditorium, the Forum, built on the land once occupied by the home of William Greiffenstein, one of the founders of Wichita. Most churches used music in their services, and it was always an exciting event when a church could purchase a new pump organ to accompany the hymn singing.

What we now call "country" music is often associated with common folks, the farmers and laborers. Beginning in the 1940s, it was sometimes called "hillbilly" music. This style of music derives from the mountain people of the Appalachians and later the Ozarks. Many of the songs and styles of musicianship can be traced back to the music of the British Isles, especially Ireland and Scotland. Subjects of songs often related to occupational experiences, such as farming and mining, or of life and death. Songs were also written from popular news stories of the day such as train wrecks, mining disasters, floods, and even the sinking of the Titanic.

As the Nation expanded and people moved west, they not only brought their music, they added to it. The songs the cowboys sang are a good example. Originally, songs were passed along orally, but eventually they were spread further by song collectors. Perhaps the most notable of those was John A. Lomax, who published his first song collection book, *Cowboy Songs and Other Frontier Ballads*, in 1910. That book, which included the words to over 150 cowboy songs, gave major public access to such ballads as "Little Joe the Wrangler," "Jesse James," "The Zebra Dun," and "Home on the Range." Many of the songs Lomax discovered were those sung by the cowboys that arrived in Wichita with the herds of Texas Longhorn cattle.

Prior to the 20th century, Wichita was part of the United States that was considered "the West." The cowboys that drove their herds from Texas to Kansas solidified that perception. Kansas cowboy, historian, and college professor, Dr. Jim Hoy stated in his book, *Cowboys and Kansas: Stories from the Tallgrass Prairie*, "Without Kansas the cowboy as we know him would never have come into existence."

Wichita's heyday as a cowtown lasted from 1872 to 1876. By 1877, most of the cattle trade had moved farther west to Dodge City, and cattle drives were mostly over by 1890. As the western part of the U.S. became settled, the concept of "the West" was redefined and divided into specific areas such as the Great Plains and the Pacific Northwest. Beginning around the turn of the century and up through at least the 1940s, Wichita was considered part of the "Great Southwest." As late as 1951, the promotional booklet of KFBI radio claimed the station's 1070 dial position as "the favorite radio spot in the Great Southwest." These days most people think of Wichita, and the entire state of Kansas, as being a part of the U.S. known as the "Midwest." It is interesting to note that even people in western Pennsylvania consider themselves to be in the midwest.

CHAPTER ONE

EVERYBODY KNEW YOUR NAME

> *Hell-bound for the Great White Way*
> *For the tawdry-bawdy burlesque stage*
> *And Wichita was miles and miles away*
> *Everybody knew your name*
>
> From "Lulu" by Natalie Merchant

Perhaps due to its connection to the southwest or just "the West," the country music of Wichita has usually taken on a more "western" flavor. Whereas the music from the mountain areas of the southeastern part of the United States often had a more "rustic" sound, Wichitans preferred the more sophisticated sounds of western swing music as exemplified by groups like Bob Wills & the Texas Playboys and Milton Brown & his Musical Brownies. Yet Wichita's first successful country music performer developed his musical foundation from a place farther west than Texas… Hawaii.

William Theodore "Billy" Burkes was born in Wichita on April 3, 1912. His mother taught him and his brother, Weldon, how to sing at an early age, and they soon began performing in the Wichita-based tent show called Brunk's Comedians, one of the most-popular theatrical tent-shows in the Southwest. When Billy was 12 years old, the family's house caught fire and burned to the ground. This event led the Burkes family to move to Fort Worth, Texas, where both Billy and Weldon learned to play instruments. They soon began entertaining at dances, parties and on vaudeville shows. They also began performing on the Fort Worth radio station, WBAP. Though the brothers mastered several instruments, Billy usually played the guitar while Weldon played ukulele. In 1929, while working at the El Tivoli Country Club in Dallas, the Burkes met Hawaiian steel guitarist, Joe Kaipo.

On August 8, 1929, Jimmie Rodgers came to Dallas to do some recording for Victor. He needed some musicians to play on the records and had heard about Joe Kaipo. Rodgers invited Kaipo to audition. Being a rather shy person, Kaipo asked Billy Burkes to tag along. The two men played for Rodgers who liked what he heard. He hired them on the spot. The following day, he also hired Weldon Burkes to play ukulele. On August 8, the group joined Rodgers in a makeshift studio in the

Jefferson Hotel for a recording session produced by the legendary Ralph Peer. The first song they recorded was the slightly risqué, "Everybody Does It in Hawaii." The Burkes brothers and Kaipo recorded six more songs with Jimmie Rodgers, and then went back to their job at the El Tivoli. That lasted for only a short time, due to Kaipo getting arrested and thrown in jail following a fight with a cab driver.

Billy & Weldon Burkes
(Photo courtesy of the University of Arizona Library Special Collections)

In September, Rodgers wrote to the Burkes brothers and told them that he wanted them, along with Joe Kaipo, to go on the road with him. He offered them each $60 a week, plus an additional $15 a week to be paid at the end of the tour. Rodgers would also pay for their transportation, food and lodging. The tour did not turn out quite the way Rodgers had hoped, but he did play a few shows in Texas. Following their final show in Port Arthur, Joe Kaipo and Weldon Burkes celebrated by getting drunk and tearing up their hotel room during a friendly brawl. Rodgers paid for the damages to keep the hotel manager from pressing charges. Though Rodgers was not happy about what had happened, he still took Kaipo and the Burkes brothers back to Dallas with him for another recording session with Ralph Peer. At that October 22 session, Rodgers recorded six songs but only used the full group on "Whisper Your Mother's Name." Exactly a week after that session came the stock market crash of Wall Street.

Jimmie Rodgers did not give much attention to national affairs, so the stock market crash was not a concern of his. He was more interested in making a film, touring, and doing some more recording. Ralph Peer had not been happy with Joe Kaipo and Weldon Burkes, following the incident at the hotel in Port Arthur, so he suggested to Rodgers that he just hire Billy Burkes instead of the entire trio. Neither was Billy happy about the group's situation, especially with Joe Kaipo's penchant for landing in jail due to drinking and fighting. Though he knew it would break up the band, Burkes, who was 17 at the time, decided to accept Rodgers' offer. In

November, the two men went back into the studio, this time in Atlanta. Among the songs on which Burkes played guitar was "Hobo Bill's Last Ride," which became a hit for Rodgers. By the spring of 1930, both brothers were back touring with Jimmie Rodgers, but this time Billy was playing the Hawaiian steel guitar, which he had learned from Kaipo. Weldon had switched to guitar and an older brother, Charlie, was brought in to play ukulele.

Near the end of his career, Jimmie Rodgers' own guitar playing was used less and less on his recording sessions. Instead, he chose to have Billy Burkes play his guitar parts in Rodgers' style. Burkes made his last recordings with Jimmie Rodgers in February of 1932. He had played on a total of seventeen of Rodgers' recordings, more than any other musician. On May 26, 1933, Rodgers passed away from tuberculosis. The three Burkes brothers continued to perform around Texas, including appearances on a radio station in Houston.

In April of 1935, Billy Burkes moved to my hometown, York, Nebraska, where he got a job performing on KGBZ. While there, Burkes formed a group called the Radio Aces, that included his wife, Dorothy, John and Eldora Slaughter, and Ted Sisco. They were kept busy and performed on as many as thirteen programs per day. In the summer of 1936, the group took a job with KFBI in Abilene and changed their band name to the Rangers. An article in the July 6, 1937 issue of the KFBI News described their thirty-minute shows as "music, song, fun and confusion." Later moves found the Burkes in Texas, Arizona, South Dakota, and Wyoming. Billy Burkes continued to play music for the rest of his life. He died of cancer in Tucson, Arizona in 1989 at the age of 77.

* * *

"Wichita" is an Indian word that comes from the tribe of Native Americans who once lived where Wichita now stands. Early settler James R. Mead claimed the word Wichita meant "scattered lodges." Whatever the name means, we know that before it was a cowtown on the Chisholm Trail, Wichita was home to various tribes of American Indians. Its location at the confluence of two rivers made the place even more special for the natives.

That makes it even more interesting when we realize that likely the first significant country music band to hail from Wichita was Big Chief Henry's Indian String Band. Not your typical hillbilly string band of the 1920s, the group was a family trio of Choctaw Indians, originally from Oklahoma. "Big Chief Henry" was fiddler Henry Hall. His sons - Clarence on guitar, and Harold on banjo and vocals - completed the group. They were a full-time band that traveled around the Country playing their music. A music promoter from Jackson, Mississippi, H.C. Speir, heard Big Chief Henry's Indian String Band at the Choctaw Indian Fair in Philadelphia, Mississippi. Speir, who became known as the "godfather of Delta Blues," was responsible for discovering most of the Mississippi Blues singers, including Robert Johnson. Though he had earlier turned down Jimmie Rodgers, Speir liked Big Chief Henry's group, and helped them land a recording contract with RCA. On October 15, 1929, exactly a week before Joe Kaipo's final sessions with Jimmie Rodgers, Big Chief Henry's Indian String Band went into a recording studio, also in Dallas, Texas, and recorded six songs which were released on RCA's Victor label. They included "Blue Bird Waltz"/"Choctaw Waltz," "Indian Tom Tom"/"The Indian's Dream" and "Cherokee Rag"/"On the Banks of the Kaney." At that time, most 78rpm records had a short description of the music. Below Big Chief Henry & His Indian String Band, were the words, "Indian fiddling and singing."

Big Chief Henry's Indian String Band
L-R: Harold, Henry, & Clarence Hall

Though the Halls were of Choctaw ancestry, they were not full-blooded Native Americans. Henry's father, Thomas Jefferson Hall, who was from Shawnee, Kansas, had been a soldier in the Union Army during the Civil War. He married Nacrissa Adaline Guellette, who was half Choctaw. Henry was born in 1877 in Shibler, Osage County, Oklahoma. On January 20, 1904, he married Sarah Susan Hager in Wichita. Sarah, who was born in Iowa, had moved to Oklahoma with her first husband, Jack Kinsey, during the Oklahoma land rush of 1889. The Halls settled in Davenport, Oklahoma and had three children, including Harold, who was born in 1901, Nellie who was born in

1907, and Clarence, who was born in 1908. Due to family issues, the Halls moved back to Wichita sometime in the mid-1920s. As Henry Hall was a fiddler, he passed along his love of music to his boys and the trio began performing as Big Chief Henry's Indian String Band. With their homemade "tour van," which

Big Chief Henry Hall and wife, Susan

was built on a truck frame, the Halls traveled around the U.S. performing their music. The pinnacle of their musical career was their 1929 recording session in Dallas.

By April of 1930, the Halls were living in Carlsbad, New Mexico, and the group had begun to expand. One of the new musicians, Orvil Harwell, lived with the Halls after they settled in Carlsbad. The family continued to move. From New Mexico, they went to California, and eventually wound up in the state of Washington. It was during their time in California that Clarence became involved with the Church of the First Born, an off shoot of the Church of the Latter-Day Saints. He brought his newfound faith home with him and the entire family was converted. Since the Church of the First Born did not condone the lifestyles of traveling musicians, Clarence, Harold and Henry all gave up music and Big Chief Henry's Indian String Band ceased to exist.

* * *

Though the Burkes brothers and Henry Hall's group were from Wichita, they had most of their success after they left town. However, the performer with the most success in Wichita, beginning in the 1920s, was a young man from Gage, Oklahoma. Named after his hometown, Gage Brewer was born in 1904, the only child of a farm couple, Charles and Mary Brewer. By the time he was a teenager, his family had relocated to Shattuck, Oklahoma, where Gage became involved in theater and music. Hawaiian music was all the rage in the U.S. during the 1920s. Many people were introduced to the music of Hawaii through a Broadway show called *Bird of*

Gage Brewer's Hawaiian Entertainers
(Photo courtesy of Wichita-Sedgwick County Historical Museum)

Paradise, which made its debut in 1912. By 1916, more recordings of Hawaiian music were sold in the U.S. than any other style. The popularity of the genre would last until well into the 1930s. Numerous musical groups from Hawaii began touring the U.S., performing at theaters across the country, including the one in the small, western Oklahoma town of Shattuck. The teenaged Gage Brewer was captivated by the sounds, and soon learned to play the guitar by studying what the Hawaiians were doing. Through diligent practice, Brewer became an accomplished guitarist.

After graduating high school, Brewer attended Northwestern Oklahoma Teachers College in Alva. Though working on his teaching degree, he continued to practice playing Hawaiian music. He even found time to travel to Los Angeles, where he met Sol Hoopii, Hawaii's best-known musician.

In 1925, Brewer, now in his early 20s, and his parents decided to move to Wichita. At that time, Shattuck, Oklahoma had a population of around 1,200. Wichita, on the other hand, was almost a hundred times larger, and appeared to be ripe for entertainment. The Miller Theater had opened on the first of May in 1922, and the Orpheum followed only four months later. Though touring musicians from Hawaii had performed in the Wichita theaters, nobody was performing the Country's most popular music on a regular basis. Gage Brewer took it upon himself to fill that gap and put together his own group to perform Hawaiian music. Finding other musicians to back him in Wichita was not easy, so Brewer began teaching others to play in his own house. He named his home studio, the Hawaiian Conservatory of Music, and he called his band Gage Brewer's Hawaiian Entertainers. The popularity of the group began to spread and before long they were performing at banquets, dances, and private parties throughout Kansas, northern Oklahoma, and eastern Colorado. Commercial radio was in its infancy, but Brewer took advantage of the new medium to promote his music. His group, which he soon dubbed, Gage Brewer's Radio Orchestra, began regular appearances on KFUM in Colorado Springs, KFXF "The Voice of Denver," and Wichita's only station at the time, KFH.

The year 1930 was a significant year for radio. The KFH facilities had been destroyed by fire in late 1929, but the station was back on the air by January. A large, "Welcome Back KFH!" ceremony was held on January 23, 1930. The featured performers at the event were Gage Brewer's Hawaiians. Less than two weeks later, the Rock Island Lumber Company sold the Shadowland Dance Club to Frederick Brother, who also owned the former Wintergarden Club, which was now called the Ritz Ballroom. The regular featured musical performers at the Ritz were Bennie Moten and his 13-piece Victor Recording Orchestra.

On April 5, 1930, Gage Brewer married pianist, Doris Buschow, in her family's home at 302 South Roosevelt. The couple then took up residence at 941 South Topeka. Shortly thereafter, Brewer purchased the Shadowland Dance Club from Frederick Brother. The Shadowland was located outside the city limits, a couple of miles south of the John Mack Bridge on U.S. Highway 81, which was also known as Lawrence Road. In late September of 1932, an event took place at the Shadowland that would have world-wide significance. It was the first time an electric guitar was featured, on-stage, anywhere in the world. This occasion occured, thanks to Brewer's friendship with guitar innovator, George Beauchamp, whose association with John Dopyera in Los Angeles led to the instrument's development.

John Dopyera was only 15 years old when his family moved from Slovakia to the U.S., where they settled in California in 1908. By that time, Dopyera had already started making violins, a skill he had learned from his father. In the early 1920s, he opened his own shop, where he made and repaired a variety of stringed instruments. In 1925, George Beauchamp, a vaudeville performer, who had relocated to California from his home in Texas, asked John Dopyera if he could help him develop a louder guitar, so his playing could be heard better by larger audiences. Dopyera took up the challenge. They eventually created a metal-bodied guitar with three resonating, speaker-like cones installed in the body of the instrument. The National guitar gained popularity due to it being the loudest guitar available. Dopyera and Beauchamp named their company the National String Instrument Corporation.

Enjoying the success, George Beauchamp began to pursue new electric technology to create an even louder guitar, abandoning acoustics entirely. His enthusiasm for the new project put him at odds with some in his company. As a result of disputes with Beauchamp, John Dopyera left National, and in 1933 formed his own company with brothers, Rudy and Emil. They called it Dobro (short for Dopyera Brothers.) Just before, Beauchamp also left National to start a company with Adolph Rickenbacher and Paul Barth, a nephew of John Dopyera. The three men called their new company Ro-Pat-In, and introduced their first electric guitars in 1932. In 1935, National and Dobro merged to become the National-Dobro Corporation, and soon moved from Los Angeles to Chicago, where many of their suppliers were based. Ro-Pat-In eventually became known as Rickenbacker International, and is still producing guitars in southern California today.

Gage Brewer had become friends with George Beauchamp, perhaps early in life when they lived in the Southwest, or maybe later when he purchased National guitars for his musicians and students. Brewer himself played a top-of-the-line National, with his name specially engraved. These connections led to Brewer endorsing Beauchamp's newly designed "electric" guitar at his Shadowland Dance Club in Wichita on that fateful day in September of 1932. That guitar, which was called the "Electro," was one of several instruments provided to Brewer by Beauchamp. One of those original Electro guitars is part of the Wichita-Sedgwick County Historical Museum's permanent collection and is featured in an exhibit exploring Brewer's story.

Gage Brewer's Country Band
(Photo courtesy of Wichita-Sedgwick County Historical Museum)

Perhaps to not let his music become stale, or to attract new audiences, Gage Brewer's Radio Orchestra began expanding their repertoire beyond just Hawaiian music. On occasion, Brewer's dance shows would take on a specific theme, and the group would perform music to fit that theme. Country or "hillbilly" music was no exception. A photo from the Wichita-Sedgwick County Historical Museum's collection shows Brewer's orchestra in an over-the-top stereotypification of a hillbilly band. The straw bales, corncob pipes, and farm animals all indicate that Brewer and his group were not all that serious about country music. Be that as it may, Gage Brewer's contributions to the Wichita music scene in the 1920s and '30s cannot be understated, and that's why he appears as more than just a footnote in this book.

On March 3, 1936, the Shadowland Dance Club burned to the ground, destroying thousands of dollars' worth of musical equipment. Fortunately, at least some of the instruments from George Beauchamp, including the Electro guitars were not lost in that fire, because by then they had begun to be replaced by newer electric instruments.

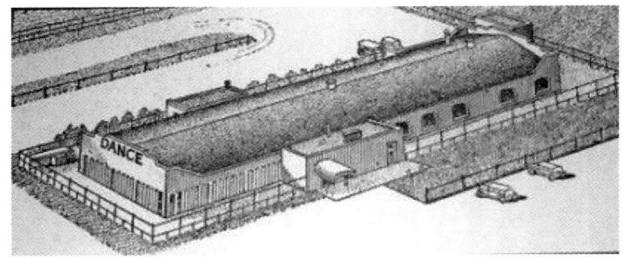

Shadowland Dance Club
(Photo courtesy of Wichita-Sedgwick County Historical Museum)

The loss of his dance club did not keep Brewer out of business for long. He acquired a large building at 2459 North Hillside, originally built as the Swallow Airplane Manufacturing Company, but had been converted for use as a nightclub. Swallow was a successful company during the 1920s that had employed such future aircraft legends as Lloyd Stearman and Walter Beech. Swallow owed much of its success to the Swallow TP, a plane which the U.S. Government used to train its military pilots in the late 1920s and early '30s. A setback came in 1927 from which Swallow would not fully recover. One of the company's principal owners, Jacob Mollendick, bet most of the company's fortune that one of his planes, the Dallas Spirit, would win the air race, known as the Dole Derby, from California to Hawaii. During the race, the Dallas Spirit, piloted by World War I flying ace, William Portwood Irwin, went down somewhere over the Pacific Ocean, never to be seen again.

Eric Cale, director of the Wichita-Sedgwick County Historical Museum, had occasion to visit the old Shadowland site on North Hillside with Gage Brewer's son, Loti. The Swallow Airplane building had already been converted to a nightclub prior to it becoming the Shadowland. Cale recalled Gage Brewer's purchase of the building as told to him by Loti Brewer. "He told me a story about the guys his dad bought the building from, that had previously run a club there. They had sandbagged machine gun turrets up in the attic on the north and south ends of the building. Sounds like a mobster racket!" Cale also mentioned that Brewer traveled and performed widely, including to places like the Arcadia Theater in New York City and the Hotel Ambassador's Coconut Grove in Los Angeles.

By July of 1936, only four months since the fire, Brewer's New Shadowland was open for business. The club continued to feature live music, based on themes and holidays. Also offered were dance lessons and free transportation. The club was especially busy during the years of World War II, when Wichita operated "24-7." In

June Frisby's Sweet Swing Sisters (June Frisby, far left)
(Photo courtesy of Wichita-Sedgwick County Historical Museum)

1950, Brewer changed the name of the venue to the Mambo Club and began catering to African Americans as well as whites. Brewer sold the club in 1965 and devoted the last years of his life to the pursuit of business interests ranging from commercial real estate to encyclopedia sales. He passed away in Wichita on May 18, 1985.

* * *

By the time Gage Brewer opened his Hawaiian Conservatory of Music in the mid-1920s, another school for musicians was already operating in Wichita, run by the teenaged June Frisby. Born Violetta Mareia June Frisby on August 12, 1905, June and her mother moved to Wichita from Missouri, following the death of June's father. Just out of high school, young June began studying music at Fairmount College, later to become Wichita University. She had hopes that she could turn her love of music into a career. She opened the doors of the June Frisby Academy of Music in 1922, while continuing her studies at Fairmount. At first, she focused her teachings on stringed instruments, especially banjo and Hawaiian guitar. Before long she added instruction in piano and dancing.

June Frisby with Country Band
(Photo courtesy of Wichita-Sedgwick County Historical Museum)

One of her annual "reviews," which featured 52 cast members, was held at Wichita's East High School on March 5, 1930. The crowd of 500 enjoyed "readings, stringed instrument selections, piano solos & duets, dancing, and solo banjo and guitar offerings." Most of the groups were in costume, with the most popular being a colonial group and a Hawaiian group. The highlight of the night was billed as, "the Only Marching Banjo Band in America." A promotional photo for the event showed 19 banjo players, along with the caption, "all banjos in picture, except 5, are Gibsons from Jenkins." Jenkins was the popular musical instrument store in downtown Wichita, located at 323 East Douglas. The June Frisby Academy became so popular that other instructors were hired, and enrollment eventually numbered 400 students. Frisby also added lessons for marimba and organ, as well as the instrument that would become her favorite, the accordion.

As enrollment increased, Frisby moved her academy to the Farmers & Bankers Life Insurance Company building at the corner of 1st and Market. Eventually she moved up the street to the building at 323 N. Market, that formerly housed the E.B. McCullough Upholstering Company. Frisby did not limit her teaching to any one style of music. She seemed to love it all. It is alleged that one of her students was

Myron Floren, the famous accordionist on the *Lawrence Welk Show*. On occasion, Frisby brought her accordion to KFH and sat in with the Ark Valley Boys, playing country music. Her contribution to country music in Wichita was not as much for her own performing as it was to the legacy she passed on through her students, one of whom was Doris Buss, who would start a lifetime career as a musician playing country music with the Ark Valley Boys. June Frisby Mullendore passed away on December 23, 1981.

CHAPTER TWO

HEADIN' OUT FOR WICHITA

It's a one-track town, just brown and a breeze too
Pack up the meat, sweet, we're
Headin' out for Wichita in a pile of fruit
From "Yea! Heavy and a Bottle of Bread" by Bob Dylan

Prior to the advent of radio, music was spread around the U.S. through recordings and sheet music. It was advertised in newspapers, magazines, and mail-order catalogs. The 1897 Sears, Roebuck & Co. catalog features a mind-boggling array of musical instruments, along with music boxes and roller organs that played mechanically produced music. Page 485 of the catalog showed a new product called a Graphophone. It was the Sears Roebuck version of the Phonograph which was invented by Thomas Edison in 1877 but did not become commercially successful until 1888. The description of the Graphophone touts, "You can hear in your own home all of the latest songs, instrumental music, speeches, etc., from the best artists in the metropolitan cities." The machine, which included an oak case, a bottle of lubricating oil, and a screwdriver, could be purchased for $25, a rather pricey sum at the time. A personal selection of twelve Musical and Talking Records (cylindrical records) cost $6. It is interesting to note that next to the listing of the Graphophone was the description of "colored slides with motion," which were made for lantern slide projectors. The first motional slide listed was "Rat Catcher: Man sleeping, awakes, swallows one rat after another in quick succession. Very laughable." It seems that folks in 1897 were easily entertained. This may have been the 19th century version of Facebook.

In 1920, things changed in a big way. KDKA in Pittsburgh, Pennsylvania signed on the air as the first commercial radio station. Other stations soon followed. By 1923, there were hundreds of stations filling the airwaves across America. Radio enthusiasts had begun broadcasting in Wichita in 1919. One of those experimenters was Charles A. Stanley who received Wichita's first commercial broadcasting license on March 3, 1922. He was assigned the call letters, WEY. Around a month later, two more stations were licensed to Wichita, WAAP and WEAH. Though WAAP received its license a month and half earlier than WEAH, technical issues forced a delay in

WAAP getting on the air until four months after WEAH had begun broadcasting. WEY lasted two years; WAAP less than a year. The WAAP transmitter was sold to the infamous "goat gland" doctor, John R. Brinkley, who moved it to Milford, Kansas where it became known as KFKB. The complete story of this station can be found in my book, *Goat Glands to Ranch Hands: The KFDI Story*. That left WEAH as Wichita's only commercial radio station. In 1925, the station was purchased by the Rigby Gray Hotel Corporation, owners of the Lassen Hotel in Wichita. The call letters were changed to KFH, which stood for "Kansas' Finest Hotel."

During the formative years of radio broadcasting, most musical entertainment was done by live performers. Not only were most radio stations not equipped to play recordings, the practice was frowned upon by the record companies. Record company owners felt that if people could hear their recorded music for free on the radio, they would not purchase the records. The federal government's broadcasting regulatory agency, the Federal Radio Commission, also tried to limit the use of recorded music. In August of 1928, the FRC cited WCRW in Chicago for playing too much recorded music. The station was fined by having their power reduced from 500 watts to 100 watts. Even as radio engineers began installing record turntables in their studios, those units were mostly used to play recorded transcriptions of the station's own musicians and singers, so they could be aired at times when the performers were unavailable. Entertainers generally performed on the radio for low pay. Their main income came from selling song books by mail order, and by advertising their live appearances in various towns within the station's broadcast coverage area. In 1937, the management at KFH hired their first cowboy singer. Robert Worley Herring was born in Lott, Texas, and began performing in medicine shows when he was 16. Herring, who adopted the name, "Dusty," worked for several radio stations in Texas before moving to Wichita to join the staff of KFH. He later got the job as a deputy in the sheriff departments of both Butler and Sedgwick counties over a period of 20 years. As his radio career evolved into television, Herring began billing himself as "Deputy Dusty" Herring. He hosted programs on KAKE-TV from 1954 to

Dusty Herring

Original Ark Valley Boys
(Photo courtesy of Rex Victory)

1964. The last move of his illustrious career came in July of 1965, when he became the farm director at KFDI radio. Herring passed away from a heart attack on May 23, 2006.

* * *

Many of the radio stations had musical groups for which they owned the name. Though band personnel might change, the band name would stay the same. Such was the case for one of Wichita's best-known radio bands, the Ark Valley Boys.

In 1939, the Ark Valley Boys were created to be the "house band" for KFH, which by then had moved to the Yorkrite building at the corner of Market and William. The ten-member group had a daily, noontime show called *Chow Time*. As the studio clock struck 12:00, the announcer would step to the microphone and say, "From seven stories high atop the Yorkrite Building, across from the *Wichita Eagle* in downtown Wichita…where it's high noon…It's Chow Time, with the Ark Valley Boys….brought to you in part by Nash's Coffee, Purina, Harvey Brothers Clothing

Original Ark Valley Boys
(Photo courtesy of Rex Victory)

Store, Ark Valley Taylor-Made Flour, Ezrie Clodfelter's Emporium, and the Yokie Penckie Pool Hall and Saloon!" Immediately, the entire cast would rip into a fast song like "Crazy to Be a Cowboy," and the show was off and running.

The Ark Valley Boys were also featured on the weekly radio show, the *KFH Barn Dance Frolic*, as well as performing three to six shows a week on the road throughout Kansas and northern Oklahoma. They were so popular that they were usually booked months in advance. The Ark Valley Boys were not only one of the top dance bands in the area, they were also known for their entertaining stage show, which included comedy routines and a wide variety of musical combinations. The band performed at lots of rodeos, and even backed Gene Autry during at least one of his Wichita appearances. In 1946, the Peer International Corporation released the *KFH Ark Valley Boys Song Book: No. 1*. The song book sold for fifty cents and included 14 of the band's favorite songs, such as "You Are My Sunshine," "When My Blue Moon Turns to Gold Again," "Dude Cowboy" and "Wichita."

Ark Valley Boys Show on KFH
L-R: Russell Cunes, Vic "Puny" Hawkins, Micki Pennington, Corky Edminster, Jack Schnipet, Curly Peavler, Darlene Williams, Dave Dawson, Roy Christinsan, Marge (unknown last name), Clarence Brown, Dave Crockett, Denny Dennis (seated)
(Photo courtesy of Rex Victory)

Front man for the Ark Valley Boys was 300-pound, former movie actor, Vic "Puny" Hawkins. Prior to becoming the manager and emcee for the Ark Valley Boys, Hawkins had worked as a character actor in many silent films, including playing the part of the sheriff in a series of movies with silent film cowboy star, Jack Hoxie. Besides carrying the nickname, "Puny," Hawkins was also known as the "Ton of Fun." During the Ark Valley Boys' shows, Puny would usually join the band, singing a song or two, doing some comedy, or even playing the drums.

Though Puny Hawkins was the manager of the band, it was not long before Leichester "Corky" Edminster joined the Ark Valley Boys and became their leader. Early in his career, Edminster played piano in the dance

Mickey Pennington & Puny Hawkins
(Photo courtesy of Rex Victory)

Corky Edminster
(Photo courtesy of Rex Victory)

band of Gage Brewer, the Wichita bandleader who introduced the electric guitar to the world. Atypical for a "country" band, Edminster was known as one of the best saxophone and clarinet players in the area. He was also responsible for the band's vocal arrangements, which often included tight, three and four-part harmonies. During World War II, Edminster left the group to join the Navy, but after the war, he resumed his position as bandleader of the Ark Valley Boys.

Cozzin Clarence

Corky's top comedian is an old timer in radio and show business having come up through the years since radio first began.

Clarence is a fine musician with both the fiddle, bass, drums and comedy voice. His comedy roles double from being a spoiled brat to loveable Grandma Brown. He has every excuse in the book for getting out of work and finally does. He originated the saying "why shore." He is a kid favorite and loved by both young and old.

Granny Brown
one of Clarence's comedy acts

Fiddler, Clarence "C.Q." Brown, also known as "Cozzin Clarence," was one of the original members of the Ark Vally Boys. He was also the main comedian in the band. Brown was a great fiddler and a singer. It was said that he knew a thousand songs. As with Corky Edminster, Brown also left to join the Navy during World War II. He too returned to the band after the war.

Bill Boggs
(Photo courtesy of Rex Victory)

Another member of the Ark Valley Boys was Bill Boggs, who became one of the best-known fiddlers in Wichita. He also left the band during the war and joined the Army where he became an Entertainment Specialist as a Tech Sergeant 3rd Class. After the war, Boggs rejoined his band mates. When television came along, Boggs got a job on KAKE-TV as "Fiddlin' Willie" on the show, *Dusty's Jamboree*, which was hosted by the popular "Deputy Dusty" Herring. In later years, after retiring from his successful sign company, Boggs often performed in a duo with Wichita guitar legend/innovator, Bob Wiley. Boggs passed away in 2012 at the age of 89.

A vital part of the Ark Valley Boys' sound was the vocal harmonies of the Victory Trio. Brothers, Oby, Bud, and Ray (also called Tex) had been singing together since they were kids. They were known for singing the Sons of the Pioneers' songs "as well as the Sons of the Pioneers themselves." The Victory family was originally from Ava, Missouri, and Oby and Ray were both born there. Their younger brother, Fred (also called Bud,) was born after the family moved to Sylvia,

Tom Noone & the Victory Trio
L-R: Tom Noone, Bud Victory,
Oby Victory, Ray "Tex" Victory
(Photo courtesy of Rex Victory)

Bill Boggs, Oby Victory, Bud Victory
(Photo courtesy of Rex Victory)

Kansas. The boys grew up singing in the Sylvia Nazarene Church. All three of the brothers played guitar, plus Oby could play the drums and Ray picked the banjo. Eventually, Ray Victory left the trio and was replaced by William "Red" McKinney.

One of the musical highlights of the Kansas State Fair in Hutchinson, during September of 1941, was the daily appearances by the Ark Valley Boys and the Moss Sisters. They performed each night of the fair at the KFH Barn Dance, which was located on the midway.

Ark Valley Boys Show on KFH
Back Row: Claude Childers (seated), Bud Victory, Corky Edminster, Roy Christinsan, Oby Victory, Denny Dennis, Snazzy Fortner, (unknown)
Front Row: Vic "Puny" Hawkins, Micki Pennington, Irene Moss, Lucille Moss, Mamie Jo Moss, Darlene Williams, (unknown), Clarence Brown (front, seated)
(Photo courtesy of Rex Victory)

The Ark Valley Boys were so popular that they could draw big crowds at Wichita's largest venue, the Forum. There was an especially large crowd on the night of November 29, 1941 where a double wedding took place on-stage. Oby Victory married Dorothy Honn, and his brother, Bud married Beulah Horrigan. The couples' honeymoons did not last long. Eight days later, the Japanese bombed Pearl Harbor, and all three Victory brothers were soon headed off to war. Bud joined the Navy, while his older brothers enlisted in the Army. Ray became a Tech Sergeant and Oby was assigned to be a medic and cook for the Army's 5th Division. He served in England, Algiers, and Italy. Like their other bandmates who had gone off to fight in World War II, the Victory brothers rejoined the Ark Valley Boys after the war ended.

* * *

Geri Mapes
(Photo courtesy of Rex Victory)

In 1939, shortly after the Ark Valley Boys began their show on KFH, they were joined by a pretty, young singer who could also yodel. Geraldine Mapes, who went by Geri, was only three years old. Her debut performance was so well received that Geri became a regular on KFH. But a year later, the radio station management changed their minds and took little Geri off the air. She chuckled as she recalled, "I began receiving unemployment checks when I was four."

After her family moved from Wichita, Mapes continued her musical career and eventually worked with Tennessee Ernie Ford. In 1971, she met steel guitar player Bud Isaacs, who is best remembered as the pedal steel guitar player on Webb Pierce's 1954 #1 hit, "Slowly." It was the first time that a steel guitar with foot pedals appeared on a recording. Patrick Carr, in his The Illustrated History of Country Music, wrote of the influence Bud Isaacs had on other steel guitar players due to "Slowly." Carr noted, "It sent scores of steel guitarists drilling holes and attaching coat hangers to their instruments trying to hook up jury-rig methods of duplicating the mind-blowing sound of the pedal steel guitar as introduced on record by Webb's steel player Bud Isaacs." Geri Mapes and

Bud & Geri Isaacs

Bud Isaacs soon married and performed together as the Golden West Singers until their retirement. Known as the Country Music Sweetheart, Geri was not only featured as a singer and yodeler, but she also played bass in the band. Her husband, Bud, was quoted in the *Fret Board Journal*: "She plays good bass. Roy Lanham (Sons of the Pioneers) says she's his favorite bass player. 'Cause she had an ear for chords. She could hit the right note. She could play a strange tune." Geri's bass playing can be heard on Bud's recordings, including his big hit, "Bud's Bounce."

In 1978, Bud and Geri Isaacs were inducted into the Colorado Country Music Hall of Fame. The couple eventually retired in Yuma, Arizona, where Bud passed away on September 4, 2016 at the age of 88.

* * *

Also, in their early years at KFH, the Ark Valley Boys often featured the singing of the Moss Sisters; Lucy, Irene, and Jody. By 1942, the girls had left KFH to tour with Ohio-based, jazz musician, Barney Rapp. Though Rapp had been a successful band leader since the 1920s, who had recorded for several major record labels, he is best-known for having discovered Doris Day.

Moss Sisters
(Photo courtesy of Rex Victory)

Other members of the Ark Valley Boys during the 1940s included Snazzy Fortner, Claude Childers, Vernon Reed, Denny Dennis, and Mark Ehart. In 1970, Ehart's nephew, Phil Ehart would become the drummer and one of the founding members of the rock band, KANSAS.

In 1943, Claude Childers, who played piano in the Ark Valley Boys, went to the home of 14-year-old accordion player, Doris McClish, and asked her to join the group. Encouraged by her mother, she had begun playing the accordion when she was seven. They lived in the same building that housed the June Frisby Academy, and Doris' mother signed her up for lessons. Besides the accordion, she also learned to play the piano, the ukulele, the steel guitar, and even the marimba. Her job at KFH came while she was in school at Cathedral High School. Her day began early. "Before school, I would go over to KFH to rehearse with the Ark Valley Boys at 6:30." Lucky for Doris, her school was flexible and allowed her to miss classes whenever she needed to play music. She recalled one of her fellow employees at KFH, Johnny Spear. "He wrote the scripts for the Ark Valley Boys shows. He was really good. Before he came to Wichita, he had written for George Burns and Fibber McGee & Molly." Besides playing in the studio with the Ark Valley Boys, Doris also played with them on the road, including the Kansas State Fair in Hutchinson. She smiled as she remembered her favorite times with the band. "I loved it when we played at rodeos. We usually played on a platform right above the bulls. That was really fun." After graduation, she married a bass player named Leonard Buss. From that point on, she was known as Doris Buss.

The year 1949 started well for the Ark Valley Boys. KFH purchased an airplane for the band to fly to their live performances in Kansas and Oklahoma. Dubbed the "Flying Ark," the Luscombe "Silvaire Sedan" had the KFH call letters and "Ark Valley Boys" painted on the side. There was also a caricature of "Cozzin Clarence" Brown. However, later that year KFH had a change of management, and the new station manager did not care for the band's music. So, on September 23, 1949, bandleader, Corky Edminster and five other key members, including Clarence Brown, Bill Boggs, and the Victory Trio, turned in their two-week resignations to KFH so they could move to a competing radio station, KANS. The name "Ark Valley Boys" was owned by KFH, so the departing musicians had to come up with a new name. With Corky Edminster still band leader, the group became known as Corky's Corral Gang. The Victory brothers, known as the Victory Trio on KFH, now became the Smokehouse Trio. Doris Buss also went along and brought her accordion.

Ark Valley Boys
L-R: Corky Edminster, Snazzy Fortner, Bill Boggs, Bud Victory, Claude Childers, Oby Victory, Clarence Brown, (unknown), Vernon Reed
(Photo courtesy of Rex Victory)

Corky's Corral Gang and Doris Buss
L-R: Corky Edminster, Red McKinney, Bill Boggs, Archie Taylor, Clarence Brown, Oby Victory, Curly Peavler (driver), Doris Buss, Bud Victory
(Photo courtesy of Rex Victory)

To no avail, the management of KFH quickly contacted the American Federation of Musicians music union to try to find replacements for the departing band members. Thereupon, they contacted Tex Ferguson, band leader at KFEQ in St. Joseph, Missouri, who agreed to move to Wichita with his four other band members and become the Ark Valley Boys. They arrived in Wichita on October 9 and signed a six-month contract, just in time to do their first performance. The next morning, they presented their transfer cards to the local musicians' union and were denied. That resulted in a landmark Kansas Supreme Court case filed by KFH against the union.

The man in charge of the local chapter of the American Federation of Musicians told the band that since they had done a performance before they transferred their membership, they could be suspended for twelve months. He also said that each member would be subject to a fine of $1,000 if they remained in Wichita. Yet, they were also told that their membership could not be transferred until they were in Wichita for six months. Band leader, Ferguson stated in court, that the band was leaving town and could not fulfill their contract with KFH because they wanted to "stay in good standing with the union....wanted to be a member. You have to be a member to work. From my experience, you can't work unless you carry a card." Ferguson also said, "In my nine years of playing as a musician, I have traveled in

Tex Ferguson & His Drifting Pioneers

Doris Buss & Corky's Corral Gang
L-R: Red McKinney, Doris Buss, Corky Edminster, Curly Peavler,
(unknown), Snazzy Fortner, Clarence Brown
(Photo courtesy of Rex Victory)

a lot of states. I have always had to go to the local where I was working and get a transfer to where I was going to move to, and there were no questions asked. If I lived there any length of time, I took my card in and showed them I was in good standing; showed them I had a transfer. Most of the time I would work a week and then go down. I have never had a reception like I got in this local in all my nine years of playing."

KFH won the suit against the musicians' union and Tex Ferguson and his band became the Ark Valley Boys for several years. In 1950, while at KFH, Ferguson signed a recording contract with 4-Star Records. He left KFH in 1953, and moved to Bay City, Michigan where he formed the group, Tex Ferguson & His Drifting Pioneers, who became regulars on the *Michigan Barn Dance*.

* * *

In 1936, Wichita had only one radio station. Several stations had been started, but only KFH had survived. However, that year Wichita gained a second station. KANS originally broadcast on 1210 KHz, but in 1941 moved to 1240 on the dial.

Dinning Sisters and the Victory Trio
L-R: *Clarence Brown, Jean Dinning, Bud Victory, Virginia Dinning, Oby Victory, Lucille Dinning*
(Photo courtesy of Rex Victory)

KFBI moved to Wichita in 1940, and in 1947, KAKE was built in Wichita. KAKE originally operated on 1480 kHz, but soon swapped frequencies with KANS. By the time Corky Edminster and his band moved from KFH to KANS, the station was broadcasting from its new spot on the dial, 1480. During the late 1940s, radio stations still relied on live performers for most of their musical programming. Even though they were no longer Ark Valley Boys, Corky and his Corral Gang continued to enjoy local popularity. They also began doing some recordings. In 1950, they released a 45rpm single with "Twin Guitar Boogie" on one side and "Don't Cry Sweetheart" on the other. This record was on the Cormac label. Next the group recorded for Wichita-based Raymor Records as Corky Edminster & His KANS Corral Gang. Their first Raymor single, released in 1954, was a somewhat risqué song called "Chili Dippin' Baby," that featured the vocals of Mary Anne McNally. The B side of the record was a mysterious song called "Shadow Rock Trail," that showcased the duet vocals of Clarence Brown and Oby Victory.

L-R: Corky Edminster, Smiley Burnette, Clarence Brown
(Photo courtesy of Rex Victory)

Corky's Corral Gang was the most-popular band in Wichita during the early 1950s, and their programs on KANS attracted large, radio audiences. For a time, the group included the Dinning Sisters. Lou Dinning and her twin sisters, Jean and Ginger were part of a family of nine children who lived on a farm, just south of Caldwell, Kansas in Oklahoma. All the kids learned to sing in church and before long, the three girls began entering talent contests. In 1939, the Dinning Sisters, still in their teens, moved to Chicago to perform on radio station WENR. Then they made an appearance on the WLS *National Barn Dance* and gained national recognition. In 1943, Capitol Records signed them for a recording contract. They became Capitol's answer to the Andrews Sisters. The Dinning Sisters had several hits, including two that hit Top 10; "My Adobe Hacienda" and "Buttons and Bows." Interestingly, their brother, Mark Dinning, made his mark in Rock & Roll. His song, "Teen Angel," written by Jean Dinning, was a #1 smash hit in 1960.

Corky & His Corral gang became friends with Smiley Burnette, who was best known as "Frog Millhouse," Gene Autry's sidekick in the movies. In 1951, Burnette requested that the group come to Hollywood to appear in one of Autry's movies. When they arrived at the movie set, they were turned down as they were not members of the Screen Actors Guild.

Oby Victory's son, Rex, recalled the days when his dad, his uncles, and Clarence Brown would hang around Oby's house, located at Seneca and 61st Street North, just across the street from the Indian Peace Treaty monument. "Those guys would get kinda crazy. One time they set up a target at the back of the garage and were shooting at it with a .22. They didn't realize how far a .22 bullet could go. One shot went through the target, through the wall of the garage, and through the window of the neighbor's house, and knocked off a skillet that was hanging on the kitchen wall.

Corky's Corral Gang with John Barrymore Jr
L-R: *Bill Boggs, Chill Wills, Bud Victory, Doris Buss, Corky Edminster, John Barrymore Jr, Red McKinney, Oby Victory, Clarence Brown (seated)*
(Photo courtesy of Rex Victory)

Corky's Corral Gang with Casey Tibbs
Back Row: *Curly Peavler, Bud Victory, Jim Shoulders, Casey Tibbs, (unknown), Corky Edminster, Bill Davis, (unknown)*
Front Row: *(unknown), Oby Victory, Clarence Brown, Red McKinney, (unknown)*
(Photo courtesy of Rex Victory)

Cap'n Bill (McLean) & Popeye (Clarence Brown)

The neighbor lady, who had been working in the kitchen, immediately called the cops. When the officer arrived, he asked the guys if they had been shooting the rifle? They admitted that they had been. The police offer said, 'Fine. But you need to move your target somewhere else.' So, they did, and the officer proceeded to shoot at the target with them." Rex also recalled a time when Smiley Burnette came to their home. "Smiley pulled up to our house in his big, fancy car. When he got out of the car, our dog bit him on the leg. Smiley never forgot that and told that story many times."

Doris Buss also has fond memories of Smiley Burnette. "Smiley took us to Hollywood where we appeared in some Armed Forces Broadcasts. I rode to California with Smiley in his car. He was so nice. He would even cook dinner for me."

Following the recording for Raymor, Clarence Brown got a job in television. KAKE-TV signed on the air on October 19, 1954. One of KAKE-TV's early shows was a cartoon program for kids, hosted by Bill McLean, who appeared as a sea captain called "Cap'n Bill." McLean's sidekick on the show was Clarence Brown, who looked just like the cartoon character, Popeye.

On Tuesday nights, KAKE-TV also had a musical program called *Dusty's Jamboree*, hosted by "Deputy Dusty" Herring. The former deputy sheriff was now presenting cowboy movies in the afternoons on KAKE, as well as doing a musical program at 6:00pm on Saturdays called *Dusty's Jamboree*. To back him, Herring put together his D-Bar-H Gang, which included several members of Corky's Corral

Dusty Herring & the D-Bar-H Gang
L-R: *Bud Victory, Bill Boggs, Clarence Brown, Oby Victory, Dusty Herring*
(Photo courtesy of Rex Victory)

Gang; Bud and Oby Victory, Bill Boggs, and "Cozzin Clarence" Brown. Eventually, Brown, as Popeye, hosted his own kids show on KAKE-TV called *Popeye & His Pals*.

Even after his Corral Gang came to an end, Corky Edminster continued to play music for the rest of his life. In his later years, he fronted a band in Wichita called the Dads of Dixieland, and played with various groups sponsored by the Shriners. He died in 2013 at the age of 96.

Doris Buss
(Photo courtesy of Doris Buss)

After a few years with Corky's Corral Gang at KANS, Doris Buss decided to try something else. She put away the accordion and decided to concentrate on the piano. Her favorite type of music was jazz so, with her husband, Leonard, on bass and Bobby Smith on drums, she put together the Doris Buss Trio. Occasionally, Cal DeBus joined in on saxophone. Highlights

Bill Wimberley and the Ark Valley Boys

of her career include a duet with Henry Mancini, touring with Bob Crosby and the Norman Lee Orchestra, and playing for the *Ice Capades*. She was one of the founders of the Wichita Jazz Festival. She was 90 when I interviewed her, and still enjoyed playing the piano at the Wichita Country Club. Doris passed away on July 5, 2020.

* * *

Though some of the original members of the band had moved to competing radio station, KANS, KFH continued to promote the legacy of the Ark Valley Boys, Wichita's original "radio" band. After Tex Ferguson had moved on in 1953, a new version of the Ark Valley Boys came together under the leadership of singer, Bill Wimberley. Among the members of the group were steel guitarist, Gene Crownover and a left-handed guitar player named Cotton Wittington. Wittington used a normally tuned, right-handed guitar and just flipped it upside down. Other members included Gene Gasaway on fiddle, Buddy Kendrick on bass, and Jack Atchley on piano. During the early 1960s, both Crownover and Gasaway joined Bob Wills' Texas Playboys.

Headin' Out for Wichita 41

Thumbs Carlille and the Black Brothers

In 1955, ABC-TV began airing a live country music program based out of Springfield, Missouri. Known as the *Ozark Jubilee*, it was hosted by Red Foley. The popular program introduced TV audiences to upcoming performers like Porter Wagoner, Brenda Lee, Leroy VanDyke, Hawkshaw Hawkins, Billy Walker, and even former Wichitan, Marvin Rainwater. Bill Wimberley also became a regular on the show. His lead guitar player was a guy who played standard electric guitar, but played it lying across his legs like a steel guitar. His name was Kenneth Carllile. Carllile was discovered, playing in a nightclub in St. Louis, by Little Jimmy Dickens. It was Dickens who gave him the nickname, "Thumbs," a name he never really liked, even though he built his career on that nickname.

Around the same time that Bill Wimberley became a part of the *Ozark Jubilee*, he was signed to Mercury Records. Several singles were released under the name of Bill Wimberley & His Country Rhythm Boys. A few of those titles included, "Black Street," "Ole Mister Cottontail," "Columbus Stockade Blues," and "Ozark Liza." He later recorded for the small Tex record label using the name Bill Wimberley's Western Swing Band. In 1958, Starday released a song called "Springfield Guitar Social" by Bill Wimberley and Thumbs Carllile. It featured Bill on vocals and Thumbs doing impressions of famous guitar players.

* * *

During his time as leader of the Ark Valley Boys, Bill Wimberley hired a young musician/singer named Frank Baughman. Baughman had recently moved to Wichita from Arkansas, and Wimberley hired him to sing in the band at the Cowboy Inn, but he wound up also performing on the *Chow Time* show on KFH as a member of the Ark Valley Boys. A lot of musicians had gone through the band since its inception in

1939. Baughman recalled, "I was number 52 or 53. We kept up a busy schedule. We did our daily shows on KFH and then headed for the Cowboy Inn where we played seven nights a week. I could play several instruments, but my main job in the group was as lead vocalist. However, I did get to play on a record by popular Wichita disc jockey, Lee Nichols. Also, Gene Crownover and I did some touring as a member of Tex Ritter's band."

Frank Baughman and his friend, Don Fowler, had begun playing music together when they were just kids in Arkansas. The boys were so good that they were invited by Upton Horn to join his country band that performed regularly at the Lamplighters Club in Branson, Missouri. This was in the days long before Branson became famous. The Lamplighter was the only night club in the sleepy, little Ozark town. Baughman recalled, "Don and I were both underage to be in that night club, so whenever the band took a break, we were ushered to a special booth where we sat and drank our Cokes until it was time for us to play again." Upton Horn and his band became well-known in the Ozarks, partly due to their regular radio show on KHOZ in Harrison, Arkansas.

Comanche Roundup Gang on KARD-TV
L-R: *Junior Jackson, Neal Sedan, Deacon Wells, Bill Davis, Frank Baughman*
(Photo courtesy of Frank Baughman)

"After I left the Ark Valley Boys," noted Baughman, "I moved back to Missouri and started my own band which I called, Frank Baughman and the Honeymoon Ranch Boys. I not only fronted the band, but played rhythm guitar, fiddle, and bass, as needed." Joining him in his new band was Baughman's old friend, Don Fowler.

By 1955, Frank Baughman and the Honeymoon Ranch Boys had relocated to Wichita. "Then we got real busy," Baughman recalled. "We played all over Wichita… places like the Trig Ballroom, Mop Hall, the Frontier Ballroom, the BEC Playhouse, the Cowboy Inn, and the Arcadia Theater." They also occasionally played square dances at Wichita's largest venue, The Forum. One of the members of the band was banjo player, Deacon Wells. Wells landed the group a job as the stars of a local TV Western series. Produced by KARD-TV, Wichita's Channel 3, the series aired every Saturday night from 10:30 to 11:00. Baughman had fond memories of that program. "The show was called *Comanche Roundup* and was based on the idea of cowboys bringing a herd of cattle up the Chisholm Trail from West Texas to Abilene, Kansas. Since Deacon was the one who got us on the show, he took the part of the trail boss. I became his 'sidekick.' We also had Neal Sedan and Bill Davis on fiddles and Junior Jackson on guitar." Kathy Dagle acted in the show as the rancher's daughter. *Comanche Roundup* was sponsored by the Comanche Meat Company of Wichita. It aired for 26 weeks with the last episode being shot in Technicolor.

In the mid-1960s, the Honeymoon Ranch Boys performed for a KFDI Christmas program at the Crest Theater. Baughman remembered that night. "Besides doing our own songs, we also backed the DJs, who were known as the KFDI Ranch Hands. Ol' Mike (station manager, Mike Oatman) liked the band so much that he asked us to become KFDI's house band. While we were with KFDI, we got to open shows for Conway Twitty, the Stonemans, and Henson Cargill." By this time, the band included Emitt Hipps on steel guitar, Doyle Richardson on bass (later replaced by Jim Bowles), Frank's son, Rex Baughman on guitar, bass and drums, along with Rex's wife, Colette on drums. Guitarist Don Fowler had been in and out of the band since the beginning. Since Baughman and Fowler began playing together as kids, they played off each other well and their twin guitar parts were especially tasty. In the mid-1970s, Baughman hired Don Fowler's two, young boys, Bucky and Scott, who later became a popular Wichita country band called, appropriately, the Fowler Brothers. Frank Baughman decided to call it quits in 1991.

*Frank Baughman & the Honeymoon
Ranch Boys at Joyland
L-R: Jason Bowles, "Arkie" Jay Hudspeth, Frank Baughman,
Tommy Sproules, Doyle Richardson*
(Photo courtesy of Frank Baughman)

The Ark Valley Boys had not been in existence for around 25 years, but in 1975, Curt Baggett licensed the name and put together a new band under the old name. The new group had more of a Southern Gospel quartet type of sound. Curt Baggett was one of the band members, along with his brother, Ron, Dean Hopkins, and others.

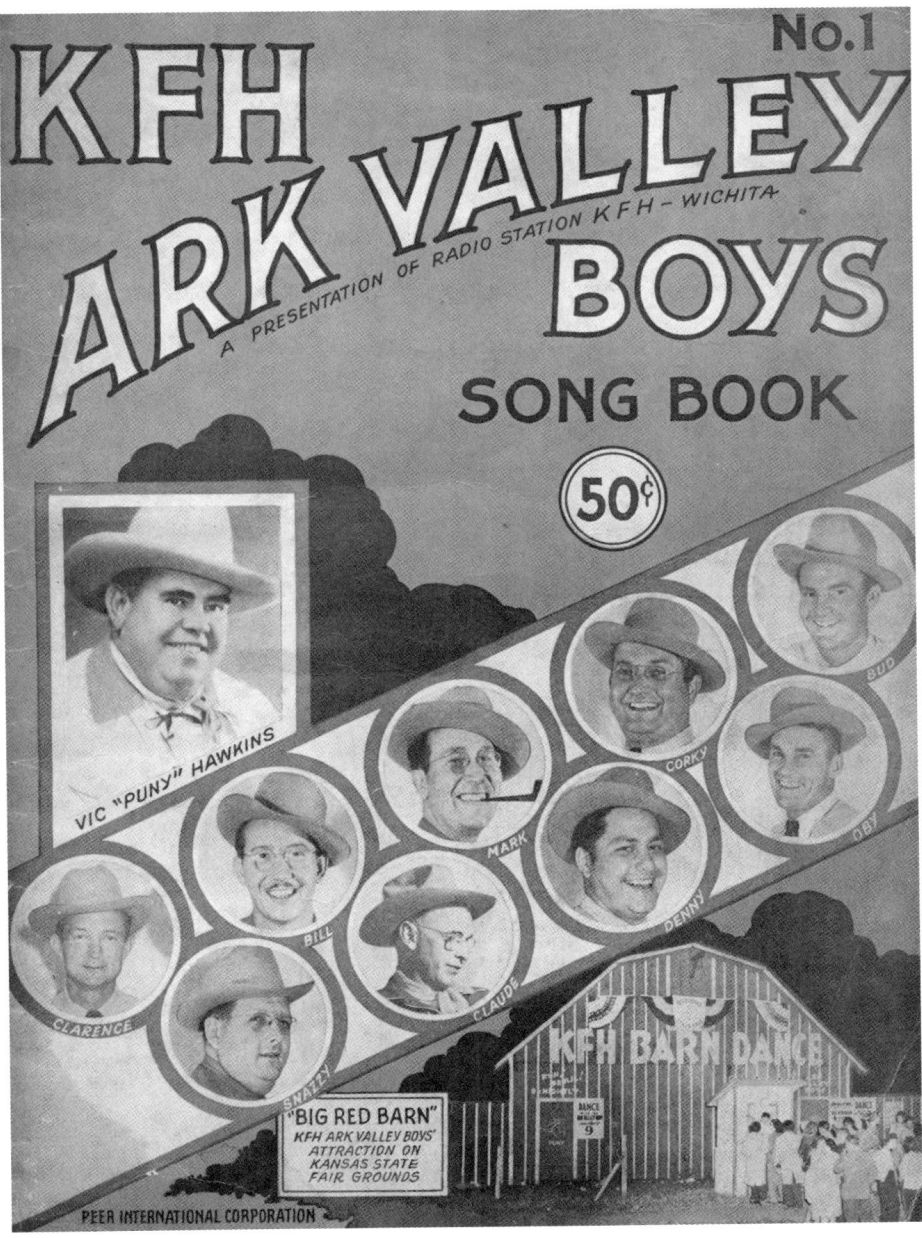

CHAPTER THREE

SHE SANG A SONG

*She sang a song about Wichita
Now I can't sit still
Went a little like this...*

From "Wichita" by Virginia Coalition

For years, KFH had a monopoly on the Wichita radio market. Though there were several other stations in the early 1920s, KFH was the only one that survived, until 1936 when KANS went on the air. In 1940, Wichita gained a third station. The Farmers and Bakers Life Insurance Company of Wichita had purchased KFKB in Milford, Kansas, in 1931, from the infamous "goat gland doctor," John R. Brinkley. The station originally started in Wichita in 1923 as WAAP. When it folded after less than a year, Brinkley bought the transmitter and moved it to Milford.

Dr. John R. Brinkley
(Photo courtesy of KFDI Collection)

Paul Harvey
(Photo courtesy of KFDI Collection)

After the Farmers and Bankers Insurance Company purchased the station, they changed the call letters from KFKB to KFBI to reflect the name of their company. Soon thereafter, they moved the station to Abilene, Kansas. Plans from the beginning were to eventually move the station to Wichita and have the studios on the top floor of their company building at 1st and Market. That finally happened in 1940, while Paul Aurandt was the Station Manager. Aurandt would later become famously known as the news commentator, Paul Harvey.

Spark-O-Life Gang on KFBI
L-R: Margaret Tivora, Helen Tivora, Bill Boggs, Ted Cook,
Bob (last name unkonwn), Sleepy Rice, Nadine Westerfield, Elmer Gray,
Ted Johnson, Zeke Williams, Pauline "Polly" Campbell
(Photo courtesy of KFDI Collection)

As with most radio stations at the time, KFBI hired live performers for their programming. At one time there were 21 musicians on the staff. They included orchestra leader, Vern Nydegger, as well as a group of "hillbilly" musicians who often performed together as the Spark-O-Life Gang, on a program sponsored by the Spark-O-Life Feed Company. Zeke Williams was the leader of the group, which also included Bill Boggs on fiddle, Sleepy Rice on banjo, Elmer Gray on bass, Ted Cook, Roy Galen and Polly Campbell on guitars, two sisters, Margaret and Helen Tivara on accordion and bass, a steel guitar player named Bob, plus a couple of additional vocalists, Nadine Westerfield and Steve Wooden. These same performers also did the noontime show as the Dinner Bell Gang. For separate programming, these musicians often did solo acts or worked in other combinations. For example, Nadine Westerfield, who was the featured singer of the Spark-O-Life gang, also did a program where she sang blues and popular songs, backed by piano, organ and drums. Roy Galen and Zeke Williams fronted a group they called the Galen-Williams' Hillbilly Band. Bill Boggs recalled his time at KFBI. "Elmer Gray and I performed as the duo, Bill & Elmer. We sang the popular duet songs of the day like those from the Delmore Brothers. Our theme song was 'In the Pines.' We would kick off our Bill and Elmer show with our theme song, but first one of us would shout to studio engineer, Les Campbell, 'Let 'er go, Les!'"

Rambling Cowboys
L-R: Zeke Williams, Elmer Gray, Sleepy Rice, Dick (last name unknown)

Band leader, Zeke Williams had come to Wichita from Texas, where he and his Rambling Cowboys had been performing on the Texas Quality Network. A native of Dundee, Texas, Williams had begun his musical career with his brother, Doyle, at a radio station in Chickasha, Oklahoma. In 1937, Williams recorded 16 songs for the ARC and Vocalion labels.

When his brother left the radio station, Zeke teamed up with Everett Stanford who played bass fiddle and called himself "Hank the Cowhand." Stanford was one of the few musicians who could play a "triple slap" on the bass. He put his talents to good use in the mid-1950s when he began playing rockabilly music. Among the songs he recorded were "Popcorn Boogie," "Fan It and Cool It" and "She's a Hum Dum Dinger." In 1964, Stanford would become one of the first KFDI "Ranch Hands," where he adopted the moniker of "Willie the Hillbilly." Following his short stint as a DJ, Stanford left Wichita and ended up in Maryland, where he died of a heart attack following a show at a county fair in West Virginia. The Rockabilly Hall of Fame lists Stanford as a "rockabilly legend."

Hank Stanford, center with guitar
(Photo courtesy of KFDI Collection)

Zeke Williams and His Rambling Cowboys

When Zeke Williams arrived in Wichita, he brought with him two of his Rambling Cowboys, multi-instrumentalist, Sleepy Rice, and Steve Wooden, who was said to play a "mean take-off guitar." Williams, himself, was an accomplished fiddler who could play harmony to his own singing. He also did a solo program of sacred songs and poems using the name, Uncle Zeke. Along with their other performing duties on KFBI, the group continued to perform as Zeke Williams & His Rambling Cowboys.

When it came time for Williams to move on, he went to Shenandoah, Iowa to become a regular on KMA radio's *Cornbelt Jamboree*. By 1946, he had moved to WMMN in Fairmont, West Virginia, where he and his old friend, Hank Stanford, started the popular *Sagebrush Roundup*. That program helped spawn the careers of Little Jimmy Dickens, T. Texas Tyler, and Grandpa Jones.

* * *

Another of the acts hired by KFBI in the early 1940s was the husband and wife duo, Guy W. "Doc" Embree and his wife, Esther. Doc recalled, "Ernest Tubb was on KGKO in Fort Worth, and he used to come over and listen to some of the other entertainers, and we got to know him quite well. Later, when Ernest went to Nashville, he wanted us to go along, but my status in the draft was so uncertain. This was in

Esther and Doc Embree on KFBI

1940 and I didn't feel like turning my wife and our little boy, John, loose in a big city like Nashville. So, around Easter of 1941 we went up to my home in Iowa. Esther's folks were living in Colorado and we thought how nice it would be to get a job about halfway between her folks and my folks. We measured, and Grand Island, Nebraska was just about halfway. So, we drove west and didn't stop until we got to Grand Island. We went to KMMJ and auditioned for Ted Johnson. In those days, radio didn't pay anything, and they didn't want you around cluttering up the airways during the summer months. They thought that people didn't listen to the radio in the summertime. So, they would 'hire' entertainers in the wintertime, and you had to go out and make your own living by making personal appearances." The Embrees were not enamored with that arrangement, so they continued to Colorado where Doc took a job as a truck driver. The couple continued playing music and often performed at resorts like those around Estes Park.

"One Friday, I was helping deliver a piano up two flights of stairs, when Esther came down waving a telegram. It was from Ted Johnson, who had moved to KFBI in Wichita. He wanted us to go to work for him, provided we could be in Wichita the following Monday." Embree immediately quit his job and left the piano on the stairs. "We piled all of our belongings in the back seat of our faithful, old Buick, put Johnny on top of them, and headed for Wichita."

At that time, radio jobs did not pay well, so Doc and five other KFBI staff members took jobs at Beechcraft, working at the aircraft plant at night and at the radio station during the day. Everything changed on December 7, when the Japanese bombed Pearl Harbor. Doc tried to enlist in the Army. "They told me, 'You're a married man with a child. They'll take cripples before they take you.'" Embree recalled one of his fellow KFBI performers, banjo player, Sleepy Rice. "He was a terrific banjo player…didn't know one chord from another…didn't know what he was playing, but he could sure play. He had an aversion to beer. In order to disguise the beer smell, which got pretty bad when we were singing trios, he would take F&F cough drops. We sang very short choruses in those days."

Among the other performers the Embrees worked with at KFBI was Perry Douthit. In 1942, Embree sang the praises of Douthit in *The Mountain Broadcast and Prairie Recorder*: "He has developed into one of the best direct selling announcers in the business. Plays a very mean lick on the guitar, likes to sing Irish songs, and play hoe-downs on a little, old, B-flat harmonica. He can also make a bass fiddle say 'howdy.'"

Doc and Esther not only performed as a duet, they each performed solo, as well as with the large hillbilly band. Esther did her solo performances as Esther Gibson, the Texas Yodeling Cowgirl. She also teamed up with Nadine Westerfield and Perry Douthit as a western trio for KFBI'S *Range Roundup* program. In the fall of 1942, for no apparent reason, Doc and the five other performers who had gone to work at Beechcraft, were fired, so the Embrees moved back to Doc's home state of Iowa and got a job on KMA in Shenandoah.

* * *

When the act of Doc & Esther moved to Iowa in 1942, KFBI needed to replace them. They especially needed another cowgirl singer, so they held a contest. Unbeknownst to Pauline Drumm, her sister submitted her name. Drumm was soon to become popular on the radio as Polly Campbell. Pauline was a pretty, young singer from Burrton, Kansas. She recalled her early years. "I graduated from high school in Sedgwick and had learned to play the guitar. I was taught a lot from a woman in Newton named Parsons. I loved western songs and enjoyed singing in public. I used to sing at local concerts and churches, and even got to do a one-time performance on a Hutchinson radio station."

Because of her sister's letter, Drumm was invited to be a part of the talent contest in Wichita. When she walked on stage and saw the huge crowd, she was "scared to death." However, she sang her song and won first place. Her prize was $10. After

She Sang a Song

*Polly Campbell,
the Singing Sweetheart*
(Photo courtesy of KFDI Collection)

that, she went back home to Burrton. Several months had passed when she got a call from KFBI. They wanted her to be a regular on the radio.

"Since I was only 18 years old, and was a single girl from a small town, my dad wouldn't allow me to have my own apartment in Wichita. So, I moved in with my grandmother." A typical day for Pauline Drumm began at 5:00am when she got out of bed. "I would dress in my cowgirl outfit, with my hat and boots, grab my guitar and head for the bus stop down the street. On cold or rainy days, I would watch for the bus from my grandmother's front porch. When I saw it coming, I would run to meet it."

Drumm usually arrived at the KFBI studios in downtown Wichita, just in time for her 15-minute show, which began at 7:30am. She sang the western classics as well as popular country songs of the time. Pauline's most popular song was the Patsy Montana hit from 1935, "I Want to Be a Cowboy's Sweetheart." That song led her to become known on KFBI as "Polly, the Singing Sweetheart." "Polly" was the nickname given to Pauline by the radio station studio engineer, Les Campbell. In March of 1943, the two were married and Pauline Drumm became Polly Campbell.

Besides her early morning "Singing Sweetheart" show, Polly was also a part of KFBI's noontime show with the station's other country and western performers. They were known as the Dinner Bell Gang. This was the same bunch of musicians and singers who performed later in the afternoon as the Spark-O-Life Gang. Campbell laughed as she recalled one of the other singers on the program. "Steve Wooden, would get so frustrated about his performances that he would launch a few swear words right before the microphone came on for him to sing his hymn."

Polly's workday usually lasted until around 3:00pm when she would catch the bus back to her grandmother's house. Once she got married, life got a little easier. "Being married to the radio station's engineer certainly had its advantages. Les was able to record my early morning show so I didn't have to go to the station so early."

Ted Johnson
(Photo courtesy of KFDI Collection)

The various music programs on KFBI, including those by the Spark-O-Life Gang and the Dinner Bell Gang, were emceed by one of the station's announcers, Ted Johnson. In 1945, the Wichita police department began an investigation of the allegation that Johnson and another KFBI employee, Ralph Varnum, were embezzling money from KFBI to purchase equipment for their newly-opened advertising agency. Police officers entered KFBI and arrested Johnson, who implicated Varnum as the instigator of the plot. But a few days later, Johnson overdosed on sleeping pills that he got from a veterinarian. After he recovered from the overdose, Johnson returned to the same veterinarian and purchased some poison for his dog. He went back to his office at KFBI and swallowed the poison himself. He was taken, by ambulance, to the hospital where his life was saved once again. The exact amount taken from KFBI was $3,116.91. Hugh Aspinwall became the new announcer.

Performing on KFBI paid off for the musicians and singers because of the bookings they received and were able to promote on their radio shows. "We played all around the KFBI listening area," recalled Campbell. "Most of us didn't play at night clubs. We would perform at events like the Pretty Prairie Rodeo or the Herington Army Airfield officers' party. We also did shows in Wichita at the Masonic Home, the VA Hospital, and occasionally for a radio station promotion at a furniture store."

Polly Campbell ended her singing career on the radio in 1952, when her son, Gary, began going to school. However, she did return to radio for a short time in 1960. She and her duet partner, Francie Railing, sang on a recorded, gospel music show on KFH called *Hymn Time*.

Later in her life, Campbell went to work for the popular Wichita clothing store, Johnston's for Men. She retired in 2014 at the age of 90. These days, Polly no longer has any family in Wichita, so she loves spending time with her friends. She still drives her own car to do her grocery shopping, and she occasionally gets out her old, Martin guitar for her own enjoyment. Polly is a true Wichita treasure.

* * *

During the latter part of her singing cowgirl time on KFBI, Polly worked with the group that had replaced the Spark-O-Life Gang. They were known as the KFBI Ranch Boys and were headed by a couple of brothers from Virginia. Jim and Jesse McReynolds were born in the small town of Carfax. They began performing together at an early age. They tried to pattern themselves after the famous brother duos of the day; the Monroe Brothers, the Delmore Brothers, and the Blue Sky Boys. In 1945, the duo disbanded as Jim, the older of the two brothers, joined the Army. In 1985, Jim McReynolds told me, "Following my time in the service, Jesse and I got back together and took up where we left off two years earlier. We got a job playing

KFBI Ranch Boys
L-R: Randy Star, Jesse McReynolds, Sonny Albright, Jim McReynolds
(Photo courtesy of KFDI Collection)

on WNVA radio in Norton, Virginia. We spent a few months there and then moved on." Like most radio performers at that time, they would base themselves at a radio station and work live shows in the station's listening area. After they had worked all the venues in that area, they would move to another radio station and start the process all over again. In 1950, Jim and Jesse ended up in Wichita at KFBI.

Jesse recalled, "We had been working with Asher Sizemore on KXEL in Waterloo, Iowa. We were also doing the Hawkeye Jamboree at a theater there in Waterloo. I remember that's where I did my first comedy show. I was watching these other comedians and decided that I could do that, so I got me this big pair of britches and put my fiddle in one of the legs of the britches. I only tried comedy a few times. I tried it once after Jim and I went to Wichita. When I came out on stage in those big britches, Jim said, 'I thought I left you in Waterloo.'"

When Jim & Jesse arrived in Wichita, their sound changed in a big way. Jesse recalled, "We knew this country singer from Cedar Rapids, Iowa named Jerry Smith, and we had done some radio shows with him on WMY. Jerry was real popular around Wichita. He told us he could get us a job in Wichita, but we would have to change our sound. He said the band could make $40 a week, but we would have to play western music."

At KFBI, the McReynolds brothers did their duet act. Jim played guitar and Jesse played the mandolin. They also became part of the station's house band, the KFBI Ranch Boys. For that group, Jesse switched to the fiddle. With the addition of Sonny Albright on steel guitar and Randy Star on bass, the group played what came to be known as Country & Western music. Jim remembered, "Jesse and I were especially drawn to the western sounds of the harmony groups like the Sons of the Pioneers. We would find all these western records in the station library and learn the songs. Our favorite group was Foy

Jim (right) and Jesse McReynolds
(Photo courtesy of KFDI Collection)

Willing & the Riders of the Purple Sage." Jesse McReynolds was a talented and innovative musician. He was impressive on both the mandolin and the fiddle. He would later become known for his invention of the mandolin style called "cross picking." In 1969, he even played on the song, "Runnin' Blue," by the rock band, The Doors. During his stint as a KFBI Ranch Boy, Jesse enjoyed playing with other musicians and could often be found at Wichita's popular, country music, nightspot, the Cowboy Inn. "That was a pretty rough place," said Jesse. "One night I was playing there, and a woman was stabbed to death." The McReynolds brothers' stint in Wichita only lasted about a year. Jesse explained the reason for their departure. "One day we discovered that the radio station had been recording us and were syndicating our shows without telling us. We didn't think they were being fair to us, so we decided to leave."

After leaving Wichita, the McReynolds brothers soon landed at the *Kentucky Barn Dance* in Versailles, Kentucky. By then the group had become a trio, with the addition of another vocalist. In 1952, Jim & Jesse signed with Capitol Records. Once a 5-string banjo player was added, the group took on more of a bluegrass sound, and from that point on, Jim and Jesse were known as a "bluegrass" act. They became regulars on the *Grand Ole Opry* and played all the major bluegrass festivals. In 1993, Jim and Jesse were inducted into the Bluegrass Hall of Fame.

* * *

Mack Sanders
(*Photo courtesy of Wichita-Sedgwick Country Historical Museum*)

Though the McReynolds brothers moved on, the Ranch Boys continued to be the featured band on KFBI. John Bozeman, who went by the stage name, Mack Sanders, soon took over leadership of the Ranch Boys. Sanders began his radio career in 1938 in Birmingham, Alabama, but had arrived in Wichita from Shenandoah, Iowa. Besides his radio career, he was also a country music performer and recording artist. He became friends with Roy Clark and Jimmy Dean, with whom he owned several radio stations. He later partnered with Jimmy Dean to start the Jimmy Dean Sausage

Mack Sanders & the KFBI Ranch Boys with Jeannie Pierson
(Photo courtesy of Wichita-Sedgwick Country Historical Museum)

Company. However, Sanders sold his half of the company to Dean before it took off.

By 1951, Sanders had moved to Wichita where he went to work for KFH radio. He worked there for a short time before moving to KFBI to lead the Ranch Boys. Among the other members of the group at that time were DeWayne Pollard, Tommie Suggs, Jack Hazen, Steve Wooden, and Sanders' wife, Jeannie Pierson. Not long after Sanders began working at KFBI, he had the chance to interview Hank Williams. On September 14, 1951, Hank performed in Wichita as part of the *Hadacol Caravan* show, which traveled the country in 17 train cars. The show included Minnie Pearl and a host of other acts, including dancers, jugglers, and clowns. The *Hadacol Caravan* was the largest show of this kind ever staged. It had been scheduled in Wichita to coincide with the city's Frontier Days Rodeo. To accommodate shift workers at the aircraft plants, a second performance was added.

In July of 1953, a new television station went on the air in Hutchinson, Kansas. That station, known as KTVH, channel 12, added a remote studio in Wichita the following year. As part of their programming, KTVH hired Mack Sanders and the Ranch Boys to do a noontime program. On TV, Sanders became known as "Kansas Mack." By the early 1960s, Sanders was starring on a Thursday evening program on KAKE-TV, Channel 10, called *Prairie Party*.

In 1958, Sanders partnered with country music star, Webb Pierce to start a new radio station in Wichita. KSIR was located at 900 on the AM dial. It was the first full-time country music station in Wichita. (That station would later become KEYN, then KBUL. It is currently known as KSGL.) Pierce and Sanders and their Pier-San Broadcasting Company then purchased KOOO in Omaha and eventually owned radio stations in nine markets. One of those stations, purchased in 1967, was KFRM, located in Cloud County, Kansas near Concordia. It also had a remote studio in the

Miller Theater in Wichita. During the 1970s, Sanders built a new FM station in Wichita at 95.1 on the FM dial. As Sanders was a pilot, he used Wichita's airport designation, "ICT," as the basis of the station's call letters, KICT. Among the DJs on KFRM was Hank Penny, a country music star from Sanders' home state of Alabama.

* * *

Herbert Clayton "Hank" Penny was nearing the end of his career when he came to Wichita. Penny had been performing since the 1930s when, at the age of 17 he got a job playing the banjo on WAPI radio in Birmingham, Alabama. After he moved to WWL in New Orleans in 1936, he became interested in the western swing music of Bob Wills and Milton Brown. He soon moved back to Birmingham where he, at the age of 19, started his own band called the Radio Cowboys.

Penny and the band began recording in 1938. The next year, they recorded the song for which Hank Penny is best-known, "Won't You Ride in My Little Red Wagon." Penny and the group were on their way to major success until 1940, when it appeared that the U.S. was on the brink of war and several of the Radio Cowboys were drafted. The band came to an end, and Penny went to work as the morning DJ on WSB in Atlanta. He was paid $35 a week, and by the summer of the next year, he had put together a new band. He worked for a short time at KXEL in Waterloo, Iowa, but was soon back at WSB. The next year, Hank moved to WLW in Cincinnati and

Hank Penny and the Radio Cowboys

Hank Penny

became a part of their *Boone County Jamboree* as well as their *Midwestern Hayride*. There he formed another band which he called the Plantation Boys. After a successful USO tour of the South in 1944, that group disbanded.

Hank Penny's next move was to California where he put together yet another band, but that group did not last long either. For a short time, Hank fronted an all-girl band in Los Angeles. In 1946, Penny was with a band called the Painted Post Rangers, named for Hoot Gibson's night club, the Painted Post. The group recorded for King Records and had two Top 5 hits with "Steel Guitar Stomp" and "Get Yourself a Red Head." After numerous band changes and radio jobs, Penny landed in the Top 5 again in 1950 with "Bloodshot Eyes." He also recorded a song called "Hillbilly Bebop," making him the first country music performer to record the bebop style of Jazz.

In 1952, Penny had his own TV show on KHI-TV in Los Angeles, but his recording career stalled. In 1954, he moved to Las Vegas where he worked at the Golden Nugget for seven years. During the last couple of those years, one of the members of Hank's band was Roy Clark. Following a few years in Carson City, Nevada, Penny moved to Nashville where he almost got a starring part in a new TV show called *Hee Haw*. Instead, the part was given to Hank's former band member, Roy Clark. So, in 1972, Mack Sanders asked Penny to move to Wichita and go to work as a DJ on KFRM. He did that for three years, then moved back to California. Hank Penny died on April 17, 1992 of a heart attack.

* * *

Another programming coup that Mack Sanders was able to pull off was getting the well-known, gospel quartet, the Plainsmen, to relocate to Wichita in 1967. Begun in 1956 as a split-off of the Stamps Quartet, the Plainsmen rose to fame and became especially noted for singing backup on Johnny Horton's 1960 #1 hit, "North to Alaska." That recording was made for the movie of the same name which starred

John Wayne. Prior to moving to Wichita, the Plainsmen were based out of Louisiana and had been working with former governor, Jimmie Davis, who was best known for his hit, "You Are My Sunshine." One of the members of the Plainsmen during that time was a young man named Sherrill Nielsen, who became known for his work with Elvis Presley under the name of Shaun Nielsen. While in Wichita, Nielsen left the Plainsmen and started his own group, Shaun Nielsen & the Good Ole Boys. When the opportunity came to join the famous Statesmen quartet, Nielsen accepted. That association led to working with Presley in a trio called VOICE. Meanwhile, the Plainsmen continued to tour around the country, while remaining based out of Wichita and KFRM until 1977, when Mack Sanders moved his operations to Nashville.

Plainsmen Quartet
Clockwise from Upper Left:
Jay Simmons, Jack Mainord,
Leon "Lee" Simmons,
Howard Welborn

KICT exists to this day, though since 1979 it has been playing rock music under the slogan "T-95." The name of Pier-San Broadcasting was changed to Great American Broadcasting and the company was eventually sold. Following the sale of his stations, Sanders turned right around and started acquiring more stations.

By 1992, Mack Sanders had moved to Hot Springs, Arkansas, where he continued to do a radio show on one of the stations he owned. Throughout most of his career, Sanders had been successfully married to Sherry Bryce, who had several duet hits with Mel Tillis in the 1970s. Mack passed away in 2003 and was inducted posthumously into the Country Radio Hall of Fame in 2005.

* * *

Harry "Hap" Peebles

From his offices in Wichita beginning in 1933, Harry "Hap" Peebles, the "Dean of Country Music Promoters," became one of the most successful promoters of country music in the nation. He was the first promoter to get county and state fairs to book country music acts for their grandstand shows, as well as being one of the first to put country and rock & roll acts on the same show. He enjoyed baseball and in the 1930s, became the publicity director for the National Semi-Pro Baseball Congress. Though Peebles also promoted rodeos, racing, and circuses, it is his country music package shows for which he is best known. Many of his Hatch Show Print posters advertising his concerts have become collectors' items. He became known for his honesty, and many performers were booked without a contract. In 1958, Peebles help found the Country Music Association in Nashville. That same year, he also complained that rock & roll was killing country music. Following a three-week tour with some of country music's biggest stars, he told The Music Reporter that he "dropped slightly over $20,000. I averaged about a thousand dollars a day loss on the tour."

Though he promoted shows throughout the U.S., Hap Peebles loved to bring country stars to Wichita. On the night of November 26, 1960, he booked one of his big, package shows in the Forum auditorium. The show, which was hosted by Mack Sanders of KSIR, featured Tex Ritter, Carl Perkins, Moon Mullican, Australia's LeGarde Twins, Gary Van & His Western Starlighters, the Plainsmen, Hawkshaw Hawkins and Jean Shepard. The highlight of the evening came when Hawkshaw Hawkins and Jean Shepard exchanged wedding vows on-stage. Ken Nelson of Capitol Records was the best man, and Hap Peebles gave away the bride. The Plainsmen provided the music for the ceremony, which was enjoyed by around a thousand fans.

Peebles also won the CMA's first award for Talent Buyer and Promoter of the Year. By 1963, the Peebles Agency was promoting 25 country music package shows in a hundred cities in 12 midwestern states. That same year, Johnny Cash presented

Hap Peebles an award for, in Cash's words, "elevating the image of country and western music throughout the U.S., and for his dedication and loyalty to country and western performers."

On January 24, 1963, a former DJ on KANS radio in Wichita, Jack Wesley "Cactus Jack" Call was on his way home from his job at Kansas City radio station, KCMK-FM. Just five minutes from home, his car collided with a truck. He died the next day from his injuries, leaving a wife and two young sons. One of Call's co-workers, Guy Smith, contacted Hap Peebles and country star, Billy Walker, about doing a benefit show for the family. George Jones was already performing in Kansas, so he was the first to sign on. Peebles and Walker felt that they needed a female star, and since Call's favorite had been Patsy Cline, they contacted her. She agreed to come. It turned out to be a huge show. Others that performed included Hawkshaw Hawkins, Cowboy Copas, Dottie West, Wilma Lee & Stoney Cooper, George McCormick & the Clinch Mountain Boys and, of course, Billy Walker. On the way back to Nashville, the small plane carrying Patsy Cline, Hawkshaw Hawkins, Cowboy Copas and Cline's manager and pilot, Randy Hughes, went down and all four were killed.

By the late 1960s, Hap Peebles was promoting over a hundred country music shows a year. He was on the CMA's board of directors for 16 years. Never one to rest on his laurels, Peebles was always ready to try new ideas, including crazy things like ostrich racing. On May 14, 1965, Mack Sanders and Hap Peebles teamed up to produce a major country music concert at two venues at the same time, the WSU Field House and Lawrence Dumont Stadium. The WSU concert began at 7pm and the concert at the baseball stadium started at 8. Performers included: Jimmy Dean, Carl Smith, Faron Young, Roy Clark, Wanda Jackson, George Morgan, Jean Shepard, Mac Wiseman, Cates Sisters, Del Reeves, Moon Mullican, and Darrell McCall.

Hap Peebles died on January 4, 1993 from a kidney ailment. He was 80. In 1980, he had founded the International Entertainment Buyers Association. In his honor, the IEBA developed the Harry "Hap" Peebles Lifetime Achievement Award. In 1998, that award was presented to a performer who had spent a lot of time in Wichita, Charlie Daniels.

CHAPTER FOUR

A ROAD IS JUST A ROAD

No matter where you go, from Waterloo to Wichita
A road is just a road that the one you love is leaving on

From "A Road Is Just a Road" by Mary Chapin Carpenter

(Mary Chapin Carpenter, John Jennings)

Another successful musician who worked at KFBI in the early 1940s was a singer/fiddler named Jimmy Hall. Born in Vinita, Oklahoma in 1921, Hall's family moved to Wichita when he was only six. By the time he graduated high school, Hall had become interested in music and had learned to play the fiddle. Though still a teenager, he moved to Salina, Kansas in 1938 and got a job playing his fiddle on KSAL. In the spring of 1940, KFBI in Abilene relocated to Wichita and needed musicians. Young Jimmy Hall saw this as an opportunity to move back home. He applied and was hired to become one of the staff musicians on KFBI. After a year or so, he moved to Tulsa, Oklahoma and took a job with KTUL. Called to duty during World War II, Hall joined the Army in 1943. Following a three-year stint, he moved back to Tulsa and took a job as fiddler and vocalist in the band of former Bob Wills & the Texas Playboys steel guitarist, Leon McAuliffe. While with McAuliffe, Jimmy Hall wrote songs like "Bitter Tears" and "TULSA Straight Ahead."

Jimmy Hall

By the early 1950s, Hall was back in Wichita, this time on KFH as a member of the Ark Valley Boys. He also put together his own band and got a job performing at Wichita's popular Cowboy Inn.

* * *

Among the band members Jimmy Hall recruited for his band was a young guitar player from Oklahoma named Tommy Allsup. Allsup had begun his career in Claremore, Oklahoma in 1949 as a member of the Oklahoma Swingbillies. A year later

Tommy Allsup and the Southernaires
L-R: Louie Tiemey, Louise Rowe Allsup, Tommy Allsup, Mansel Tierney, Danny Lucas, Chuck Caldwell

he joined the band of Miami, Oklahoma fiddle player, Art Davis. Before long, he got the call from Jimmy Hall in Wichita. After a couple of years playing with Hall at the Cowboy Inn, Allsup moved to Tulsa to become a member of Johnnie Lee Wills and His Boys. However, his tenure with Wills lasted only a short time. In 1953, Allsup decided to form his own band which he called The Southernaires. For five years, they were the house band at the Southern Club in Lawton, Oklahoma.

Allsup also began making records under his own name. In 1958, he went to Norman Petty's studio in Clovis, New Mexico. While there, he met Petty's most-successful client, Buddy Holly. Holly had recently split with his band, The Crickets, so he talked Allsup into joining his new band as lead guitar player. Holly also hired a young Waylon Jennings to play bass. Buddy Holly's career ended on February 3, 1959 in a plane crash near Mason City, Iowa, which also took the lives of J.P. Richardson (The Big Bopper) and Ritchie Valens. Both Allsup and Jennings were scheduled to be aboard that plane, but Jennings gave his seat to the ailing Richardson and Allsup "lost" his seat in a coin toss with Valens.

Tommy Allsup

Tragically out of a job, Allsup moved to California where he went to work for Liberty Records as their Country & Western A&R Director. While at Liberty, he began producing records. Among the first performers he worked with were Bob Wills and the Texas Playboys. In May of 1963, Wills and his band recorded 14 songs for Liberty at the Radio Recorders studio in Hollywood, California. Tommy Allsup not only produced those recordings, he also played rhythm guitar and bass. The Texas Playboys at the time included two other former Wichita musicians, Gene Crownover and Gene Gasaway. Ten years later, Allsup produced Bob Wills' final album, *For the Last Time*. He also played bass during the session. During his time at Liberty, Allsup produced dozens of artists, including Tex Williams and Willie Nelson. In 1972, he met Ray Benson, leader of the band, Asleep at the Wheel, and the following year he produced the group's debut album, *Comin' Right at Ya*, for United Artists. When Asleep at the Wheel moved to Capitol in 1975, Allsup again became their producer and worked with them on four albums. He continued to produce albums by the Original Texas Playboys, Hank Thompson, and others until he died on January 11, 2017 following complications from hernia surgery. He was 85. I once visited with Tommy Allsup in the KFDI record library. We were both drinking coffee and I accidentally took a sip from Tommy's coffee cup. I'm not sure what he had put in his coffee, but it was the worst tasting liquid I had ever put in my mouth.

* * *

When African American jazz and blues guitarist, Berry Harris moved to Wichita he got jobs playing music in all sorts of different clubs, even those that were not in his usual element. Like Jimmy Hall and Tommy Allsup, Harris sometimes worked at the Cowboy Inn on West Street. In an interview with Wichita historian, Pat O'Connor, Harris noted, "We had to play a lot of country music. I was familiar with it, having grown up with it." Harris was born and raised in Oklahoma where one of the few radio programs he heard on a regular basis was the *Grand Ole Opry*. He went on to become somewhat of a local legend as a blues guitarist and continued to play right up until just before he died on April 6, 2020 at the age of 90.

Berry Harris

CHAPTER FIVE

WICHITA JAIL

*'Cause in thirty more days I'm goin' back home
To see that gal of mine, but the Wichita jail is a long, long way
From the Tupelo County Line.*

From "Wichita Jail" by Charlie Daniels

Following World War II, one of the most popular dance clubs to emerge on the scene in Wichita was the Hi-Ho Club, where "every night is a Saturday night." Located near the northwest corner of Broadway and 47th Street South, the Hi-Ho was originally known for big band and swing music. Though guest performers were often featured, groups like Wichita's own Esquire Jumptette, played at the Hi-Ho on a regular basis between 1946 and 1949. As the 1950s came along, music at the Hi-Ho shifted to country music and rock & roll. Bobby Koefer, who was from Clay Center, and had been a member of Bob Wills' Texas Playboys, played at the Hi-Ho for five years during the 1950s.

The mixture of music, dancing, and alcohol can sometimes lead to violence. The Hi-Ho Club was no exception. For undetermined reasons, a homemade bomb blasted the rear of the Hi-Ho at 2:47 on the morning of November 9, 1959. The blast shook houses six blocks away. A second bomb, made from four sticks of dynamite, failed to explode.

Among the various groups performing at the Hi-Ho in the early 1960s was the rock & roll band, Billy Joe & His Confidentials. Billy Joe went on to record as a solo artist for labels like Paula and Jewel, using his full name, Billy Joe Young. Several of his songs were written by another regular performer at the Hi-Ho during the 1960s, Charlie Daniels. Charlie Daniels & the Jaguars were more of a rock & roll band that played mostly the pop hits of the day. Daniels fondly recalled his time in Wichita. "We'd come into town and play regularly at the Hi-Ho for a few weeks or even a few months at a time. Then we'd leave and go to Tulsa for a while and come back to Wichita and do it again. That was in 1963 and 1964. We always stayed at a little Hawaiian-themed place called the Aloha Motel. When we first came to Wichita,

Charlie Daniels and the Jaguars
L-R: Charlie Daniels, Buddy Davis, (unknown), Vic Catalino

folks wanted us to do western swing like Bob Wills. We had heard of Bob Wills, but we didn't know any of his music. But we soon learned some and started doing some of his stuff."

Tom Green, who became somewhat of a rock & roll legend in Wichita, recalled Charlie Daniels from his days at the Hi-Ho. "I was with a band called the Squires. Our main gig was at the Hi-Ho Club, which is where Charlie Daniels & the Jaguars used to play. The Jaguars were a great band and Charlie was killing it with his fiddle back then, as he does today." Other members of the Jaguars were Buddy Davis on drums, Vic Catalino (aka William Vickers) on tenor sax, and Joey DiGregorio on the Hammond B-3 organ. DiGregorio, who was later known as Taz, became a longtime member of the Charlie Daniels Band.

Daniels recalled an incident that took place while he was playing at the Hi-Ho. "One night the police came in the club and picked up a friend of mine, and they took him to jail for something that had happened. I'm pretty sure it was the same day that John F. Kennedy was shot. (November 22, 1963) And I went down to get him out. I was hollerin' outside the jail, 'Hey Jack!' The cops told him later, 'We almost put that big guy in jail.' I almost ended up on the wrong side of the bars in Wichita. So that's where I got the idea for 'Wichita Jail.'" That song was released in 1976 and became Charlie Daniels' third chart record. Three years later, he hit #1 and was awarded the Country Music Association's Single of the Year for "The Devil Went Down to Georgia."

Though Tom Green played at the Hi-Ho as a member of one of Wichita's premiere rock & roll bands, the Squires, he cut his teeth on country music. "When I was very young, and underage, I would

Tom Green

play the animal circuit (Moose and Elks Clubs) with Clay Cerday's country band. Clay knew my dad from Boeing and asked my folks if they would let me play guitar in his band, if he would take care of me and be responsible for me. That's where I developed my love for the classic country music of the '50s, including the amazing Ray Price. Another friend of the family was a real good country guitar player named Ray Shores. He used to take me to the country jam sessions around Wichita and let me sit in with the bands."

* * *

Some performers, like Charlie Daniels, would come to Wichita to play in clubs like the Hi-Ho and stick around a while. Others, such as Roy Clark, would only stay in town for a short time. In September of 1962, Clark, who had recently signed with Capitol Records, worked at the Hi-Ho Club for two weeks. Immediately following his stint in Wichita, Roy moved to Las Vegas to become a headliner in the casinos. In 1963, he became the first Country performer to host the Tonight Show.

Roy Clark

Sometime in the late 1960s, the name of the Hi-Ho Club was changed to the Western Swinger. Though still a popular dance spot, the music tended to focus more on country and western swing, though occasionally rock & roll bands were featured, such as Mike Finnegan's band, the Serfs.

* * *

Not far from the Hi-Ho Club, on the east side of 47th and South Broadway, was another popular night spot. Like most clubs of the day, the Stardust showcased not only local bands, but also touring acts. One such performer was rockabilly singer, Chuck Miller. Charles Nelson Miller was born in Wellington, Kansas on August 30, 1924. As a child, he learned how to play the piano. His idols were jazz pianist, Fats Waller, and Moon Mullican, the "King of the Hillbilly Piano Players." Miller also enjoyed singing, so he honed his craft and moved to California in the mid-1940s and became a part of the Los Angeles music scene. In 1953, Miller was signed by Capitol Records, where he recorded such boogie-woogie songs as, "Hopahula Boogie" and "Idaho Red." When performed by country artists like the Delmore Brothers, Tennessee Ernie Ford, and Red Foley, boogie-woogie music began to be called hillbilly boogie or just country boogie. This soon led to the style of music that crossed country music with rock & roll. They called it "rockabilly." Chuck Miller fit right in with this category of music.

Chuck Miller

In 1955, Miller moved from Capitol to Mercury where he had his first big hit with "House of Blue Lights," a song that had first been sung in 1946 by Ella Mae Morse when she sang with Freddie Slack's band. Chuck Miller's recording of "House of Blue Lights" became a Top 10 pop hit. Other singles followed with little success. However, the following year Miller recorded a song that had just been released by a newcomer, Leroy VanDyke. It was called "The Auctioneer." VanDyke recorded for the small Dot label which was based out of Gallatin, Tennessee. Chuck Miller was on the big, Chicago-based Mercury label.

Logic suggests that Miller should have had the bigger hit with "The Auctioneer" but it wasn't to be. Though Miller's version made it to #59 on the pop charts, VanDyke's original version made it to #19 on the pop charts and all the way to #9 on the country charts. Chuck Miller never had another hit after that, but he did continue to tour the country and perform on a regular basis in places like the Starlight in Wichita.

B.W. Norris of Wichita, a cousin of Chuck Miller, recalled meeting Miller at a family reunion in Wellington. "My only firsthand recollection of Chuck probably happened around 1957, '58 or so. I would have been five or six years old. There was a family event at Lake Wellington. I still remember seeing a car pull up, and this hep cat looking dude gets out……all decked out in a suit and Ray Ban type sunglasses……sort of the original 'sharp dressed man' look. Of course, I was drafted to go over to his table to ask him to sing us a tune. He just looked down at me over the top of his shades and said, 'I'm a night bird baby.' I am not sure I really understood his reply at the time, but even at that young age I was pretty impressed."

Chuck Miller continued to play music for the rest of his life, moving to Boise Idaho and then to Alaska. For a while he played at a club at Lake Tahoe, and eventually ended up in Hawaii, where he played at Maui's The Whales Tale. He died in Maui in 2000 at the age of 75.

CHAPTER SIX

GUITAR MEN

Night after night, who treats you right, baby, it's the guitar man
Who's on the radio, you know, baby, it's the guitar man
When he comes to town and you see his face
And you think you might like to take his place

From "Guitar Man" by Bread

(David Gates)

One of the most successful country music bands in Wichita in the early 1950s was a group composed mostly of kids. The band, known as Bobby Wiley and the Rhythmaires, was led by 11-year-old steel guitar player, Bobby Wiley. Wiley's parents, Milo and Grace, were the owners of a music store. For a time, Milo Wiley had played ukulele in the band of country music star, Jimmie Davis. Wiley was a part of Davis' touring band during the time of his successful campaign for Governor of Louisiana. After moving to Wichita, Milo and his wife, Grace, started a music store originally called South Sea Island Studios. Wiley loved to play the steel guitar, especially on Hawaiian music. It was the love of that music that led to the name of the store.

In 1947 Milo Wiley became one of the first Fender guitar dealers. Leo Fender had started his guitar company the previous year, specializing in steel guitars. It was Wiley who suggested to Leo Fender that he make steel guitars with the tuning keys facing upward instead of out the side of the peghead like standard guitars. This suggestion by Wiley made it much easier for steel guitarists to tune their instruments. In 1950 Leo Fender began making electric "standard" guitars, that he soon called Fender Telecasters.

Growing up in a musical family whose parents owned a music store, it was only natural that young Bobby would become a musician. By the time he was 10, he spent his summer playing with Smiley Burnette, who was best-known as the movie sidekick of Gene Autry, Roy Rogers, and Charles Starrett, the Durango Kid. Though known more for his role as a comedy sidekick, Burnette was a talented musician who could play dozens of instruments. Bobby Wiley performed with Burnette for two summers.

Bobby Wiley and the Rhythmaires
L-R: *Bobby Wiley, Jim Vetter, Bernie Rozell, Bob Smith, Jerry Hahn*
(Photo courtesy of Jerry Hahn)

While he was back in Wichita, he got with some friends and they started the group which was billed as Bobby Wiley & the Rhythmaires. They were soon playing dances in the small town of Kechi, just north of Wichita. Besides Bobby Wiley, who was 11 at the time, the group also included two 11-year-old rhythm guitar players, Bernie Rozell and Jerry Hahn. A third guitar player, Jim Vetter, played lead guitar until Jerry Hahn took over that position. The group was rounded out by Bob Smith on bass and fiddle.

Bobby Wiley

Wichita's first television station, KEDD, went on the air in 1953. Bob Olander, who appeared on TV as a cowboy named "Cheyenne," (not to be confused with the TV cowboy portrayed by Clint Walker) hosted a program called the *Bar 16 Ranch*. He invited Bobby Wiley & the Rhythmaires to become part of the show. By that time, the group had added Mac McKinzie on drums. McKinzie was later replaced by Jimmy Knight, who was then replaced by Jerry Hahn's best friend, Ronnie DeGrant. Bobby Wiley's cousin, Diane Hamilton was also added as a vocalist. The group performed on KEDD for three years and underwent a couple more personnel changes during that time. Anita "Hoppy" McCune was added as a singer and guitarist. She brought some credibility to the *Bar 16 Ranch*, as she owned her own horse and considered herself a real cowgirl. Gary Andrus also replaced Bernie Rozell.

Besides performing on the weekday *Bar 16 Ranch* show, the band eventually got their own program, *The Bobby Wiley Rhythmaires Show*, which aired on Thursday nights. Major country music stars often appeared on their show, including Hank Williams, Hank Thompson, Hank Snow, Little Jimmy Dickens, and others. Broadcasts on KEDD ended in 1956, due to the station being on UHF channel 16. Most television sets in Wichita and around the country at that time only had VHF receivers which could go no higher than channel 13. The KEDD studios in north Wichita became the home of KTVH (now KWCH) which operated on channel 12.

In 1959, Bobby Wiley switched from steel guitar to standard guitar so he could play jazz and pop music. Like his father, Wiley also became an innovator and inventor. In 1967 he came up with a gizmo that made a guitar sound like an organ. He called it the Guitorgan Guitar Synth. In 1973, he invented the Auto Orchestra, which could make a guitar sound like a variety of different guitars and even other instruments. In later years Bobby could be found playing swing and jazz with fiddler Bill Boggs, who had been a member of the Ark Valley Boys. Even at the time of his passing in 2014, Wiley was in the process of world-wide marketing of his unusual invention known as the Ministar guitar. The Ministar was mainly a guitar neck without a body. Because of its small size, the Ministar was starting to become popular among musicians who traveled on planes.

Jerry Hahn

* * *

The 11-year-old guitar player, Jerry Hahn, also went on to bigger and better things. He started playing guitar when he was only seven and ended up making a career of it. After studying at Wichita State University, Hahn moved to California in 1962 and became an in-demand, jazz guitarist. He worked with jazz saxophonist, John Handy, and jazz vibraphonist, Gary Burton. He even toured as a member of the band for the pop group, 5th Dimension. Hahn formed his own group called the Jerry Hahn Quintet, and later put together another band, which featured the keyboards and vocals of fellow Wichitan, Mike Finnegan. The group was called the Jerry Hahn Brotherhood. In 1970, they released an album on Columbia. The music was a fusion of rock, jazz, blues, and even a bit of country. One of the songs on the album, "Captain Bobby Stout," was later covered by the British rock group, Manfred Mann's Earth Band. Jerry Hahn went on to become one of the most revered jazz guitarists in the world.

He was still playing country music in 1956 when 16-year-old Jerry Hahn went to Nashville to perform on the Ernest Tubb Midnight Jamboree at Tubb's famous record shop, playing guitar for Wichita country singer, Sammy Hart. Born Ralph Krenzer in Susank, Kansas on September 18, 1930, the boy who would become known as Sammy Hart moved to Wichita with his family when he was twelve. He got an early taste of country music by listening to Corky Edminster's band on a regular basis. "I was only 12 or 13 and I got a job as an usher at the Nomar Theater. Corky's Corral Gang from KANS played there once a week. I think it was Thursday or Friday night."

Sammy Hart at Ernest Tubb Record Shop
Jerry Hahn (far right)
(Photo courtesy of Ralph Krenzer)

Following a variety of jobs, Ralph's father, Mathew, established a barber shop inside the Eaton Hotel on East Douglas. After World War II, the Krenzer family purchased a farm near Olpe, Kansas. When Ralph married his wife, Betty, the couple moved to Wichita where he got a job working for Boeing until he decided to follow in his father's footsteps and become a barber. By that time, Krenzer loved country music, especially western swing. He enjoyed singing and taught himself to play the guitar. He recalled his beginnings as a musician. "I walked into a pawn shop in downtown Wichita and saw this old guitar hanging there, so I bought it. It was probably a terrible guitar. The neck was all bowed." Owning a guitar was one thing but learning how to play it was another. "I went down to see Milo Wiley at his music store to take lessons. At the first lesson, he handed me a piece of paper and told me to learn these notes. I took a look at that piece of paper, left the store, and never went back for a second lesson."

After a while, Krenzer had taught himself enough guitar that he felt comfortable enough to start a band. He was encouraged by his brother-in-law, Tom Kerby, who was a popular DJ on KANS radio. Kerby suggested to Krenzer that he should change his name. "He said that nobody would remember 'Krenzer'. He already called me Sammy anyway, so we just chose the name Sammy Hart. I started my first band around 1954 or '55. I just called it Sammy Hart and His Western Swing." It was a band name that he would use on and off for years while occasionally pursuing other musical ventures. Early band members included Webb Tipton on lead guitar, Ira Newton on steel guitar, Al Casey on fiddle, saxophone, and upright bass, and Dub

Tom Kerby's KANS Corral Gang
L-R: Sammy Hart, Mac McKinzie, Webb Tipton,
Dale Cantrell, Jerry Sisk, Al Casey
(Photo courtesy of Ralph Krenzer)

Tom Kerby's KANS Corral Gang
L-R: Ira Newton, Webb Tipton, Mac McKinzie,
Sammy Hart, Al Casey, Dale Cantrell
(Photo courtesy of Ralph Krenzer)

James on bass and drums. Besides working with his own band, Hart also became the front man for steel guitarist, Tony Rico, and his band the Moonlighters. Along with Rico and Hart, the Moonlighters also included Royal McCaskey on lead guitar and brothers, Dub and Chuck James on bass and drums, respectively.

Since 1949, Corky Edminster had been performing on KANS with his band, Corky's Corral Gang, following their controversial exit from KFH. In 1955, KANS was purchased by former vaudeville entertainer, Frank Lynch, and his partner, Ken Brown. Edminster and his band soon moved on. Though often referred to as Corky's Corral Gang, the full name of the group was Corky's KANS Corral Gang. Under the Frank Lynch ownership of KANS, the band was led by Tom Kerby, even though he was not a musician nor a singer. Still, the band was renamed Tom Kerby's KANS Corral Gang. Lead singer and front man for the new version of the band was Kerby's brother-in-law, Ralph Krenzer, aka. Sammy Hart. Besides Hart, the band once again included Webb Tipton on lead guitar and Al Casey on fiddle, sax, and bass. The group was rounded out by Jerry Sisk on steel guitar and Mac McKinzie, formerly of Bobby Wiley & the Rhythmaires, on drums. They performed live on KANS weekday mornings at 6:00.

It was while he was working for KANS that Hart went to Nashville to cut a record at the Ernest Tubb Record Shop. Unfortunately, nothing happened with that record. "I always wanted to make it big time, but I raised twelve children, so I thought I kind of needed to stay around. I think the good Lord knew where I needed to be."

In 1958, Frank Lynch and Ken Brown sold KANS to a California group who changed the call letters to KLEO and began programming Top 40 music. In 1962, Lynch returned to Wichita and purchased the former KFBI from Hollywood stars, Mary Pickford and Buddy Rogers. The celebrity couple had been operating the station as a pop station, using the call letters, KIRL, for the last two years. Lynch changed the call letters to KFDI and began doing a lot of sports and religious programming, along with a healthy dose of country music. Among the DJs he hired was Tom Kerby. Soon Sammy Hart and his band were also on KFDI, this time as the Country Rhythm Boys.

Besides playing clubs, such as the 505 Club on East Douglas, Sammy Hart and his band were regulars in Derby, Kansas, at the *Derby Barn Dance* and the *Big D Jubilee*. Hart worked with a lot of musicians over the years, including Dale Cantrell, Earl Clothier, Jack Crandall, Rusty Rector, Bobby Koefer, Curly Lewis, and many others. Occasionally the band got to back nationally known artists, like Marvin Rainwater.

In the early 1980s, Hart formed the High Country Show Band with once again brothers Dub and Chuck James, along with Billy Helms on lead guitar. As band members retired or passed away, Hart taught himself how to play the piano. Even now, though in his 90s, Hart continues to perform at area VFW clubs, using his real name, Ralph Krenzer. He loves to play golf and still gives haircuts to his old friends.

CHAPTER SEVEN

GONNA FIND ME A BLUEBIRD

Gonna find me a bluebird, let him sing me a song
'Cause my heart's been broken much too long.
From "Gonna Find Me a Bluebird" by Marvin Rainwater

"Whatever happened to Marvin Rainwater?" That was one of the most-asked questions of country music disc jockeys in Wichita during the 1970s and '80s. Born Marvin Karlton Percy on July 2, 1925 in Wichita, Rainwater was sometimes called a "one hit wonder." But that one hit was a smash. "Gonna Find Me a Bluebird" made it to #3 on the Billboard country music charts and became a million-seller. It is likely that the only reason the song did not make it to #1 was because Ferlin Husky held that spot for ten consecutive weeks with his hit, "Gone."

Marvin Rainwater

Rainwater used his mother's maiden name as his stage name. He would sometimes perform on stage wearing a full Native American headdress. His early publicity emphasized that Rainwater was a full-blooded Cherokee. In fact, Marvin's mother was half Cherokee, making him one fourth Native American. Though he did not live in Wichita for long, some locals claim to have known him during childhood. At the age of eight, Marvin began playing classical music on the piano. As a teenager, he lost part of his right thumb in an accident so his classical music skills on the piano ended. He attended Washington State University where he majored in mathematics. He had planned to become a veterinarian but that changed when World War II broke out and he joined the Navy. It was there that he picked up the guitar and began performing for his shipmates.

After two years in the Navy, Marvin moved to Oregon and became a tree surgeon in the logging camps. While there he fell in love with the music of Roy Acuff, the King of Country Music, and started writing country songs. He moved to Virginia and performed country music with his brothers. He began to emphasize his native heritage by changing his last name to Rainwater and wearing a buckskin jacket and Indian headband on-stage.

In 1946 Rainwater went into a local studio and recorded 50 songs. Some of those records were heard by Red Foley. In 1954, when Foley began his Springfield, Missouri based, *Ozark Jubilee* TV show, he invited Marvin to appear as a guest performer. That led to a recording contract with 4 Star Records and later for Coral Records. None of the records Rainwater recorded for those companies did much. However, the next step was a 1955 TV appearance on *Arthur Godfrey's Talent Scouts*. There he sang "Gonna Find Me a Bluebird." He was brought back for four straight weeks, which led to him performing on Godfrey's morning radio show.

Things were starting to move fast for Rainwater. He got a job performing at the Shamrock Club in Washington, D.C. and then became a cast member of the WWVA *Wheeling Jamboree* in Wheeling, West Virginia. From there it was back to Springfield, Missouri, where he became an official cast member of Red Foley's *Ozark Jubilee*. A recording contract with MGM Records soon followed. Rainwater's songwriting was also starting to pay off. One of his songs, "I Gotta Go Get My Baby," was a Top 10 hit for country music singer Justin Tubb, and then became a pop hit for Teresa Brewer.

Rainwater's stardom rose to the top in 1957 when MGM released "Gonna Find Me a Bluebird," which became an instant hit. The song spent 28 weeks on the country music charts. It also made the Top 20 on the pop charts, making Rainwater one of the first

Marvin Rainwater (center) with Sammy Hart and his Band
(Photo courtesy of Ralph Krenzer)

country music performers to cross over to pop. Several other songs landed on the country music charts but he never had another Top 10 country hit. "Whole Lotta Woman" and "Nothin' Needs Nothin' (Like I Need You)" both made the Top 20, and "Whole Lotta Woman" even became a #1 pop hit in Great Britain, which made Rainwater an international star. Much of the music he was recording was what was called rockabilly. For the most part, his records were not doing all that well on the country charts, but his songs eventually would. One of his songs, "I Miss You Already (And You're Not Even Gone,)" was a big hit for Faron Young in 1957. It also became a hit for Jimmy Newman in 1960 and Billy Joe Royal in 1986. Carl Smith had a minor hit with Rainwater's "Be Good to Her" in 1965. Rainwater also had songs recorded by Harry Nilsson and Petula Clark.

In 1959, Rainwater had his last Top 20 record with a song written by John D. Loudermilk called "Half Breed." He was also the first to record another Loudermilk composition called, "The Pale Faced Indian." Though Rainwater had limited success with that song, it became a #1 pop hit in 1971 for Paul Revere & the Raiders under the new title, "Indian Reservation."

Marvin Rainwater toured extensively during the latter part of the 1950s, but by 1960 he had developed calluses on his vocal cords and lost his voice. An operation helped, but it was four years before he would record again. He also had problems with the IRS because of his songwriting royalties. During the 1970s, he spent a lot of time in Britain where he was still a big star. Rainwater spent his final years living in Minnesota where he operated a small grocery store called Bluebird Corner. He passed away in Minneapolis in 2013 of heart failure.

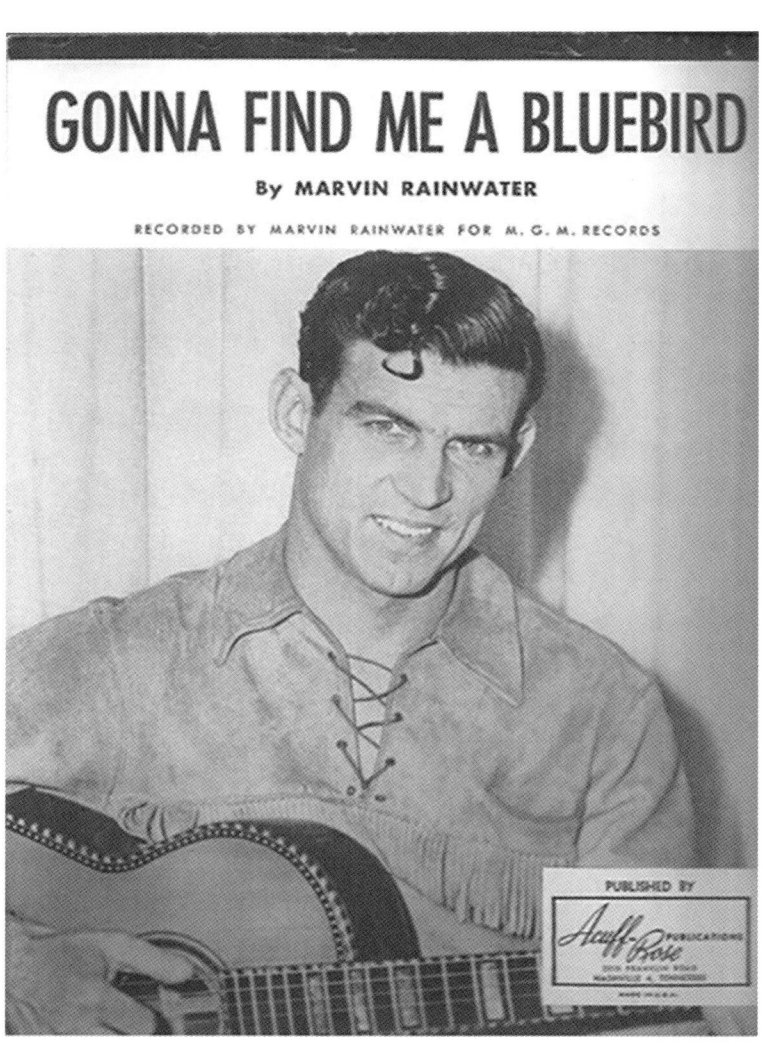

CHAPTER EIGHT
GROWING UP IN WICHITA

*He said, "I grew up in Wichita
In a Mayberry kind of town"
He never liked overalls
Or haulin' hay 'til sundown*

From "You're Not in Kansas Anymore" by Jo Dee Messina
(Jo Dee Messina, Tim Nichols, Zack Turner)

Live music seemed to be happening everywhere in Wichita during the 1960s. Inspired by the "British Invasion" with groups like the Beatles and the Rolling Stones, rock & roll bands were being formed in garages in seemly every neighborhood in the Air Capital. Though the heightened popularity of rock & roll may have been affecting the popularity of country music on a national level, it did not seem to make much of a difference in Wichita. Country bands were playing everywhere, from large ballrooms to tiny dive bars. The year 1968 is a good example of what was going on in Wichita. The Western Sunsets were playing at the 4Ls, the Southland Playboys were working at Jody's Hitching Post, the Country 4 were at John & Ada's, and the Lucky 7 Outlaws were the house band at the Lucky 7. Joe Wycoff & the Melody Playboys were working at the Hillcrest Lounge in 1968. Joe's group had been around for years playing at places like the Rock Castle, which had been renamed the Hobble-De-Hoy. The Melody Playboys were also the first band to play at the Mint Club when it opened in 1962.

Though many night spots came and went, the Mint Club was around for many years. One of the bands that performed there for quite a few of those years was Carl Adams & the Longbranch Boys, a group that even had a television show on KTVH Channel 12. When Japanese fiddler, Shoji Tabuchi first arrived in Wichita, the first band he joined was Carl Adams & the Longbranch Boys. By 1978 Adams had moved to Branson, Missouri where he opened a couple of restaurants.

Johnny Bee had a trio that played at a little dive near 21st and North Broadway called the Doghouse. Dwain Terry described the place as a "classic dump." He also recalled the time when Marvin Osborn and his band made a live recording at the Doghouse.

The April 18, 1968 issue of a Wichita entertainment paper called *Country Music News*, listed 23 country music bands performing in various clubs throughout the city. Paid advertisements in the paper showed Gene Anderson & His Honky Tonkers at the Golden Knight, the Chaparell Playboys at Thelma's No. 1, Jimmy Johnson & the Country Playboys at the Bonanza, Bill Boyd & His Buckshots at the Frontier Ballroom, and Ted Scott & His "Famous" Western Drifters at the Double D Lounge. Colburn Hamilton & his Country Western Swingers also performed at the Double D, as well as at Al's V-Bar-7. Fiddle and guitar player, Vern Beery was a 7th grade school teacher who had a trio that played at the Emperor Club.

Bands came and went. Some groups were around for years, though usually with regular personnel changes. Some bands lasted less than a year. Honky-tonks and beer joints did not fare much better. When one bar would close, another one would open, sometimes in the same spot. Dwain Terry recalled a dive on Orient Boulevard called Dave's Cave. "That was a rough place in the '60s. If you wanted to see a fight, you'd go to Dave's Cave." Terry also mentioned a downtown bar called Oakies. "That place didn't have air conditioning, so they would leave the door open in the summer. One night as Ray Barker's band was playing, two motorcycles drove right in on the dance floor."

Owen McCarty & his Troubadours were regulars at the Draw One Lounge. McCarty considered himself to be a good friend of Ernest Tubb and likely borrowed his band name from the "Texas Troubadour." In 1968, the band recorded "Key to My Heart" on Wichita's Kanwic label. The song shows a strong Ernest Tubb influence. Back in 1951 McCarty had recorded "She Done Moved to Kansas City," a blues number that featured Punk Rhyne on lead guitar. A year after his Kanwic release he recorded "It's Too Late for You and Me" under the name Owen McCarty and his Emeraldites on the Air Cap label. In the early '70s he moved to Nashville to try to make it in the music business. In 1972 he released "Another Lonely One" on his own Emeraldite label.

Growing Up in Wichita 89

Ted Scott Show in 1960
(Ted Scott in Cowboy Hat)
(Photo courtesy of Dwain Terry)

Ted Wayne Scott was born in Atlanta, Kansas on October 4, 1932. He loved playing country music but to support himself he got a job at Boeing as a mechanic. Sometime in the 1960s he formed his own band called Ted Scott & His Western Drifters, which for a time included husband and wife duo, Loyd and Millie Sledge. Ted and the band released singles on two Wichita labels, Chet-Mark and Cher'O-Key, as well as a single on the Albuquerque, New Mexico-based Vantage label. His song "Unwanted," which was released in 1960, received airplay on KFBI during the time the station was owned by Hollywood Stars Mary Pickford and Buddy Rogers. For a time, Scott had a weekly show on KJRG in Newton, and soon was touring the Midwest with big-name stars like Ray Price, Carl Belew, Marty Robbins, and George Morgan. In later years Ted Scott did some singing with the Powder River Band. He passed away on May 19, 2008.

* * *

Vernon Oxford was born near Rogers, Arkansas on June 8, 1941, but his family moved to Wichita in the early 1950s. It was a musical family and his father had gained a reputation as a fine old-time fiddler. Growing up in Wichita, Oxford learned to play the fiddle and guitar and sing country music. For a while in 1960, though still

Vernon Oxford

based out of Wichita, Oxford spent some time playing in a club in Utah. Returning to Wichita, he began doing a lot of club dates and square dances.

In 1964, Oxford moved to Nashville. With his hard-core, traditional, honky-tonk sound, he was considered "too country" by most country music record company executives, who were more interested in the smooth, modern, "Nashville Sound." However, he did become friends with one of Nashville's top songwriters, Harlan Howard, who was able to help him land a contract with RCA Records. Seven singles and an album were released but no hits resulted. It looked like Oxford's music career was over until he was discovered by country music fans in Britain who went crazy over his traditional country sound. RCA released a double album of Oxford's music in the United Kingdom. It did so well that RCA gave Oxford a new contract.

Though he never had a Top 10 hit, Oxford did land seven songs on the Billboard country charts including "Shadows of My Mind" and "Your Wanting Me Is Gone." His biggest hit, which made the Top 20, came in 1976 with the release of "Redneck! (The Redneck National Anthem.)" Around 1978 RCA released Oxford again, so he began recording for smaller independent record labels like Rounder and Rich-R-Tone.

In the early 1980s Oxford had minor parts in the films, *Coal Miner's Daughter* and *The Thing Called Love*. He also switched his emphasis to gospel singing and even did a little preaching. He still performs both in the U.S. and Europe.

CHAPTER NINE
THE WICHITA WAY

Every night I dream of Wichita
That's the price I pay
Show the world I ain't no quitter
That's the Wichita way

From "Wichita Way" by John Cowan

(John Cowan, Fred Koller)

Despite the growth of rock & roll, country music remained popular in Wichita throughout the 1960s. Popular night spots, such as Frankie's Lounge, featured country music six nights a week, usually from 9:00pm to one or two o'clock in the morning. Among the band leaders at the time were folks like Merlin Gooch, Ron Maynard, Jimmy Johnson, and June Riddle the wife of another popular Wichita entertainer, Tommy Riddle. Tommy had led a western swing band from the 1950s through the 1980s. Among the better-known musicians that played in Riddle's band were keyboard player Sid Barnes and fiddlers Gene Gasaway and Curly Lewis. Both

Barnes Brothers Band
(Photo courtesy of Dwain Terry)

Guy Vincent Band
(Photo courtesy of Dwain Terry)

Elmo B and the Other 3

Gasaway and Lewis had been members of Bob Wills' Texas Playboys, but Gasaway had also been in the bands of Ray Price and Mel Tillis, while Lewis was best-known for playing fiddle for Johnnie Lee Wills.

Sid Barnes had previously played with Wynn Stewart's West Coast Playboys in California following a stint in Wichita playing in Guy Vincent's band. His career in country music began in the 1940s when he and his four brothers formed a band at their family home just north of Cedar Vale. Living in a small community in southeastern Kansas did not provide a lot of opportunities for a country group, so the Barnes Brothers packed up and moved to Wichita. Sid Barnes started out on steel guitar but eventually switched to the piano. His brother, Bob was also a piano player who later found success fronting his own group, Bob Barnes & the Country Boys. During the 1960s the band was one of the regulars at Frankie's Lounge.

Most local band members held day jobs but loved playing music so much that they did not mind spending their nights in a smoky bar, even though they played for six nights for a total sum of $125. It was not about the money. After a hard day's work, Wichitans wanted to let loose, so before they went to bed, they would head over to their local night spot and dance to their favorite band. Among those bands were Lucky Fail & Mod Country, Ray & the Countrymen, the Bob Brooker Band, and Elmo B & the Other Three. In the early 1960s, Elmo Barnett and his group played at Frankie's Lounge, before relocating to the Maples Club, which was owned by Gene and Marge Lovell who later started the Wagon Wheel Club. Lucky Fail was an innovative guitar player who used his volume pedal to get a steel guitar effect. He continued to perform around Wichita until his passing in 1999.

* * *

Bill Parker (not to be confused with Billy Parker, country music performer and DJ from Tulsa) moved to Wichita from Howard, Kansas. Around 1960 Parker and his wife, Wanda, formed the Billy Parker Western Swing Band. One of the band members was steel guitarist and songwriter Duane Bass, who had some of his songs recorded by Leon McAuliffe of the Texas Playboys. The Billy Parker Western Swing Band played at many of Wichita's popular night spots, including Johnny & Bonnie's

*Billy Parker Western Swing Band 1960-61
L-R: Dwayne Bass, Dale Arnold, Wanda Parker,
Bill Parker, Bob Barnes, (unknown)*
(Photo courtesy of Dwain Terry)

Ballroom, the Sands Klub, and the Hut. During the late 1970s Parker reduced the size of his band to four members. In the early '90s, he developed brain cancer but continued to perform almost to the end of his life.

Local country musician Dwain Terry recalled another band that was working the same time as Parker's. "Clay Cerday was a Native American country singer. Billy Parker would get so frustrated with him. He (Cerday) didn't have his own band, but he would book a job and then hire the musicians to back him. He would borrow musicians from other bands, including Billy Parker's. It used to make Billy really mad."

During the 1960s most country musicians were not able to make a living by just playing music. Performers such as Grant Helmer would work a day job and then play music at night or on weekends. Helmer was born in Tampa, Kansas but grew up in El Dorado. For a time, he did the morning show, playing country records on El Dorado's station KBTO. His band, the Swing Aires, included Dan Spoonhour on steel guitar, Dwight Sullivan on second guitar, and Butch Foust on drums. Foust's father also led a group called the Joe Foust Western Swing Band. The group, which was active in Wichita in the late 1950s and the early '60s, often played at the Hut on K-42 highway.

Grant Helmer & the Swing Aires
L-R: Dan Spoonhour, Grant Helmer, Butch Foust, Dwight Sullivan
(Photo courtesy of Dwain Terry)

Kenny Pruitt and his wife, Rosa, formed a band in 1967. A year later, the band's name was changed to Kenny Pruitt & the Oakies. Other members of the band included Jimmy Hall, Bill Powell, Larry Gordon, Arnold Bolen, and Ronnie Bolen, who was later replaced by Monty Baker. They often performed at the Stardust, which was located on East 47th Street South on the other side of Broadway from the Western Swinger. Gene & Dottie Hensley, Joe Wycoff, and Bill Dry & the Rhythm Riders also played at the Stardust on a regular basis.

Dwain Terry
(Photo courtesy of Dwain Terry)

* * *

In 1958, Dwain Terry of Grenola, Kansas reached the age of 17. He loved music and longed to play in a band. One night in Pittsburg, Kansas, he stumbled across a band made up entirely of African American musicians. Looking back, Terry could not remember the name of the band. "They played mostly rock & roll and a few pop standards, with a little bit of country like Don Gibson's 'Oh Lonesome Me.' They let me sit in with them, just singing." Terry was inspired to learn the guitar, and four years later he met a man in Arkansas City who had a band. "The guy owned the Singer Sewing Center in Ark City. His band had a booking to play a dance in Newkirk, Oklahoma and needed a rhythm guitar player so I said I'd go. When we arrived at the club in Newkirk, we were told that the place had double booked, and they were going with the other band. We noticed another bar across the street, so we went in and asked if we could play. The owner said we could, but we would have to play for tips. We each made three dollars that night."

Others may have called it quits after that but not Dwain Terry. He soon put together his own band. "I just called it Dwain Terry Western Swing. There were five of us. We mostly played dances there in Grenola." Terry had a fondness for western swing music, a style he would lean on throughout his entire musical career. As he continued to play, he soon went from being a rhythm guitar player to playing lead. In 1964, he joined the Billy Parker Western Swing Band. This six-piece group kept busy playing fairs, clubs, and private parties in towns like Sedan and Howard. They also played for the Coleman Employees Club near Wichita.

Dwain Terry played guitar for Bill Parker on and off for a couple of years. Occasionally, he would fill in for Bob Brooker who had the Brooker Brothers Band with his brother, Donnie. In 1967 Terry landed a solo gig at the Emperor Club located at 1100 South Seneca in Wichita. "I played six nights a week from April through October. I played mostly western swing, even though it was just me." Around that same time, Terry also filled in on guitar with Marvin Osborn & the Rhythm Gamblers, who mostly played at the "new" Cowboy Inn at Central and St. Paul in Wichita and at a joint just north of Wichita in the little town of Park City.

Like most country bands in Wichita, Marvin Osborn & the Rhythm Gamblers moved around from club to club. Sometimes a band would play regularly at the same joint for weeks or even months. Often bands were relegated to one-night stands. James Smith grew up in Wichita and has been a fan of country music his entire life. "My family loved to go to the clubs. We called it 'goin' honky-tonkin'.' Us kids would sit in the car while mom and dad and grandma would go into the club. After

The Wichita Way 97

Dwain Terry & the Continentals
L-R: John Fain, Dwain Terry, Bill Pokorny
(Photo courtesy of Dwain Terry)

a while, they'd bring us some chips and a bottle of pop. Sometimes we'd sneak into the club so we could listen to the music. I loved to watch Marvin Osborn. He could play guitar and dance with his wife at the same time." Smith recalled a time, later in life, when he went into a club and saw his grandmother sitting at the bar. "I walked up to Grandma and started hugging on her. This big guy came up to me and yelled, 'Find your own woman!' I didn't understand him, so I said, 'What?' So, he yelled it again. 'Find your own woman.' Then he came at me. I hit him as hard as I could, and he fell back into the booth. So, Grandma hollered, 'Stop! That's my grandson!'"

In 1968 Dwain Terry formed his Continental Western Swing Band, which he later shortened to the Western Continentals. The group played the same circuit of clubs that most of the other country bands in Wichita were playing. Among them were Swingland, the Cypress Club, the Pirates Cave, the Sands Klub, the Carriage Inn, the Hangar Club, The Eye, the Tiki Club, the Little Missouri, Lucky's Club, the V Bar 7, the Rock Castle, and the Maples Club, later known as the Wagon Wheel. One night

Dwain Terry & the Continentals at the Hangar Club
L-R: Jan Smith, Tommy Wise, Dwain Terry
(Photo courtesy of Dwain Terry)

in 1976 Dr. Hook & the Medicine Show were in Wichita for a concert. The group was known for the hits, "Sylvia's Mother" and "The Cover of Rolling Stone." After the concert, Ray Sawyer, who was known as Dr. Hook, showed up at the Wagon Wheel. Dwain Terry recalled the occasion. "Dr. Hook was in town for a concert, and after his show, he came down to the Wagon Wheel and sat in with us. He was a big George Jones fan, so he sang George's songs all night." For a while, Dwain Terry & the Western Continentals played at the Mary Carter Club, a venue on West Maple that was owned by the people who had the Mary Carter Paint Store. On at least two more occasions Terry and the band were joined by national celebrities. *Grand Ole Opry* stars, George Morgan and Ernie Ashworth both sat in with the band following their concerts in Wichita.

Besides playing lead guitar, Dwain Terry was also the lead singer. That became a problem for him in 1981 when he started having major problems with his voice. He was diagnosed with paralyzed vocal cords. The original prognosis was that he might never sing again. He recalled, "Since I couldn't sing, I decided to disband the Western Continentals and just become a guitar player in other people's bands." Eight

Yesterday's Playboys at Caprice Ballroom
L-R: Wyatt Long, Dwain Terry, Ron Maynard, Jess Moore, Joe Wycoff
(Photo courtesy of Dwain Terry)

years later, Terry discovered an operation that gave him the possibility of getting his voice back. His normal voice did return but he never quite got back the vocal range he possessed prior to the paralyzed vocal cords. In 1998 Terry felt like it was time to start another band. He formed Yesterday's Playboys, a group that once again relied heavily on western swing with a little bit of standard country, big band, and pop thrown in.

Yesterday's Playboys not only kept up a busy schedule on their own, they often were the backup musicians for others, including KFDI morning DJ, Dugg Collins. Collins, a member of the Country Music Disc Jockey Hall of Fame, had come to Wichita in 1999 to replace the retiring Mike Oatman. Like Oatman, Collins also loved to perform country music, especially western swing. Yesterday's Playboys were a perfect fit to back Collins. On another occasion the group was called upon to back country music legend Hank Thompson. Thompson, who was sometimes billed as the "King of Western Swing," often worked with pickup bands in his later years. Harold Widdup, who would later become a part-time DJ on KFDI, was a friend of Hank Thompson's. Widdup told Dwain Terry, "You know, Hank doesn't like to feature his musicians so tonight you'll just have to play backup fills." However, unbeknownst to Terry, Widdup mentioned to Thompson, "That Dwain Terry is a real good, Merle Travis-style guitar player." Perhaps that sparked something within Thompson that night. Merle Travis was his favorite guitar player and the two of them had made some recordings together, including their big 1955 hit version of "Wildwood Flower." As the show began, Dwain Terry settled in on guitar, content to be in the background behind one of America's biggest country stars. Then it happened. Terry explained, "During one song, Hank looked over at me and told me to take a lead. He must have liked it because pretty soon he had me do it again." Still another time, Yesterday's Playboys performed at a dinner theater in El Dorado, playing backup for Albert Brumley Jr. Brumley was a successful country and gospel performer whose father, Albert E. Brumley, was best known for writing songs like "I'll Fly Away," "Turn Your Radio On," "Jesus Hold My Hand," and many more. In 2012 Dwain Terry decided it was time to quit, and Yesterday's Playboys disbanded. Now in his late 70s, Terry still enjoys playing music and sitting in with country bands.

During the time that Dwain Terry & the Western Continentals were playing at the Mary Carter Club, there was a bartender who enjoyed their music and loved to sing along, especially entertaining those at the bar. Terry Crane remembered those fun times. "I was the bartender at the Mary Carter Club for around two years. I had a great time singing along to those people at the bar. Finally, one night, Dwain hollered, 'Hey, Terry. Since you like singing so much, why don't you just come up and sing with the band.' I really enjoyed singing with Dwain, but in late 1972, I left and decided to put together my own group, Terry Crane & the Blue Diamonds." Crane and his band worked many of the joints in Wichita before deciding to take their show on the road. "I took a page from Greg Stevens and the Wichita Linemen. The Linemen were having a lot of success playing in different towns in Kansas. I decided to follow their route and play in the same places they played. We'd follow them to Hutchinson, Concordia, Dodge City and other places. Greg Stevens was a big influence on me. He told me that we needed to do more than just play our songs. We needed to entertain." Crane took entertaining to heart. In 1980 he moved to Eureka Springs, Arkansas and built a thousand seat theater, the Country Shindig. Country music stage shows were presented six nights a week and featured ten musicians and a comedian, all hosted by Terry Crane.

Chuck Yockey was somewhat of a rarity in the Wichita country music scene. Though he fronted a band and did some singing, Yockey was mostly known as a comedian. During the 1960s and into the '70s, the Chuck Yockey Show was a fixture on the local country music scene, especially at places like Swingland on North Broadway. One of the local entertainment tabloids said of Yockey, "This clown is not happy unless he's performing for somebody, somewhere." The writer went on to say, "Chuck plays pretty fair rhythm guitar and his booming baritone keeps the cash customers awake and jumping."

Chuck Yockey
(Photo courtesy of Dwain Terry)

Swingland featured country music almost every night of the week. The Chuck Yockey Show was usually presented on Monday and Tuesday nights. On Thursday nights, the spotlight fell on Hap Clark & his Log Cabin Boys. Clark fronted the band and played bass. He was backed by Dick Rinehart on rhythm guitar, Wayne Brockman on lead guitar, and Emmett Hipps on steel guitar. Besides their gig at Swingland, the Log Cabin Boys also performed regularly at the local Elks Club and American Legion Halls.

Hap Clark
(Photo courtesy of Sam Bidwell)

When it came to country music bands in Wichita, it seems that the only constant was change. Bands not only moved from club to club, but musicians moved from band to band. Some bands lasted only a short time., while others continued performing for years. Larry Oakman started his band in the late 1960s and was still performing into the '90s. Among the favorite spots to find the Larry Oakman Band were the Sportsman Club, the Wagon Wheel, and the later Cowboy Inn, located on St. Paul Street.

CHAPTER TEN

WICHITA LINEMEN

And I need you more than want you
And I want you for all time
And the Wichita Lineman is still on the line.

From "Wichita Lineman" by Glen Campbell

(Jimmy Webb)

He called himself, "Ol' Tee-legged, Toe-legged, B-legged, Bow-legged, Curly-headed, Pee Williker, Mike," but usually just shortened it to "Ol' Mike." Though he combined that "hillbilly" name with a "good ol' boy" persona, Mike Oatman was one of the most-savvy radio broadcasters in the history of country music radio. This country singer and DJ from Texas went on to become the most-successful radio broadcaster in Wichita history. There is even a street at Wichita State University named after him.

Michael Clifton Oatman was born in Marfa, Texas on September 4, 1939. He fell in love with country music and put together his first band when he was 14. Even though he was barely in his teens, he called his band Ol' Mike and the Trailblazers. By the age of 17, Oatman and the band were performing on radio and television. His love of country music and performing led him into a career as a radio DJ. When he was 20, Oatman began working with KHEY in El Paso. He soon became the station's program director and sales manager. As he would do throughout his entire career, Oatman not

Mike Oatman and son, Andy

only held down a managerial position, he also did a regular, early morning on-air shift as a DJ. At the same time he kept up a busy performance schedule with his band, renamed Ol' Mike and the K-HEY Riders. In the early 1960s, this popular El Paso band hosted their own Opry-style, live radio show on KHEY.

In 1962 an Oklahoma broadcaster and former vaudeville performer, Frank Lynch, purchased KIRL in Wichita from Hollywood actors Mary Pickford and Buddy Rogers. Prior to using the KIRL call letters, to promote the association with Mary Pickford, the "girl with the golden curls," the station had a 30-year history as KFBI. Due mostly to poor management by Pickford's husband, Buddy Rogers, KIRL was not successful. Lynch hoped to return the station to its glory days and revive the call letters, KFBI. However, legend has it that J. Edgar Hoover, director of the Federal Bureau of Investigation, personally turned down the re-issuance of the KFBI call letters due to abuse of the "FBI" letters by previous KFBI sales staff members. Lynch was forced to find other call letters. He chose the ones that sounded as close to KFBI as he could…KFDI. Lynch got his son, F.F. "Mike" Lynch to take over the daily operations of the station. At the beginning, the KFDI format was block programming. Mostly there were blocks of religious programming or sports, such as major league baseball games. Times not taken up by sports or preachers were filled with gospel and country music. Mike Lynch did not feel that the block programming was successful and convinced his father that KFDI should be a full-time country music station. Neither father nor son felt qualified to program such a format, so they placed an ad in the trade papers, searching for a program director. Mike Oatman, who had recently had a disagreement with the owners of KHEY in El Paso, answered that ad. On September 1, 1964, just three days before his 25th birthday, Ol' Mike signed on the morning show on KFDI. He also took on the same managerial positions he had left at KHEY, program director and sales manager. The following year, Mike Lynch purchased KFDI from his father and became president and general manager. Before long, the younger Lynch formed a partnership with his

F.F. "Mike" Lynch

Ol' Mike Oatman and the Wichita Linemen
L-R: Carl Hendricks, Mike Oatman, Greg Stevens, Robin Harris (hidden)
(Photo courtesy of KFDI Collection)

ambitious employee, Mike Oatman. The two men, known locally as Mike and Mike, would eventually purchase radio stations in other markets under the corporate name of Great Empire Broadcasting. Prior to the major corporate radio station buy-outs, which began in the late 1990s, Great Empire was the largest chain of country music radio stations in the world.

Though he had left his band behind in El Paso, Mike Oatman continued to enjoy playing his guitar and singing. His busy schedule precluded him from fronting or even being a part of a regular band. Yet, he never had to be coaxed to get on stage to sing a few songs at KFDI events, such as the station's annual anniversary party, held each summer at Wichita's Joyland amusement park. He also kept his sunburst Gibson J-45 guitar and his gold-plated Gibson Mastertone banjo in instrument stands right next to his desk at KFDI. To ease the stress of making corporate decisions, Oatman could just reach over and grab his banjo and pick a few tunes. Country music stars, both legends and newcomers, would often stop by KFDI to promote their concerts or their latest record. After visiting on the radio with whichever "ranch hand" was on the air at the time, the "star" would usually be invited into Oatman's office, where the two would discuss the music and often sing a few songs together.

On August 19, 1998, Mike Lynch and Mike Oatman sold their corporation, Great Empire Broadcasting, to the Journal Broadcast Group of Milwaukee, Wisconsin for just under $96,000,000. Oatman's last show on KFDI took place on June 4, 1999. He planned to retire, play golf, and travel with his wife, Jane. Unfortunately, Jane died less than a year later. Eventually, Mike Oatman remarried, but died of liver cancer on January 27, 2003. He was 63.

Where most radio stations hired disc jockeys for their radio expertise, Mike Oatman felt that it was important to hire on-air personalities who had a genuine love for the music they were playing. He also preferred hiring musicians. At the end of what seemed like a successful job interview, a potential employee would be asked by Oatman, "Well, do you happen to play an instrument?" If there were two potential employees vying for the same position, the ability to play an instrument would usually tip the scale toward the musician. One such person was a guy who became known as "Little Donnie Do Dad."

* * *

In 1965, a country music singer named Don Walton, drove to Wichita from his home in Newton, bringing his first recording. The 45rpm record on the Dixie label was called "Another Heartache." Walton felt pretty good about his record and hoped he could get it played on the radio. "I first stopped by KSIR, the well-established radio station owned by Mack Sanders. I played my record for the music director, but he turned me down. He told me that the station didn't play local artists. I was disappointed but there was one more station I could try, which was located on the north end of Wichita, right on the way back to Newton."

Walton went to KFDI and met Mike Oatman. Oatman not only liked Walton's record and said he would play it on KFDI, he hired Walton on the spot. So, on February 1, 1965, Don Walton became the newest KFDI "Ranch Hand." He was a perfect fit. The Yates Center native had begun singing country music in the early

*Don Walton alias
Little Donnie Do-Dad*
(Photo courtesy of KFDI Collection)

1950s, and though Walton did not have his own band, he often sat in with bands at various country music night spots around Wichita. "I was singing one night with the band at the Water Hole, which was located near the corner of 37th & Broadway, not far from KFDI. I even got paid. That night I made five dollars."

Walton's regular job at KFDI was doing a midday shift on the air, as well as programming the station's music. He loved country music, especially the classic country sounds that featured fiddles and steel guitars. One of the places he liked to frequent was the Western Swinger, which was located just west of Broadway at 47th Street South. Formerly called the Hi-Ho Club, the Western Swinger had been the home of popular Wichita country performers like Red Young and Vern Laswell. No matter who was in the group, the house band for the club was usually called the Western Swinger Band. Laswell had previously led a group known as the Silver Star Playboys, who performed at Frankie's Lounge six nights a week. He had also released a record on Wichita's Kanwic label.

In 1969, KFDI "Ranch Hand," Don Powell was the steel guitarist in the Western Swinger Band. The group at the time also included guitarist Dana Lovelady, drummer Robin Harris, and a fiddler from Japan, Shoji Tabuchi. Though they usually played every night of the week at the Western Swinger, the band occasionally got a break to do something else. One September they performed at the Farm Bureau Arena at the Kansas State Fair in Hutchinson. Don Walton was the emcee and fronted the band. "Dana Lovelady told me that he enjoyed my singing, so he suggested that I should join the group. He told the band that they should hire me and leave the Western Swinger." Lovelady, who sounded a lot like country music star, Wynn Stewart, felt that they could each make more money if they left the Swinger and started their own band. Shoji Tabuchi had a family to support and was not ready to give up a steady income at the Western Swinger to gamble on the possible success of a new band. Robin Harris and Don Powell, along with Don Walton, decided to join Lovelady and, with the addition of Carl Hendricks on lead guitar. a new band was formed, the Wichita Linemen. Lovelady, whose idea it was to start that band, only lasted two months so Hendricks switched from bass to lead guitar. However, that meant that the Linemen needed a bass player. Walton found Greg Stevens playing in a jazz group in a club called The Eye located on South Broadway. "I talked Greg into becoming the new bass player and vocalist for the Wichita Linemen. After a short time, he switched roles with Carl Hendricks. Greg took over as lead guitarist and Carl switched to bass." Stevens also became the primary lead vocalist while Hendricks developed into a comedy character.

By 1971 Don Walton became too busy with his duties at KFDI. Besides being one of the on-air, "Ranch Hands," he had also become the station's program director. Playing with the Wichita Linemen, while working at KFDI and trying to raise a family was just too much, so he left the group. However, due to the involvement of Walton and another KFDI Ranch Hand, Don Powell, the Wichita Linemen soon became KFDI's "house band" which led to them becoming one of the most successful country bands in Wichita. Where most bands were making a few hundred dollars a show, the Linemen eventually were making a few thousand. They performed at most of KFDI's annual, signature events such as the Anniversary Parties, the Listener Appreciation Shows, and the sponsor barbecues. The Linemen also played at many concerts and dances at the Cotillion Ballroom, both as headliners and as the backup band for nationally known performers. They were known for their tight, high-quality stage show, and for playing four hours straight, without taking a break.

* * *

While becoming the front man for the Wichita Linemen, Greg Stevens also worked for Phil Uhlik at Uhlik Music, on West Douglas in the part of Wichita known as Delano. Growing up in Fremont, Nebraska, young Phil Uhlik became interested in the accordion. Sometime in the late 1950s he went into the military service. When he came back to Kansas in 1959, he moved to El Dorado and got a job selling accordions and started an accordion school. In 1969 Uhlik felt like it was time to expand his market, so he moved to Wichita. Uhlik Music opened on February 1, 1972. Phil became known in Wichita as a supporter of the local country musicians.

Wichita Linemen 1984
L-R: Carl Hendricks, Robin Harris, Jerry Powell, Jimmy Powell, Greg Stevens
(Photo courtesy of KFDI Collection)

The store is now located on East Douglas in Wichita and Phil Uhlik continues to support local musicians. You can sometimes find him playing his accordion in the store or hanging out with another accordion player, Ron Binkley. For a time, Uhlik Music was managed by yet another accordion player, Wes Trinkle, who played mostly country music. Trinkle, who now makes his home in Arkansas, had learned to play the accordion from Leona Balman, who was a graduate of the June Frisby Academy. Besides accordion, Balman also taught guitar, piano, mandolin, organ, and violin.

CHAPTER ELEVEN

FIDDLIN' MAN

And I ran off to be a fiddlin' man
Momma threw a fit bangin' pots and pans
Said she'd better never ever get her hands
On that no good fiddlin' man

From "Fiddlin' Man" by Michael Martin Murphey

The Japanese fiddler Shoji Tabuchi, who had declined the offer to become one of the members of the Wichita Linemen, remained at the Western Swinger for a short time. Born in Daishoji, Ishikawa, Japan on April 16, 1944, he began to learn the violin at the age of seven, using the Suzuki Method. Young Shoji fell in love with country music and made plans to someday come to America. During college he started a bluegrass band called the Bluegrass Ramblers, which won a national talent contest in Japan. A defining moment in Tabuchi's life came when he attended a concert by the "King of Country Music," Roy Acuff. Tabuchi remembered, "I met Roy Acuff, his fiddle player, Howdy Forrester, and 'Bashful Brother' Oswald. Howdy Forrester played 'Listen to the Mockingbird,' and I loved it. I grew up playing classical music and had never heard the violin played like that." Shoji decided right away that he wanted to play country music. Acuff encouraged him and told him to "look me up if you ever come to America." Tabuchi was soon on his way.

When Tabuchi arrived in the U.S., his first stop was San Francisco. He and a guitar-playing friend named Kenji put together a duo act. "We called ourselves the Osaka Okies," laughed Tabuchi. "The first show we played was at the famous club called the Hungry I. We opened for the Dillards." Rodney Dillard remembered it a little differently. "Shoji and his friend had just gotten off the plane and they came to the Hungry I where we were playing. We already had an opening act, but we invited the Osaka Okies, on-stage, during our show." After a year in San Francisco, Tabuchi moved to Kansas City, Kansas and landed a steady job at the Starlight Club in Riverside. The next year, Shoji found himself in Wichita. "I moved to Wichita to take a job at St. Francis Hospital in 1969," he recalled. "I worked in the radiology department with Dr. Lyle Ackerman."

Though Tabuchi now had a steady job, he still wanted to continue playing the fiddle in country bands. "When I got to Wichita, I was listening to KFDI. They were doing a remote broadcast from Schofield Pontiac, so I drove there and met Don Powell." During their conversation, Powell, one of the KFDI radio "ranch hands," discovered that Shoji was a country music fiddler. Powell was also playing steel guitar for a band at a popular Wichita club at 47th & South Broadway. "It was called the Western Swinger," noted Tabuchi. "It was right next to the T-Bone Steakhouse. The Western Swinger Band was led by Gene Hensley and his wife, Dottie. Don Powell was on steel guitar and Robin Harris played the drums." Harris recalled the night that Don Powell introduced the band to Shoji Tabuchi. "One weekend we were playing at the Western Swinger and Don told us that he wanted a guy to sit in with us that night. Well, we had this policy where we would let guest musicians occasionally sit in with the band, but not on Friday and Saturday nights. Since this was a weekend...I can't recall if it was Friday or Saturday...we reminded Don that we didn't allow anyone to sit in with us. Don informed us that he brought a 'fiddlin' cowboy from Japan, and that we were going to make an exception to our rule this time. So, Shoji got up and played 'Orange Blossom Special' and the crowd went nuts." After a response like that, Gene Hensley offered Tabuchi a steady job with his Western Swinger Band.

Shoji Tabuchi

In July of 1972, Tabuchi performed at the 8th Annual KFDI Anniversary Party at Joyland Park. Headliners at that event were country music stars, Billy Walker and Faron Young. Tabuchi recalled how he met Young. "Terry Burford from KFDI introduced me to Faron Young and his manager, Billy Deaton. When Faron got back to Nashville, he told Tillman Franks about me. Tillman was managing David Houston. David was needing a fiddle player, so I auditioned for him and got the job. I played with David Houston and the Persuaders for five years." Tabuchi's next job was backing a professional football player.

Terry Bradshaw was a successful quarterback for the Pittsburgh Steelers. In 1976 during the middle of his football career, Bradshaw decided that he also wanted to be a country music star. He landed a contract with Mercury Records which immediately produced a Top 20 hit with his cover of the Hank Williams 1949 classic, "I'm So Lonesome I Could Cry." Bradshaw put together a band and hired Shoji Tabuchi to play fiddle. "I was with Terry Bradshaw for seven months and then he just quit." No longer with a band and out of a job, Tabuchi decided to try to make it as a solo act. "I went on the road and played with pickup bands for a few years."

For a while Tabuchi lived in Bossier City, Louisiana and did some performing on the Johnny High show in Grapevine, Texas, while continuing to take his show on the road. One of the regular spots on his schedule was the Ocean Opry in Panama City, Florida. The venue was owned by Wayne "Bud" Rader, who had moved to Florida from Wichita, where he had a family gospel group known as the Riverside Boys. Bud Rader's son, Dennis, recalled, "Our friendship with Shoji goes back a lot of years. My fondest memories are from 1979 through around 1985, something like that…We booked him every year as a single…did a late afternoon rehearsal…opened the doors to let the crowd in, and then did the show. One of the funnest gigs ever was getting to play behind Shoji." Eventually, Tabuchi landed in Branson, Missouri and played on a couple of shows there before opening his own theater. He became one of the most successful performers in the history of the Ozark town and was dubbed the "King of Branson." Currently, Shoji Tabuchi still performs at his elaborate theater in Branson.

CHAPTER TWELVE

PLEASANT VALLEY SUNDAY

The local rock group down the street is trying hard to learn their song
They serenade the weekend squire who just came out to mow his lawn
Another pleasant valley Sunday, charcoal burning everywhere
Rows of houses that are all the same and no one seems to care.

From "Pleasant Valley Sunday" by the Monkees.

(Carole King, Gerry Goffin)

Denzil Alcorn was born in Wichita on October 24, 1943, but most of his childhood years were spent in Missouri. However, when he was in high school, his family moved back to the Pleasant Valley area of Wichita. As a teenager, Alcorn became fascinated with the guitar and spent a lot of time on the front porch of his family's home. He put together his first band, the Golden Jubilees, while still attending West High School in Wichita. Alcorn also entered and won the talent contest at a Wichita venue called the Midwestern Jamboree, which was located on South Hydraulic.

After graduating high school, Alcorn formed the Pleasant Valley Playboys and started playing the local clubs around Wichita. They recorded their first record, "Let's Dance," for Wichita's Aircap Records in 1965. The recording had the feel of Hank Williams with a little Buddy Holly thrown in. It paved the way for the honky tonk sound that would prove to be Alcorn's mainstay. Alcorn was particularly taken by the music of Johnny Horton; whose career took off in 1956 with "Honky Tonk Man." Following a string of hits like "The Battle of New Orleans," "Sink the Bismarck," and "North to Alaska," Horton was killed in 1960 when his car was hit by a drunk driver. A few years later Denzil Alcorn became acquainted with Tillman Franks who had been Johnny Horton's manager. Franks was the talent manager for the famous *Louisiana Hayride* on KWKH in Shreveport. He thought Denzil had potential. Alcorn recalled, "Tillman Franks told me that he thought I could be the next Johnny Horton. Johnny had been one of my favorites and I guess I sounded like him. I was pretty excited for a while, but then he (Franks) went with David Houston." It was Franks who got David Houston signed to a Nashville recording contract. Houston went on to have over 60 hits, including several duets with Tammy Wynette and Barbara Mandrell.

Denzil Alcorn and the Citations

Denzil Alcorn and the Pleasant Valley Playboys continued performing at many of the Wichita night spots that featured country music, including the 81 Club, the Pirates Cave, and the Bonanza. Sometime during this era the group was invited by Clay Allen to perform on the *Big D Jamboree* in Dallas, Texas. The *Big D Jamboree* was Dallas' answer to Nashville's *Grand Ole Opry* and Shreveport's *Louisiana Hayride*. The jamboree was hosted by KRLD-TV, which broadcast a 30-minute portion of the program on Saturday nights. Both Clay Allen and his partner, Dewey Groom, discussed hiring Denzil Alcorn to be a regular on the show but for some unknown reason it fell through.

Alcorn enjoyed many kinds of music, but especially rockabilly, the hybrid cross of country music and rock & roll. Another of Alcorn's musical heroes was Conway Twitty, who scored nine Top 40 pop hits before becoming a big star in country music. Twitty's first hit, "It's Only Make Believe," had gone all the way to #1 on the pop charts. Twitty moved to Oklahoma City in the mid-1960s, and while there, he decided to make the complete switch from rock & roll to country music. He soon became the star of the *Channel 13 Barn Dance*, a country music program on Oklahoma City's public television station, KETA. At that time Denzil Alcorn fronted the Wandering Okies who were able to land a guest spot on Conway Twitty's Barn Dance program. Twitty liked the band so much that he invited them to be the opening act for his concerts.

In 1968, after recording several songs in Wichita and sensing that his star was on the rise, Alcorn went to Nashville. He hired producer Tommy Hill of Starday Records. Together they recorded the single, "Big Blue Baby Eyes," along with the B side, "The World Is Filled with Lovers." Hill not only produced the session but also played rhythm guitar. Other musicians on the record included Nashville stalwarts, Pete Drake on steel guitar, Jerry Smith on piano, Jerry Shook (Carl Smith's guitar player) on lead guitar, and Elvis Presley's drummer, D.J. Fontana. The backup singers were the Four Guys from the *Grand Ole Opry*. The record was released on Nashville-based Camaro Records, a small subsidiary spin-off label of Starday. Though the record was never a big hit, it proved to be Alcorn's biggest recording success. In 1973, following a temporary move to Enid, Oklahoma to perform at the Bamboo Club, Alcorn re-released the record on Enid's Gemini label.

Vince Baker got his start playing drums for Denzil Alcorn in 1968. Born on February 8, 1944 in Wichita, Baker soon became interested in music. In 1966, he started hanging out at Saturday morning jam sessions at the Bloody Bucket, located in the 2400 block of South Meridian. On one particular day, no drummer showed up for the jam, so someone suggested that Baker give it a try. "I wasn't very good at first, since I had never played drums, but I picked it up pretty fast." Baker took to the drums and soon Denzil Alcorn asked him to join his band. "I worked for Denzil for about a year and then Bill Powell asked me to join a new band that he and some friends were forming. Bill Powell played steel guitar, and was the father of Jimmy and Jerry Powell, who later became members of the Wichita Linemen. When we started our new band, it was just four of us…Bill Powell, Ira Newton, Arnold Bolen, and me on drums."

Vince Baker's next move was to the Longbranch Club where he joined Bill Jordan & the Longbranch Jamboree. "I played there for eight months to a year. We did a TV show, plus we had a KFDI night and a night for Mack Sanders' station (KFRM.)" At one point, the band hired a 17-year-old fiddler from Alamogordo, New Mexico named Hiram Posey. Posey was a hot fiddle player which led him to leave

Wichita to travel the country and enter fiddle contests. He won the National Fiddle Contest in Weiser, Idaho two years in a row (1981 & 1982.) The following year, he was a judge in the contest and was inducted into the National Fiddler's Hall of Fame. Having played the violin since the age of nine, Posey became proficient in various styles of music including classical, jazz, bluegrass, blues, western swing and, of course, country. He moved to Nashville in 2004 where he still performs.

In 1969, following his stint at the Longbranch Jamboree, Vince Baker became the drummer for Bob Brooker & the Velvatones. Having become a successful drummer, Baker became interested in the piano and began playing at the Kansas Country Music Association jam sessions at the Wagon Wheel. That led to him playing piano for Marvin Rainwater, who made a guest appearance at the Wagon Wheel. Then in 1975, he helped form the progressive country band, Oklahoma Sunshine, and remained with the group until 1979. Baker still plays, often with his old friend, Bob Brooker, but these days he plays mostly keyboards instead of the drums.

Denzil Alcorn continued to play his music all the way to the end of the 20th century. For a time, he had a band called the High Plains Drifters, which included Lloyd Sledge, Kenny Clevenger, and Gary Cornelius. The group played a regular schedule at the Moose Club in Hutchinson and the Elks Club in Wichita. Prior to retiring from music in 2000, Alcorn's final band was called Denzil Alcorn & the Citations. Alcorn died on May 4, 2018, shortly after being interviewed for this book. A part of his legacy was inspiring and influencing other musicians in Wichita. He recalled giving some guitar tips to a kid down the street. That young man would go on to become a successful country music performer in Wichita, himself. His name was Sam Bidwell.

CHAPTER THIRTEEN
SAM'S PLACE

There's a place down the street we call Sam's Place.
It starts a-jumpin' every evening when the sun goes down.
You can always find me down at Sam's Place,
For that's where the gang all hangs around.

From "Sam's Place" by Buck Owens.

(Buck Owens, Don Rich)

Sammy Bidwell became interested in singing and playing the guitar when he was just a child. Like many kids who were born in the 1950s, Sammy fell in love with the music of Elvis Presley. His mother played the guitar and both she and his father encouraged his musical interests. Bidwell's mother used to tell him that he "could sing before he could walk." By the time he was ten, Sammy was performing on-stage at a place called Hill Billy Paradise, just northeast of Wichita near Benton. Among the regular performers were Ted Scott & the Western Drifters and Norman Harvey & the Westerners, which included Marvin Osborn and his wife, Donna, along with Darrell Fleming on lead guitar, Dennis Brown on drums, and several female vocalists.

Hill Billy Paradise was billed as an "open-air dance platform." It was basically just a performing stage that was setup in a farm pasture. Later, an old boxcar was moved in to serve as a bar. Hill Billy Paradise was run by a character who called himself, "Wild Bill" Elliott (not to be confused with the Hollywood cowboy star) or "Hill Billy Bill." Elliott also ran a Wichita venue called the Midwest Jamboree, located in the Wichita Sports Arena at 540 North Hydraulic. Wild Bill was known for playing a single-string instrument he called the One-string Pitchfork, which was an actual pitchfork with a fret board, electric pickup, and one string. Bidwell recalled that Elliott "would shove one of the tines of the pitchfork through his belt loop and then twang away." An advertising flyer from that time reads like a wanted poster: "Wanted for Murder. Bill Elliott. Alias Hill Billy Bill. This man has murdered more country music than anyone known to the music world." An article in a small Wichita entertainment newspaper called *Country Music News*, touted Elliott as "the only entertainer that started at the very bottom and is still there." The writer also

Ted Scott and His Western Drifters
(Photo courtesy of Dwain Terry)

suggested, hopefully with tongue in cheek, that "He really hasn't got much talent. He just has a lot of guts." Hill Billy Paradise is long gone, but the site is now the location of the Chisholm Trail Gun Club.

In 1966, Sammy Bidwell turned 11 and met a group that called themselves Traveling Strings. Band members included Troy Welch, Jesse Young, and Keith Wright. "They needed a guitar player," recalled Bidwell, "so they invited me to join the band." Among the other popular Wichita bands at the time were Ted Scott & the Western Drifters and Hap Clark & the Log Cabin Boys. During that time, Bidwell's parents encouraged him to enter a talent contest at the Midwest Jamboree. There he competed with other would-be country stars in Wichita, including his older neighbor, Denzil Alcorn. Bidwell won the contest and was featured on the cover of the very first issue of *Show Biz*, a weekly entertainment paper published by "Skidrow Joe" Moody.

One evening, Bidwell and his parents were having dinner at the Golden Chance Steak Saloon at 4205 South Seneca. They noticed a small stage at one end of the room. Bidwell recalled what happened next. "My dad told the waitress that he wanted

Sam Bidwell & Ted Scott
(Photo courtesy of Sam Bidwell)

to speak to the owner. The waitress told Dad that he was pretty busy. Dad finally convinced her that it was important. When owner, Carl Murrell, finally came to our table, he wasn't very happy. His apron was filthy, and he was covered in sweat. Murrell explained that his cook had failed to show up for work, so he was having to cook. Dad got right to the point. He told the owner, 'See that stage over there? You need my son singing on that stage.' The owner told my dad, 'I don't need any entertainment in here.' Dad ignored that comment. He just said, 'Sammy, go out to the car and get your guitar.' So, I grabbed my guitar and got up on that stage and started singing. I ended up singing on that stage every Saturday night for two years."

Even into his teen years, Bidwell's mother encouraged her son, now using the older sounding, "Sam," instead of "Sammy" to enter talent contests. At the age of 17, Bidwell won a contest at the Longbranch Club, located in the lower level of the Seneca Square shopping center. The house band, led by steel guitar player, Jerry Sisk, was called Bill Jordan & the Longbranch Jamboree. Though blind, Jordan played bass, sang lead, and was the front man for the group. Sue Ericson also sang and played keyboard. Other members included Hiram Posey on fiddle, Roger Newton on guitar, and Vince Baker on drums. The band had weekly radio shows on both KFDI and KFRM, along with a TV show on KWCH, Channel 12, called the *Longbranch Jamboree*. When the band suddenly fired Jordan, they asked Sam

Sam Bidwell
(Photo courtesy of Sam Bidwell)

Bidwell to take his place. He remembered, "I had never played bass, so I learned on the job. Sometimes we backed big-name singers, like Lefty Frizzell and Hank Thompson, usually with no rehearsal. On my first night with the band we had to back Wynn Stewart. I was stumbling all over, trying to figure out the notes, when in walked Greg Stevens, bass player for the Wichita Linemen. Jerry Sisk mentioned to Wynn Stewart that a great bass player had just walked into the room. Wynn smiled and gave Greg a big introduction. Greg came on stage and I gladly passed my bass to him. It worked out pretty good for Greg because Wynn Stewart later recorded one of his songs." That song, "Paint Me a Rainbow," became a Top 50 hit for Wynn Stewart in 1972.

On another occasion, the Longbranch Jamboree backed singer, Ronnie Sessions. Sessions had recently had his first chart record with a country cover of Three Dog Night's pop hit, "Never Been to Spain," a song written by country music singer/songwriter, Hoyt Axton. After listening to Sam Bidwell sing, Sessions suggested that he should come to Nashville and he would help him get into the music business. Though Bidwell turned down that opportunity, the seed had been planted. He eventually picked up the phone and called former Wichitan, Frank Dycus, who had become a successful Nashville songwriter. Bidwell recalled their conversation. "I got Frank Dycus on the phone and said, 'My name's Sam Bidwell. You probably don't remember me.' Frank said, 'I sure do remember you. You're that **** kid who used to beat me in the contests.' I asked Frank if he would help me if I came to Nashville. He asked me, 'Are you any good? If you're good, come on down. If not, stay home.' So, in October of 1985, I went to Nashville and I guess Frank liked what he heard because he took me into the studio. He told me to pick who I wanted to play on my sessions." The musicians Bidwell chose were members of what was often considered to be Nashville's A-Team. Hargus "Pig" Robbins was on piano and Sonny Garrish played steel guitar. Fred Newell and Jimmy Capps were on guitars, Joe Osborn and Larry Paxton played bass, and Eddie Bayers played the drums. Two fiddle players were called, Rob Hajacos, who later became known for his playing on many of Garth Brooks' hits, and the legendary, Buddy Spicher. Over the years, Spicher had played on records by virtually every major country star. However, when he began playing on Sam's session, Bidwell did not care for what he was hearing. "I called Jeff Pritchard in Wichita and asked for his advice. He told me, 'I used to play in a lot of fiddle contests with this friend of mine. He just moved to Nashville and is looking for work. His name is Mark O'Connor.' Mark came in and played on one song. He was so good that he ended on playing on four more songs. When he was done, I asked Mark, 'What do I owe you?' Mark said, 'How about 50 bucks? Is that OK?'" Mark O'Connor would soon become the most in-demand fiddler in Nashville. His credits can be found on more than 450 albums.

Returning to Wichita, Sam Bidwell went to a place called Biggies. This country music night club at West Street and 47th Street South had been previously known as the Wagon Wheel. The house band at Biggies was a group called Nite Shift, that featured the vocals of Cheryl Bellew. Other band members were Gary Wall, Jerry Powell, Tony Sanford, Paul Riggs and Jeff Pickering. Sam Bidwell joined Nite Shift, and they soon decided to enter the regional *Marlboro Country Music Talent Roundup* to be held on October 15, 1986. They won the contest, which included $5,000 and a chance to open for George Strait, Merle Haggard, and Ricky Skaggs at the Kansas Coliseum.

However, Bidwell soon set his sights on a national TV talent contest as a solo performer and temporarily stepped down from Nite Shift. The TV contest, known as *You Can Be a Star*, aired on TNN (the Nashville Network) and was hosted by *Grand Ole Opry* star, Jim Ed Brown. Though Bidwell was edged out of the top spot, his credibility increased among local fans back home. Wichita club owner, Bill Selby liked what he heard and hired both Sam Bidwell and the band from Biggies for his new club he named Fox Canyon. The band became known as Sam Bidwell & Nite Shift.

In 1993 Bidwell decided that it was time to open his own club which he named Sam's Place. Buck Owens had a #1 hit back in 1967 called "Sam's Place," so it was the perfect name for a country music nightclub run by a guy named Sam. Sam's Place was located at Broadway & 47th Street South in a building that had lots of country music history as the Hi-Ho Club, the Western Swinger, the Saddle Boogie Saloon, and Kit Shickers. Band personnel had changed a bit. Cheryl Bellew and Jeff Pickering were still members of Nite Shift, but Tony Sandford was now on drums, with Randy Raines on lead guitar, Doug Kimble on bass, and Jimmy Russell on keyboard. Things were going along just fine, but Bidwell was soon forced to change the location of his club. The building that had hosted so much music for 40 years, including Roy Clark, Charlie Daniels, Willie Nelson, Kitty Wells, and even Elvis Presley, was going to be torn down to make way for a new Dillon's supermarket. Bidwell packed his things and moved farther south on Broadway to near 71st Street South. Band members remained the same, except that Scott Henderson replaced Pickering on steel guitar, as well as playing the fiddle.

* * *

Before Sam Bidwell joined Nite Shift, most of the lead singing was done by Cheryl Bellew. Born in Wichita, Cheryl fell in love with music and began singing in the school choir and in small, vocal ensembles. After graduating high school, Bellew began going to various clubs around Wichita, looking for a group that was needing a "girl singer." One of those clubs was E.J.'s Red Lion on East Kellogg, that featured Bob Shepherd. Sitting at her table, listening to Shepherd, Bellew began singing along. She recalled that night. "I was singing along, in harmony, and Bob heard me. He invited me to come up and sing with him." Shepherd liked what he heard that night and hired Bellew. "I sang for tips and sang with Bob Shepherd for 2 ½ or three years. After that, I joined Nite Shift and was there for 9 ½ years." During that time, Nite Shift opened for 13 major country artists, including Hank Thompson, Marty Stuart, Shelley West, and Asleep at the Wheel. In 1990 the group won a KFDI band contest and got to open for Charley Pride at KFDI's Listener Appreciation Show. The station held a contest again the next year which Cheryl Bellew won as a solo performer. This time she got to open the show for one of her favorite singers, Waylon Jennings.

*John Denver, Cheryl Bellew
& Johnny Western (hidden)
Kansas Coliseum 1995*

Bellew next sang for about a year with the house band at a place called the Rodeo, at Pawnee & Meridian. Then, in 1997, Jerry Hardman was putting together his second version of the Saddleboogie Band. "Jerry hired me to be his 'chick' singer," recalled Bellew. "The other band members were Beau Richards, W.C. Edgar, Howard Bedient, and a drummer, usually Hugh Leslie or Dave Windsor." Bellew sang with Jerry Hardman for around a year and then formed her own band, Cheryl Bellew & Boys on the Side. That group also lasted for around a year until Bellew had to give up singing due to troubles with her vocal cords.

* * *

Born and raised in Payson, Utah, Jerry Hardman loved rodeos. By the time he was a teenager, he began entering rodeo competitions. He planned a career in professional rodeo. That did not happen. Hardman also loved music and he changed career directions to focus on country music. After high school he put together a country band he called Nite Life. They began touring the country and, in 1972, their agent booked them for two weeks at the Western Swinger in Wichita. The band was back on the road when Hardman got a call from Paul Schultz, owner of the Western Swinger. He wanted Jerry Hardman and Nite Life to be the full-time band at his club. The offer was too good to pass up, so the band headed back to Wichita. This time, instead of playing at the Western Swinger for two weeks, they ended up staying there for two years, after which they went back on the road.

Around 1978, Hardman got another call from Wichita. This time it was from the owner of the Mint Club, located at Seneca & 31st Street South. Nite Life took the job, which lasted another two years until 1980. At that time Hardman decided that it was time to go back home to Utah. Then, two years later, Wichita called again. The Western Swinger had been sold and the new owner wanted Jerry Hardman and Nite Life to be his band. The group came back to Wichita but this time they only lasted six weeks. Hardman and the new owner did not get along, so they parted ways. The band then went back to the Mint Club, where they stayed another year. By this time Hardman had begun to appreciate Wichita. "I loved the people," he exclaimed. And the people loved him and came to see him and the band. He attributed that to KFDI. "Wichita was a bigger country music market than most, thanks to KFDI."

The Western Swinger went up for sale again in 1983. This time Jerry Hardman purchased it and changed the name of the club. Hardman explained his reasons. "Chris LeDoux was a friend of mine. The name of his band was the Saddleboogie

*Jerry Hardman (in ball cap) and his Saddleboogie Band
backing Kathy Mattea and Orin Friesen
KFDI Open Air Concert at A. Price Woodard Park*

Band. When Garth Brooks made him famous and Chris signed a major label deal, he changed the name of his band to Western Underground. So, I talked to Chris and asked him if I could use Saddleboogie Band. He said, 'Absolutely.' So that's how that came about. Then I changed the name of the Western Swinger to the Saddleboogie Saloon. That lasted until 1987."

Hardman's next move was to the South Forty Dance Hall, located at 5700 South Broadway in Haysville. Once again, the band received a name change. They were billed as the River City All-Stars. Besides Hardman, band members included Gary Hilton on lead guitar, Johnny Helms on steel guitar, Del Cady on bass, and Merlin Bone on drums. After a while, Cady was replaced by Beau Richards and Bone was replaced by Gary Cornelius. The River City All-Stars were together almost a decade. Drummer, Gary Cornelius now plays in Mickey Gilley's band, while Johnny Helms plays steel guitar for Johnny Lee. Ever since the *Urban Cowboy* days, Mickey Gilley and Johnny Lee have done lots of shows together, so Cornelius and Helms still get to hang out together at those concerts.

Yet, Hardman was not finished. In 1997 he put together the new version of the Saddleboogie Band with Cheryl Bellew. Finally, in 1999, after spending most of his music career in Wichita, Hardman decided to call it quits. He moved back to Utah to take over operation of his family's tour bus company. When asked about all the time he spent in Wichita, Hardman replied, "I didn't choose to move to Wichita, but I chose to stay."

These days, Jerry Hardman is enjoying semi-retirement back home in Utah. He still loves country music and often performs solo, billed as the Classic Country One Man Band.

Wanted FOR MURDER

Bill Elliott

Alias Hill Billy Bill

This man has murdered more country music than anyone known to the music world. Every Friday & Saturday night he plays a one String Pitch Fork, with some other country western musicians, at the Hill Billy Paradise open air Dance.

Located ¼ mile East of 143rd street on 69th street or 6 miles East of Kechi 1 mile North and ¼ East or 14700 East 69th street North. Adults $1.00 Children always Free

CHAPTER FOURTEEN

GONNA GET A LIFE

I'm gonna get a life. That's what I'm gonna do
So startin' now, you can find one too.

From "Gonna Get a Life" by Mark Chesnutt

(Frank Dycus, Jim Lauderdale)

Occasionally, some country music performer's pathway to success will start by winning a talent contest. One such person was Marion Frank Dycus, who was born on December 5, 1939 in Hardmoney, Kentucky. In 1955, Dycus moved to California where, at the age of 16, he joined the United States Air Force. During his service, he formed an Everly Brothers-style duo with a friend, Don Gonzalez. Following their stints in the Air Force, the duo got a job performing on KPEG in Spokane, Idaho. While there, Dycus met stars like Buck Owens, Jim Reeves and Ray Price. In 1962, he briefly moved to Nashville but could not get anything going with his music. He soon moved again, this time to Wichita, where he got a factory job at Boeing. He also kept on singing and began doing the early morning show on KAKE radio. In 1966 Dycus won KFDI's first-ever talent contest. Concert promoter, Hap Peebles, who was based in Wichita, caught Dycus' performance and the two became friends. Peebles introduced Dycus to *Grand Ole Opry* stars, Minnie Pearl and Lonzo & Oscar. Encouraged, Dycus moved back to Nashville the following year. Country singer Tommy Hill suggested that Dycus try writing songs. Hill, himself, had become a successful songwriter, penning such #1 hits as Webb Pierce's "Slowly" and Red Sovine's "Teddy Bear." Dycus' first cut as a songwriter was a truck driving song called "White Lines and Roadside Signs" which was recorded by the Willis Brothers. His first song to hit the Top 20 was "Lilacs and Fire," which made it to #17 for George Morgan in 1970. In 1972, while continuing to write songs, Dycus went to work for Porter Wagoner and Dolly Parton. He ended up managing their recording studio. His next hit song was "He Can't Fill My Shoes" which made it to #8 on the charts in 1974 for Jerry Lee Lewis. Porter Wagoner and Dolly Parton also hit #8 with the Dycus-penned "Is Forever Longer Than Always."

While running Porter Wagoner and Dolly Parton's Fireside Studios, Dycus met 19-year-old Dean Dillon. The two became friends and Dycus hired Dillon to work in the studio. He even allowed him to sleep in the studio. Dillon was destined to become one of Nashville's most-successful songwriters, penning numerous hits for George Strait, Keith Whitley, Willie Nelson, and others.

Though he had a steady job in the music business and was becoming a successful songwriter, Dycus still had the desire to perform on-stage. He put together a group he called Lonesome Frank & the Kitchen Band. It was somewhat of a novelty band as they used pizza boxes for drums and had a bass made from a tea chest. Though the group's recordings received quite a bit of airplay in Texas and Oklahoma, not much else happened. In 1976 Dycus resigned from Fireside Studios and decided to do some traveling. He went to Sweden in 1979 and did some recording and performing over there. Returning to the U.S. the following year, he got together once again with Dean Dillon. The two began collaborating on their songwriting. Their first success as co-writers came with "Unwound," the first single for a country music newcomer named George Strait. They soon followed that with another George Strait hit, "Marina Del Rey." It looked like Frank Dycus had finally hit his stride. RCA even offered him a recording contract in 1986, but before anything could be recorded, Dycus got sick. He ended up having heart surgery. To recover, he left the music business again and moved to the mountains. He returned to Nashville in 1989 and decided to give up songwriting and focus on music publishing. But one day he was inspired by a row of rocking chairs on his front porch, so he sat down and wrote "I Don't Need Your Rockin' Chair" which became a hit for George Jones in 1992. After that success, Dycus continued to write songs and was twice voted SESAC's Songwriter of the Year. He died in 2012 at the age of 72.

* * *

Frank Dycus may have been the first person to go on to country music success by winning the KFDI Talent Contest, but he was not the last. KFDI's annual contest was held at the station's anniversary party which took place at the Joyland Park amusement center in south Wichita. The winner of the 1967 contest was a young man from Burlingame, Kansas who went by the name, Kenny Starr. Born Kenneth Trebbe in Topeka on September 21, 1952, Starr began performing when he was only five years old and had put together his first band, the Rockin' Rebels, by the age of nine. His next band was called Kenny & the Imperials, a group that toured in surrounding towns. When young Kenny turned 16, he became interested in country music and started a new band called Kenny Starr & the Country Showmen. When he came to Wichita, he won the KFDI talent contest by singing the Ray Price hit "I Won't Mention It Again." Hap Peebles caught Starr's performance and hired him to open for Conway Twitty and Loretta Lynn at a concert in Wichita. Lynn loved Starr's performance and encouraged him to move to Nashville. Though still a teenager,

Kenny Starr

Starr made the move to Music City in 1968 and went to work in Loretta Lynn's touring show. Lynn also helped him get a recording contract with MCA where she was recording. Starr landed three minor hits on the charts, and then hit it big in 1975 with a cover of the David Geddes pop single, "The Blind Man in the Bleachers." Starr's record made it all the way to #2 on the country charts and crossed over to the pop charts. With the success of that song, Starr decided to leave the Loretta Lynn Show and try to make it on his own. Though he placed nine more singles on the charts, none of them made Top 20.

CHAPTER FIFTEEN
ONE NIGHT

It's like I've waited my whole life
For us to be together this one night
Let's make it last forever, now

From "One Night" by Martina McBride

(Martina McBride, Claude Kelly, Tommy Lee James)

The Fowler brothers, Bucky and Scott, started playing music around 1970, when they were kids. Bucky was ten and Scott was nine. The boys were sons of Don Fowler, who was originally from Belfort, Arkansas, a little town just outside Harrison. He had learned to play the guitar by hanging out with Hugh Ashley, the owner of Ashley Music, a guitar studio in Harrison. Ashley, who also had a daily radio show, became a mentor to young Fowler. Don became friends with another musician his age, Frank Baughman, and the two of them forged a musical friendship that would last until Fowler's passing.

By the age of 14, Bucky Fowler was already becoming an accomplished country music singer. He decided to enter the KFDI Talent Contest, which was held at Joyland Park in celebration of KFDI's 10th Anniversary. That 1974 event was headlined by Johnny Cash's brother, Tommy Cash. Other acts on the show included Freddy Weller, and Leona Williams, who would later marry Merle Haggard. Weller, who rose to fame in the pop group, Paul Revere & the Raiders, had become a successful country music singer in 1969 with the release of his first hit "Games People Play." For the talent contest on that hot July day, Weller was one of the judges. Bucky Fowler and his brother, Scott, had put together a little band they called Century III, so they signed up for the contest. Century II Auditorium in Wichita was just five years old at the time and the Fowlers needed a band name for the contest, so they just adapted the name from that of the auditorium. The band placed third in the contest.

In 1975 Bucky and Scott Fowler joined their father in Frank Baughman's Honeymoon Ranch Boys. Scott became the bass player and Bucky played the steel guitar. Four years later Don Fowler and his boys decided to leave Baughman's group and start their own band which they named The Fowlers. The group originally included Don, Bucky, and Scott Fowler, along with drummer, Brad Renollet. Bucky and Scott were the singers in the band, and they loved to harmonize. They talked their brother, Brent, into joining the band on keyboards, mainly because they wanted a third vocal part. A fourth brother, Greg, became the band's soundman. The Fowlers did shows all around the Wichita area and became a tight band. Eventually Don Fowler decided to step aside and let his boys carry on without him. He played his last show with his boys at the Eagles Lodge on North 69th Street on New Year's Eve of 1983.

The reorganized country band, now made up of the three Fowler brothers and Renollet, felt they needed a new name. but they could not come up with anything they liked. Their fans had been referring to them as the Fowler Brothers, and the name stuck. They became the Fowler Brothers Band.

In 1984 it was announced that a country music talent contest, called the *Marlboro Country Showdown*, would take place at various locations throughout the U.S., including Wichita. The preliminary round was held at the Wagon Wheel club in southwest Wichita. Bucky Fowler recalled, "A friend suggested that we enter the contest, and since the prize was $5,000, we decided to give it a try." But first they needed a recorded demo to enter. They found a little studio run by Gary Scheer and made a recording. This led to acceptance into the opening round of the contest at the Wagon Wheel. That night the field was narrowed down to four or five bands, one of which was the Fowler Brothers Band.

The Wichita finals of the *Marlboro Country Showdown* were held at a bar called Podnuh's, in downtown Wichita on St. Francis, just south of Douglas. The Fowler Brothers Band came out on top. They won the $5,000 and, as part of their prize, the band got to open for Ronnie Milsap, Merle Haggard, and Ricky Skaggs at the Kansas Coliseum.

KFDI had been the official Wichita radio station sponsor of the *Marlboro Country Showdown* so it would have been only natural for the Fowler Brothers Band to become more closely associated with Wichita's main country music station. "Unfortunately for us," stated Bucky Fowler, "KFDI already had a house band, the Wichita Linemen. They were using the Linemen for all their special events and to back major country singers. They didn't really have a place for us." However, in 1985, KFH-FM was programming country music, and their program director, Pete Brier, offered an association with the station to the Fowlers, which they accepted. KFH-FM's country music format did not last long, but on Valentine's Day of 1986 another Wichita station began programming country music. KZSN became known as "Kissin' Country," or simply "Kissin'." "KZSN was looking for an official band," recalled Fowler, "so they put on a band contest. We won the contest and became their band."

In 1988 Brent Fowler decided to leave the group. "Scott and I had originally drafted Brent into the band because we needed someone to sing the third vocal part," said Fowler. There were dozens of country bands in Wichita during the 1980s. Most of them featured great pickers backing a lead vocalist. "Our main strength was our vocal trio. No other band around could come close to matching our tight, trio harmonies." With Brent Fowler gone from the band, they hired a female singer to take over Brent's part, but it was not quite the right fit. Not long after that the Fowler Brothers Band was booked to play a Saturday night at the Cotillion Ballroom. Since playing at the Cotillion was a big deal, the group felt like they needed to hire a soundman. Bucky recalled, "A friend of mine told me to call a local sound company called MD Systems, which was run by John McBride. So, I called John and explained the situation to him, and he said it would be perfect. He had to run sound for an event at the Cotillion on Friday night, so he would just leave his equipment set up for Saturday night and cut us a deal." After the show, McBride told the Fowlers how much he loved their show. A friendship was formed, and John McBride began doing sound for all the Fowlers' shows.

After running sound for the Fowlers for around six months, McBride approached the band following one of their shows. He told the group, "You guys sound great, but you should hire my wife." Not much thought was given to it until the next show. McBride once again said, "You guys really need to hire my wife. She's singing with this rock and roll band called Lotus and she's ruining her voice."

John McBride's wife grew up in a musical family in the small town of Sharon, Kansas, just down the road from Medicine Lodge. Martina Schiff was born on July 29, 1966 to Daryl and Jeanne Schiff, a couple who owned a dairy farm. Daryl was also a cabinet maker who loved country music. He passed that love to his children, and as they grew up, Schiff put together a band called the Schiffters, which featured the talents of his kids, Marty, Steve, and Martina. Young Martina's vocal talents became apparent to everyone who heard her sing. She entered KFDI's annual talent contest in 1980, shortly before she turned 14. A total of 95 performers entered the contest and Martina made it into the top 10. The Schiffters made several successful forays into Wichita, including performances at one of the early Wichita River Festival concerts and the opening of the Kansas Coliseum in 1977. Expectations were high for the Coliseum's opening weekend. Following a soft opening on Thursday with the Bill Gaither Trio, the main events were a Charley Pride concert on Friday night with Bob Hope headlining on Saturday. Activities took place throughout the weekend. Though she was not yet a teenager, Martina McBride still remembered that weekend. "We (Schiffters) played at the Kansas Coliseum on Friday afternoon." Her father, Daryl Schiff also recalled that day. "They said we could do anything we wanted except touch Charley Pride's piano." Martina confirmed, "Yeah. That was off limits."

When she got older, Martina moved to Wichita and joined a rock group called The Penetrators. Her next move, in 1987, was to the popular Wichita rock and roll band, Lotus. "When I was with Lotus, we played at the Fireside Club. The other guys in the band were Bill Landrum, Don Lovell, Sean Matthews and, of course, Donny Overstake." Overstake had formed the band in 1972. During Martina's time with Lotus, the group was looking for a rehearsal space and found MD Systems. They were able to rent the space they needed from the company's owner, John McBride. The audio engineer and the young, rock and roll singer soon hit it off, and the following year they were married.

One night, Lotus was playing at the Airport Hilton in Wichita. The Fowler Brothers band happened to be performing at a large private party in another ballroom in the same hotel. During one of her breaks, Martina came over to watch the Fowlers. This was the chance for which John McBride had been hoping. As the band's soundman, he requested to the Fowlers that they ask Martina to sing a song with them. The guys figured, "What could it hurt?" Besides, their soundman had been pushing for this for months. When Martina took the stage, the band asked her, "What do you want to sing." Martina asked, "Do you know 'Crazy?'" Front man, Bucky Fowler replied, "Well, we've never played it, but we know it." Fowler remembered that she was "extremely good." The performance of that one song is what planted the seed for Martina to possibly join the Fowlers. The band set up an evening for an audition. The Fowler brothers had grown up with country music with their guitar-playing father, Don. Martina was also steeped in classic country music because of the time she spent playing in the Schiffters with her father, Daryl. The audition turned out to be more of a jam session. Bucky Fowler recalled, "I knew Martina had the job after the first song, but we ended up singing with her for several hours. We discovered that we all knew the same classic country songs."

Martina McBride did her first show as an official member of the Fowler Brothers Band at the Moose Lodge in Hutchinson, Kansas. She ended up performing with the band for a year and a half. Near the end of that time, Martina entered and won the 1989 KFDI Talent Contest at Joyland Park. Part of her prize was a recording session with KFDI's band, the Wichita Linemen. She recorded two songs with the Linemen, "Your Cheatin' Heart" and "Hello Love, Goodbye." KFDI-FM's program director, "John Boy" Speer felt that Martina had what it would take to "make it" in the music business. So, the McBrides packed everything they owned into a U-Haul truck and their old Plymouth and headed for Nashville. "John and I went to Nashville on January 1, 1990," recalled Martina. "I had a demo tape that I had made and was shopping it around to record companies. I wasn't having any luck so I did whatever I could. I was a waitress, I worked in stores, and did various jobs." It was her husband who had the first success in the music business. "John happened to run into an up and

*Martina McBride performs with the Fowler Brothers Band
at the Cotillion Ballroom*
(Photo courtesy of Bucky Fowler)

coming singer from Oklahoma named Garth Brooks, who was trying to put together a crew to take his show on the road." Brooks hired John McBride to run sound, and Martina went along. "I sold t-shirts at the concerts for Garth," she said. All the while, she continued working on her own country music ambitions. She finally landed a recording contract with RCA Records and released her first single, "The Time Has Come," in 1992. The song made it to #23 on the Billboard country charts. After a couple of more chart singles, Garth Brooks offered Martina the job of opening act on his shows. Her career took off from there. Martina's fourth single, "My Baby Loves Me," went all the way to #2 and she never looked back. She became the most successful Kansas country music performer, ever.

Following Martina McBride's departure from the Fowler Brothers Band in 1989, the group again needed someone to sing the third part in the vocal trios. They first hired Adam Hughes and then Kim Stancer. After Stancer left, they began another search to find a replacement. Bucky Fowler then asked his wife, Karla, if she could fill in until they found a permanent replacement. As it turned out the search ended there. Karla Fowler became the band's newest member.

Eventually the Fowler Brothers Band and KZSN dropped their exclusive agreement and the band was finally able to reconnect with KFDI. In 1995 the group performed at the KFDI Open Air Concert. That night they added three new members…Kristine (age 10,) Kelcy (age 8,) and Kandace (age 5)… the daughters of Bucky and Karla Fowler. Bucky smiled when he remembered. "The girls kept telling me that they wanted to sing with the band. I just brushed them off. I had seen too many kids that weren't very good, being put on stage by their parents. I didn't want that. Karla called me into the house one night and said, 'You better listen to this!' Unbeknownst to me, the girls had been working on a song…the old Patsy Cline song, 'Back in Baby's Arms.' I couldn't believe it when I heard it. They had perfect three-part harmonies. So, I put them on that KFDI show. They did 'Back in Baby's Arms' and that old McGuire Sisters song, 'Sincerely.' The audience went crazy. They loved it."

In 2001, Scott Fowler left the band but remained in the music business. Since that time, he has been the road manager for Garth Brooks. These days, the group now known as the Bucky Fowler Band often includes musicians like Rob Loren on

Bucky Fowler Band and Southern Charm
L-R: Pat Keitel, Kristine Fowler, Kelcy Fowler, Rob Loren, Kandace Fowler, James Hocutt, Karla Fowler, Kurt Graber, Bucky Fowler

fiddle, Pat Keitel on drums, Dude Stewart on bass, Nick Havel on steel guitar and, of course Karla on vocals. The girls, Kristine, Kelcy, and Kandace, also became permanent members of the show as the Fowler Sisters. More recently the trio started calling themselves Southern Charm. For five years the Bucky Fowler Band and the girls did regular Opry-style shows, both at the Fox Theater in Newton, Kansas and the Poncan Theater in Ponca City, Oklahoma. The group knows hundred (perhaps thousands) of songs which they perform mostly in Kansas and Oklahoma. Bucky grinned, "We never do the same show twice."

* * *

The success of a band often depends on the musicians in the band. A band leader can be a fine singer and an excellent musician, but his or her music will only be as good as the other members of the band. Great musicians can raise the perceived talent of the band leader. By the same token, mediocre or poor musicians will lower the perception. Successful band leaders search out the good musicians. Bucky Fowler is a great example. He always has great musicians in his band. One of those musicians, who has performed in the Bucky Fowler Band since the mid-1990s is fiddler, Rob

Ray Price and Rob Loren
(Photo courtesy of Rob Loren)

Loren. Loren grew up near Portland, Oregon, but moved to Albuquerque, New Mexico in 1976 to study music. For a while, Loren was a member of the band Starberry, and later a group called DJ Cookin'. He also worked with Jim Meek & the Country Showmen, which included Wade Kirby, the son of successful country music songwriter, Dave Kirby. After the Kirbys moved to Nashville, Wade heard that Ray Price was looking for a fiddler, so he called Rob. Loren auditioned with Price by playing a show with him, and he got the job. He was a member of Ray Price's Cherokee Cowboys during the last couple of months of 1982 and all of 1983. In Albuquerque, Loren also met his wife, Connie. In 1990 the couple found jobs in Wichita, so they relocated to Kansas. Rob began teaching orchestra and elementary strings in the Wichita public schools.

As his reputation spread, Loren became the most in-demand fiddler in Wichita. His skill set was such that he could play almost any kind of music. He could play classical, jazz, bluegrass, and of course, country. In the mid-1990s Loren joined the Fowler Brothers, and later Tina Dunnegan & Thunder Road. Often he was called to back nationally known performers, including Charley Pride, Merle Haggard, and Michael Martin Murphey, and became a member of Hank Thompson's Brazos

Valley Boys at the end of Thompson's career. Though Thompson died in 2007, Loren had fond memories of playing with him. "I played the very last two shows he ever did." One of the most memorable times for Loren was when he performed with Charlie Daniels. "I was playing with the Bucky Fowler Band and we were going to back Charlie Daniels at the KFDI Stars for Starkey concert at the Airport Hilton. Before the concert, Charlie said to me, 'We're going to do 'Devil Went Down to Georgia' and you're going to be the Devil.' When we got done, one of the band members told me, 'You beat him!' Charlie just stared at me, and then he took his fiddle bow and knocked my bow out of my hand. Then he laughed." In 2019 Rob Loren was inducted into the Northwest Western Swing Music Society's Hall of Fame. He continues a busy performing schedule, playing the fiddle, the mandolin, and even doing some singing.

CHAPTER SIXTEEN
WICHITA SKYLINE

Down at the train they go to Independence everyday
But anywhere else now seems like a million miles away
And I must have been high to believe that I would ever leave
Now I'm just a flat fine line like the Wichita Skyline

From "Wichita Skyline" by Shawn Colvin

(Shawn Colvin, John Leventhal)

Another country music radio station signed on the air in Wichita on August 12, 1974. Operating at 900 KHz on the AM dial, it was the station previously licensed by country music singer and businessman, Mack Sanders as KSIR. In 1967, the station had been purchased by Wichita broadcaster, Bob Freeman, and Lowell Denniston, owner of the supermarket known as Mr. D's. It went on the air with a Top 40 format, in direct competition with Wichita's only other Top 40 station, KLEO. Its call letters were KEYN.

In 1968, while attending a Spanish class at WSU, I met Larry Waggoner who was chief engineer at KEYN. He was also one of the DJs, and went by the name of Alan McKay. Larry told me that KEYN was about to launch a new FM station and asked me if I was interested in a job. I was taking 17 hours of classes at WSU and was already working three other jobs, but I said, "yes." So, in November of that year, KEYN-FM went on the air and I was the evening newsman. The staff did not think that Orin Friesen was a good "air" name, so they had me become Doug Stevens. That was the only time in my 50+ years in broadcasting that I ever used a name other than my own.

KEYN-FM was one of the first FM stations in America to feature Top 40 pop music. As the station, and FM in general, began to get more popular in Wichita, the owners, which by that time also included Pizza Hut founder, Frank Carney, along with Freeman and Denniston, decided to do something else with the 900 AM frequency. They chose a country music format, to compete with AM country powerhouse, KFDI. Successful salesman Shelly Davis was hired away from KFDI to manage the station.

Originally the call letters of the re-formatted KEYN AM were going to be KGNE, a play on KG&E, the power company, Kansas Gas & Electric. A new logo was drawn, featuring a likeness of KG&E's mascot, "Ready Kilowatt," wearing a cowboy hat. However, after KG&E threatened a lawsuit, that idea was dropped. Instead, the station became KBUL, also known as "K-Bull." The logo featured a graphic representation of a longhorn bull. Larry Waggoner, once again as Alan McKay, was assigned to do the morning show. I did a two-hour, all-request, country music oldies show from noon to 2pm. Following me, in the 2 to 6pm shift was Mike Hoyer.

* * *

Hoyer had begun his radio career in 1945 at the age of 17. He had done eight years on KMA in Shenandoah, Iowa but in 1965 he became known for his "Country Music USA," all-night, truckers' show on 50,000 watt WHO in Des Moines. Each night he would sign on the air with, "From border to border and coast to coast and then some..." Hoyer was also a songwriter. His biggest success came with "Looking at the World Through a Windshield," a Top 5 hit for Del Reeves in 1968. The song was also covered a few years later by California country-rock band, Commander Cody & His Lost Planet Airmen. Hoyer is also credited with being the first person to begin taking bus tours to Nashville. He was inducted into the Country Music Disc Jockey Hall of Fame in 1995 and passed away in 1999.

Getting Mike Hoyer to move to Wichita was quite a coup and was what KBUL needed to even begin to compete with the well-established, highly successful KFDI. My noon to 2pm shift was my first daily DJ job in commercial radio. The "all request" format of my show allowed me to interact

KBUL's Jody Carter, with Mike Oatman and Mike Hoyer
(Photo courtesy of KFDI Collection)

with my listeners and to share my knowledge of country music. It was during that time that I also began my weekly program of bluegrass music, which continues to this day.

* * *

Across town, KFDI had a "house band" to assist with their promotions. Since 1971 that position had been held by the Wichita Linemen. Not to be outdone, KBUL management also wanted a band of their own. They got the Nashville News, which was led by steel-guitarist Stan Holmes, who sometimes went by the nickname, "Sherlock." He even had an image of Sherlock Holmes on the front of his steel guitar.

Holmes began his musical career by learning to play the resonator guitar, which is more commonly known by the trade name, Dobro. He recalled his first instrument. "It was a handmade dobro with a wooden faceplate. I found it in a trash can in an alley in Pratt. I still have that guitar." As his skills improved, Holmes felt like he needed a better instrument. "Around 1962 or '63 I bought an old, metal National (resonator guitar) for $29.95. I showed it to Clif Major who owned a guitar store. He asked me if I would sell it to him and I told him I wasn't interested in selling. Then he offered me $600 so I sold it to him on the spot. I found out later that Clif sold that guitar within a week for $1,500."

Later, while visiting Nashville, Holmes ran into Shot Jackson. Harold "Shot" Jackson, a successful steel guitarist on the *Grand Ole Opry*, had started a steel guitar manufacturing company with another legendary steel guitarist, Buddy Emmons. They called their company Sho-Bud. After a few years, Shot Jackson also began building dobros, which he called Sho-Bros. One of those instruments was played by "Bashful Brother Oswald" Kirby of Roy Acuff's Smoky Mountain Boys. "Shot was showing me around his shop. He pointed to an old guitar case and said, 'Man. There's a dobro you ought to have!' On the side of the case were two pieces of tape, which had the words 'Brother' and 'Oswald.' I looked inside and saw this beautiful, Sho-Bro dobro. I asked Shot what he wanted for it. He said, 'Well, I'd have to have $400 for that one.' I could hardly get my checkbook out fast enough. I said, 'Sold,'

Nashville News 1975
L-R: Stan Holmes, Mike Copeland, Kenny Pruitt, Monty Baker
(Photo courtesy of Stan Holmes)

and handed him the check. Shot immediately reached down and pulled off those two pieces of tape. I said, 'Shot, what did you do that for? I wanted Oswald's name left on there.' Shot said, 'Well, I can only refund your money.'"

In 1962 Stan Holmes became the dobro player in Kansas' first bluegrass band, Jack Theobald's Bluegrass Country Boys. After a short stint playing bluegrass, he switched his interest to the pedal steel guitar, and helped form the country band, Nashville News. Other members included Kenny Pruitt on bass, Mike Copeland on drums, and Monty Baker on fiddle and lead guitar. Later Roger Mattingly was added on lead guitar so Baker could stay on fiddle. They played country dances at Moose Lodges, Elks Clubs, and American Legion halls across Kansas and Oklahoma. One night they did a show in Pickway, Kansas that was emceed by Gary Hightower and Jody Carter, who had taken over the morning show on KBUL from Larry Waggoner. At the show, members of Nashville News met KBUL station manager, Shelly Davis, who told the guys that he would like to get them to be KBUL's house band. The group accepted and began performing at various KBUL events.

One of those events took place on September 19, 1976. Billed as the "KBUL New Faces Show," it featured six of country music's most-promising, up-coming stars in concert at Century II Auditorium. Hosted by famed country DJ, Biff Collie, the lineup included Gene Watson, Ed Bruce, Darrell McCall, Jo-el Sonnier, Carmol Taylor, and former Wichitan, Vernon Oxford. Nashville News lasted until 1978. During the last two years of the band's existence, Stan Holmes also played dobro with Buster Jenkins, a bluegrass and old-time fiddler who was based out of Denver. Following the disbanding of Nashville News, Holmes played steel in the reformed Ark Valley Boys, a country gospel group that was headed by brothers, Curt and Ron Baggett. In 1982 he helped form a new group called the Flatland Band. Other members of the group included Sam Bidwell, Doug Rowland, Jeff Pritchard, Brad Oxford, and Don Neal. This group did quite a bit of work for KFDI, including opening for the big stars at the KFDI Country Club Dances at the Cotillion Ballroom. The Flatland Band lasted until 1987.

* * *

Jeff Pritchard had already established himself as one of Kansas' best fiddlers long before he joined the Flatland Band. I first encountered Jeff around 1971 when he was 14. His mother, Mary, brought him to where I was living. She said, "My son plays violin in the Junior Symphony and he wants to learn to fiddle." I had no clue how to play the fiddle, but I could play chords on the guitar so Jeff could play along. It was obvious even back then that Jeff's talents would soon take him way beyond my abilities. Pritchard continued to hone his skills by practicing for fiddle contests. He began competing in, and winning, local and regional fiddle contests. In 1973, he won the very first Walnut Valley Old Time Fiddle Championship in Winfield. Pritchard was held to the #2 spot the next year, being bested by 13-year-old, child prodigy, Mark O'Connor, but in 1973, Jeff took home top honors again.

Pritchard's fiddle playing career almost came to an end in 1979 due to a power saw accident. The saw completely severed the middle finger of his left hand and badly injured two other fingers. A surgeon was able to reattach the severed bones, ligaments, and tendons, but no one, except Pritchard, thought he would ever play the fiddle again.

Charlie Daniels, Jeff Pritchard and Rob Loren
(Photo courtesy of Rob Loren)

By 1982, he felt ready to enter the *Grand Master Fiddler Championship*, which was held at Opryland in Nashville. That first year, Pritchard placed 6th. Winner of the contest that year was once again, Mark O'Connor. Pritchard placed 7th the following year, 3rd in 1984, and finally hit his stride in 1986 by winning first place.

Over the years, Pritchard has lent his fiddle playing talents to numerous Wichita country bands, including the Wichita Linemen, Terry Henry's Rockin' Rowdy Country Band, the CrawDaddies, Doug Rowland & the Fireglows, Tony Rico & the Moonlighters and, of course, the Flatland Band. He even spent two years playing in Country Music Hall of Famer, Hank Thompson's Brazos Valley Boys. A modern-day renaissance man, Pritchard has become a successful businessman, real estate developer, and pilot. He also has a boat with which he and his friends are trying to navigate all the major waterways in the U.S. He still enjoys playing the fiddle whenever his busy schedule allows.

CHAPTER SEVENTEEN
URBAN COWBOYS

But then one night in Wichita
I was just comin' off the stage
Folks all lined up screamin' for my autograph
And Lord I was a national rage

From "Sure Hit Songwriter's Pen" by Bobby Bare
(Shel Silverstein)

A major event took place in America that gave country music a huge shot in the arm. On June 6, 1980, the movie *Urban Cowboy* was released. The film, which starred John Travolta and Debra Winger, was based around Mickey Gilley's Pasadena, Texas dancehall called Gilley's. Due to the success of that movie, country music was suddenly the hottest thing going in the U.S. Wichita was already a hotbed for country music, but *Urban Cowboy* made it even hotter. Nationally, the Urban Cowboy craze spawned hitmakers like Johnny Lee, Ronnie Milsap, and especially the group, Alabama. Where before, when most country hits were by solo artists, Alabama made it popular to be a band, not unlike the Beatles, and play country music. The garage band phenomenon that created countless bands in wake of the success of the Beatles and many other rock & roll bands of the 1960s, had now shifted to country music. Country music bands were being formed throughout the U.S. and Wichita was certainly no exception. This trend continued throughout the 1980s and well into the '90s.

Along with the new bands and the massive popularity of country music came the bars and dance clubs that catered to the country music crowds. Jesse's Supper Club was located at 425 East 61st Street North. A look at their calendar from March of 1989 shows bands like Slim Chance, the Country Rip Riders, Nite Shift, Leather & Lace, Mixed Company, and Midnight Rose, formerly known as Dusty Rose. Midnight Rose was also performing at the Cockeyed Cowboy Club which was located at 300 South Greenwich Road. Another popular night spot was the South Forty Dance Hall at 7426 South Broadway, just south of Wichita in Haysville, home to the River City Allstars. To the west of Wichita was the Westgate Fun Center & Dance Palace. This venue, located at 13000 West Highway 54 often featured the popular band, Slate Creek.

* * *

Formed by 16-year-old Terry Henry and his friend, Phil Ray, Slate Creek also featured the talents of Donny Ramsey, Don Raymer and Ronnie Mills. The group won the 1989 *Kansas Battle of the Bands*. The next year, Slate Creek entered a national country music talent contest called the *True Value/GMC Truck Country Showdown*. They made it to the final round and performed on the stage of the *Grand Ole Opry*. Slate Creek entered the contest again in 1991, and once again made it to the finals. Both appearances were televised, nationally, and the group shared the *Opry* stage with several nationally known entertainers, including Kathy Mattea, Sawyer Brown, and Restless Heart.

In 1992, after eight years, Slate Creek lead singer, Terry Henry, decided to strike out on his own. He became friends with a local, songwriting couple, David and Cindy Love. One of the songs the Loves wrote for Henry was called "Rockin' Rowdy." That song became the name for Terry Henry's Rockin' Rowdy Country Band. The Loves not only provided songs for Henry, but David became the band's manager. His son, Mike, joined the band, and would eventually receive co-billing. As he had done with Slate Creek, Henry entered his Rockin' Rowdy Country Band in several talent contests. Though the band had only been together a few months, they were one of the finalists for the KFDI talent contest which took place at the station's 28th Anniversary Party at Joyland Park. Henry and his group won that contest and earned an all-expense paid trip to the *Country Music Awards Show* in Nashville.

Slate Creek with Willie Nelson
L-R: Terry Henry, Donny Ramsey, Willie Nelson, Donny Raymer, Ronnie Mills, Phil Ray

Having twice made it to the finals of the *True Value/GMC Truck Country Showdown*, Henry entered his new band in the 1992 contest. Band members included Pat Kelly on drums, David Kilgore on bass, Kurt Graber on steel guitar, either Steve Falke or Jimmy Russell on keyboards, and award-winning fiddler, Jeff Pritchard. The group made it all the way to the Midwest Regionals by winning the state contest, which was held at the *Ellis County Fair* in Hays. By the following year, the band, now called Terry Henry, Mike Love & the Rockin' Rowdy Country Band, became a full-time touring band, performing at venues coast to coast, including the famous Golden Nugget in Las Vegas. When they were back home in Wichita, they often performed at McGraw's, a club owned by Bill Selby.

* * *

Monty Coble was born in Wichita in 1961, and by the time he was seven, he began learning how to play the guitar. Not long after, Monty's family moved to Arkansas City, Kansas. When Coble was in junior high, he put together his first band, a typical rock & roll garage band. During his late teens, he became interested in country music and joined some friends at Norm's Club in Ponca City, Oklahoma where they formed a band. "I got together with Rick Anderson and Joel Day. Then we found a bass player, and later added Rick Palsmeier on fiddle. Troy Walburg and Ben Russell joined later on. We didn't have a band name until one night when somebody hollered, 'Whiskey River,' so we became the Whiskey River Band."

Though the group was based out of Arkansas City, they occasionally played in Wichita at places like the Saddleboogie Saloon. Among their other Wichita performing highlights were a Shriners Convention and KFDI's 26th Anniversary

Whiskey River Band at Wichita Union Stockyards in 2019
L-R: Joel Day, Kim Schmidt, Dan Graves, Monty Coble,
Donny Ramsey, Jon Irsik

Party at Joyland Park in 1990. "We disbanded in 1998 but a few years ago I decided to reform the Whiskey River Band." Members of the re-formed band, besides Monty Coble, included Jon Irsik on lead guitar, Donny Ramsey on bass, Joel Day on steel guitar, and Zach Wiederstein on drums. Rick Palsmeier, from the earlier version of the Whiskey River Band, returned to the group in 2020, once again playing fiddle.

* * *

Bands continued to come and go in Wichita. Some of the other country bands at the time included Double Take, the Firewater Band, Strawboss, and a band called Wichita* that featured the vocal talents of Cheryl Wayne. Wayne, whose given name was Cheryl Madison, began performing in 1978, when she was still a child. At the age of 14, she entered her first talent contest. Wayne competed in contests for seven years, sometimes in competition with another young singer from Kansas, Martina Schiff, who went on to become famous as Martina McBride. In 1985, Wayne won the talent contest at KFDI's 21st Anniversary Party at Joyland Park and went on as a state finalist in the *True Value Country Showdown*. Other members of the Wichita Band included Mike Tripp on lead guitar, John Evans on bass, Jason Martin on piano, and Wayne's husband, Hugh Leshley on drums.

* * *

One of the most popular country music night spots in Wichita was located at 5327 East Kellogg. It opened in 1980 and was simply called The Cowboy. The place was large enough to accommodate not only local bands, but also featured occasional nationally-known touring acts. On nights when bands were not featured, the music was showcased by the club's DJ, "Cowboy Joe" Sparks. In 1994, The Cowboy relocated to 2nd & Mosley in Wichita's Old Town district. At 24,000 square feet, the new location was three times the size of the original club. My personal favorite memory at The Cowboy in Old Town was visiting with Marty Stuart and having him hand me his Fender Telecaster guitar. That guitar had been previously owned by Clarence White of the rock group, the Byrds. It was the prototype for the original Parsons-White string bender. Inside the body of the guitar was a mechanism that allowed White to "bend" the B string of the guitar, very similar to the way strings

---

*Author's Note: This is a different "Wichita" than an earlier band of the same name, which will be discussed in Chapter 20.

are "bent" by a pedal steel guitar. The device was invented by Gene Parsons, who played drums and banjo in the Byrds with Clarence White. That Telecaster is one of the most-iconic guitars in Country and Rock & Roll music. It remains Marty Stuart's main guitar to this day.

* * *

KFDI Radio, which had used the Wichita Linemen as their "house" band since the 1960s, became home to another country music band formed within the radio station by "Ranch Hand," Andy Oatman. Following a short-lived band called Detour, Oatman enlisted fellow Ranch Hand, Scott Piper, along with Brad Stevens, Tracy Presnell, Fritz Davis, and Tom Boulanger to form the Ranch House Swing Band. Boulanger had the most experience, having played steel guitar in the band of Wichita radio personality, Mack Sanders.

Oatman, the son of KFDI owner/manager/morning DJ, Mike Oatman, began his radio career by mowing the lawn at KFDI on weekends when he was still in school. He originally did not consider a career in radio. "I didn't want to follow in the footsteps of my father," Andy said. After spending time in Argentina as an exchange student, Oatman considered majoring in Spanish in college. But not wanting to be

Ranch House Swing Band at Cain's Ballroom in Tulsa, OK
L-R: Paul Chavez, Andy Oatman, Eddie Macy Jr. (hidden),
Scott Piper, Pat McJimsey
(Photo courtesy of Michelle Oatman)

a teacher and finding few opportunities for a career as a Spanish major, he changed his major to business, graduated with a degree in radio and television, and began reconsidering a career in radio. He explained, "It finally got through to me that whatever I did, I was going to be following somebody's footsteps. And, if I had to follow somebody's footsteps, I could do a lot worse than follow my dad's." Andy began working part time in 1983, doing the all-night shift on weekends. He became a full time "KFDI Ranch Hand" in 1985.

Oatman's co-founder in the Ranch House Swing Band, Scott Piper, was already an established "Ranch Hand," having worked at KFDI since 1983. Piper had also started at KFDI doing the midnight to 6:00am shift. Like Andy, Piper had not planned on a career in radio. Though he had worked part time at a radio station in Hutchinson, Kansas during high school, he set his eyes on becoming a teacher. He attended the University of Kansas where he earned a degree in English literature. Piper remembered, "I got sidetracked when I learned to play the guitar and started playing in bands at KU. When I graduated, I joined a country-rock band called Tree Frog. We played professionally for about four years or so and toured quite a lot."

Tree Frog
L-R: Jim Fey, Eric Elder, Gary Durrett, Lynn Piller, Scott Piper
(Photo courtesy of Scott Piper)

Though based out of Lawrence, Tree Frog played some shows for KFDI in Wichita. It was at one of those shows where Piper met KFDI-FM Program Director, John Speer. Piper was also familiar with KFDI because of his friend and fraternity brother, Dave Quillen. Quillen had become a successful advertising agent and had married Cindy Lynch, the daughter of Great Empire Broadcasting's majority owner, F. F. "Mike" Lynch. The flagship station of Great Empire was KFDI. Those radio connections sparked a bit of interest in Piper, who found a job working for KOFO, a small radio station in Ottawa, Kansas. Piper reminisced about his early days in radio at KOFO. "It was one of those stations where you get to do a little bit of everything. I did late night DJ work. I cleaned the place out. I did some news, production, writing, sales. Eventually I was Operations Manager. It was a good experience."

After five years at KOFO, Piper decided that it was time to move on. He set his sights on Nashville. "I wrote songs for the band. I played guitar and fiddle. I thought that it would be nice to work at a radio job in Nashville, while pursuing some of this other stuff on the side." He sent his resume to around 30 stations in the Nashville area. He included Mike Lynch of KFDI as a personal reference. In return, Lynch asked for a copy of Piper's resume. A call from Nashville never came, but one from Wichita did. Piper was soon doing the midnight to 6:00am shift on KFDI, replacing "Uncle Dick" Houser who had passed away one night on his show. That was in 1983. Two years later, Piper was doing the midday shift from Noon to 3:00pm on KFDI AM. Shortly after arriving at KFDI, he had begun sitting in with Andy Oatman's band, Detour. "I found that I wanted to play again," said Piper. Detour had been

Ranch House Swing Band
L-R: Andy Oatman, Tommy Boulanger (seated), Tracy Presnell, Rick Meyers, Pat McJimsey, Paul Chavez (seated), Scott Piper, Eddie Macy Jr.
(Photo courtesy of Michelle Oatman)

doing a variety of styles of music, from pop to rock to country. When a couple of members left, the band decided to become focused on country music and changed their name. The Ranch House Swing Band recorded their first album at the KFDI studio. They called it *World Tour '86*. In 1989, they released their second album, *Caught in the Act*, which they put together from a live performance they did at Sheldon Coleman Jr.'s Big Dog Studios in downtown Wichita, currently the site of Cabaret Oldtown.

Band personnel continued to change. For a while, the lead guitar player in the Ranch House Swing Band was James Garver. However, Garver soon left to move to Nashville where he became a member of Garth Brooks' band. He remained in Garth's band until Brooks decided to retire in 2000.

As the more "country" players in the Ranch House Swing Band decided to pursue other interests, they were replaced by several of Wichita's key rock and blues players, including Pat McJimsey, Ricky Meyer, Ed Macy, Jr., Paul Chavez, and Bob Hartley.

* * *

During the 1990s, country bands in Wichita came and went. Sometimes groups changed members due to personality clashes or because the music was taking a different direction. Musicians moved from band to band. Band names were dropped from the scene. New names were added. A list from 1991 shows groups like the Full House Band, Under the Gun, Rhythm 'N Heart, Lodestone, Steel Diamond, Cactus Jack, Dakota, Rapid Fire, and Marvin Osborn & the Rhythm Gamblers.

A good example of the Wichita bands from the early 1990s is Southern Exposure. Bass player/singer Joe Worrel grew up in Texas and learned how to play the bass when he was only seven. During his teens, he joined a young band that toured across the U.S. Following high school, Worrel joined the Air Force and ended up being stationed at McConnell Air Force Base in Wichita. His love of country music propelled him to form his own band. He enlisted guitar player, Fred Austin, and drummer, Richard Broz. They soon added Darla Presnell on keyboards and vocals, after hearing her sing at KFDI's Anniversary Party at Joyland Park in 1991. Besides playing the area night spots, Southern Exposure gained good exposure by opening

Urban Cowboys

Southern Exposure with Kansas Senator Bob Dole
L-R: Darla Presnell, Rick Caywood, Bob Dole, Joe Worrel,
Richard Broz, Fred Austin
(Photo courtesy of Joe Worrel)

for Eddy Raven at his Wichita concert, and by appearing on a couple of local TV shows. Like most of the country bands from the '90s, Southern Exposure had their run and then split up to do other things. Band leader, Joe Worrel eventually moved to Atlanta, Georgia where he now performs as a solo act.

Still more new country bands came along in the early to mid-1990s. Groups like Bits & Pieces, In Kahootz, Heartland, and the Donnie Huffman Band were performing in country night spots around Wichita. Country bands continue to perform in and around Wichita to this day. Perhaps the best known are the Whiskey River Band, and those bands led by Matt Engels, Rusty Rierson, and Bucky Fowler.

CHAPTER EIGHTEEN

WHERE THE GRASS GROWS TALL

Goin' back to where the grass grows tall
And the fields burn in the fall
You can still hear the night birds call
Back in Wichita.

From "Wichita" by Gillian Welch

Originally, bluegrass and western music were a part of country music, but as the "Nashville Sound" came into vogue, those sub-genres were moved into categories of their own. Bluegrass is a type of acoustic music based around the 5-string banjo, mandolin, fiddle, acoustic guitar, and bass. The resophonic guitar (dobro) is also usually considered to be the sixth bluegrass instrument. Bluegrass, or "Blue Grass," as its founder preferred, was begun in the 1940s by Bill Monroe. The music got its name from Monroe's band, the Blue Grass Boys. Monroe named the band for his home state of Kentucky, often known as the Blue Grass State. Other bands evolved, both directly and indirectly, from Monroe's bands. They included Lester Flatt, Earl Scruggs & the Foggy Mountain Boys, the Stanley Brothers, Jimmy Martin & the Sunny Mountain Boys, and the Osborne Brothers.

It did not take long before bluegrass bands were popping up across the southeastern part of the United States, and even in New England. However, it took longer for the music to reach Kansas. The first bluegrass band in Kansas was put together in 1962 by guitarist and singer, Jack Theobald. Theobald had been dabbling in bluegrass and old-time country music with fiddler, Buster Jenkins, and later became part of another duo with fiddler, Richard Povenmire, as the Country Boys. In 1963, Theobald decided to put together a full-fledged bluegrass band. With his son, Mike, on 5-string banjo and Emitt Hipps on fiddle, he formed a group he called Jack Theobald & the Country Boys. The name was soon changed to Jack Theobald & the Bluegrass Country Boys. As the band gained popularity, Mike's name was added to that of his father's and the group became Jack & Mike Theobald & the Bluegrass Country Boys. A few years later, the "boys" was dropped from the band's name altogether. Among the early members of the group were Joe Payton on mandolin and fiddle, Jack Jarman on fiddle, Dan Kocks on bass, and Stan Holmes on dobro.

Bluegrass Country Boys
L-R: Jack Theobald, Jay Yount, Dan Kocks, Mike Theobald, Joe Payton
(Photo courtesy of Mike Theobald)

Later members included fiddlers, Jay Yount and Fred Morton, mandolin players Coleman Stephens, Orin Friesen, Mike Keyes, and Stan Greer, dobro player, Greg Hissem, and guitarist, Fred Austin. Jack Theobald lived in the small town of Belle Plaine, not far south of Wichita, so Bluegrass Country was based there. However, the band always included members from Wichita, and the group played in Wichita quite often. For example, they played the KFDI Anniversary Party shows at Joyland Park every July. Throughout the 1960s, Jack and Mike Theobald's band was the only bluegrass band in Kansas. Bluegrass festivals were becoming popular in the '60s, but the closest ones to Wichita were in Missouri or Oklahoma. In 1967, the Walnut Valley Folk Festival took place at Southwestern College in Winfield, Kansas, and the bluegrass music of the Theobalds was included there.

The Theobalds also hosted regular bluegrass concerts at the American Legion building in downtown Belle Plaine. Many aspiring bluegrass musicians got their start at these concerts. I am one of those people. I met Mike Theobald in 1966 in one of my classes at Wichita State University. I was doing a folk music show on the WSU radio station, KMUW. One time I noticed that Mike was carrying a banjo case. I thought, "folk music," so I invited Mike to play the banjo on my radio show. He agreed, but brought along his father, Jack, to accompany him on guitar. I recorded them doing seven banjo instrumentals. Mike informed me that this music was called "bluegrass." From that point on, Mike began to teach me about bluegrass music. He brought me records by Flatt & Scruggs, the Stanley Brothers, Jim & Jesse, Bill Monroe, and a group that became my favorite, the Dillards. My folk music program soon became more of a bluegrass show, which is the forerunner of the show I still do today on KFDI, which I call *Bluegrass from the Rocking Banjo Ranch*.

Even though I was new to bluegrass, I started a little bluegrass trio at WSU around 1967. Mike Theobald was on banjo, Chris Taylor played bass fiddle, and I played guitar and sang. I started singing regularly at the Theobald's Belle Plaine concerts. Around that time, WSU began presenting concerts at the Campus Activity Center. One of those concerts was a solo performance by banjo player, John Hartford. At the time, Hartford was best-known as the composer of Glen Campbell's breakout hit, "Gentle on My Mind," and for his appearance on the Byrd's *Sweetheart of the Rodeo* album. Since I was playing bluegrass on KMUW, I decided to do an interview with Hartford. It was the first of hundreds of interviews I would end up doing during my 50+ years in radio. It was also the first time I had ever been around somebody

Bluegrass Trio at WSU
L-R: Orin Friesen, Chris Taylor,
Mike Theobald

smoking marijuana. I was shocked to be interviewing John Hartford while he lit up a joint and smoked it, right there in the CAC on the WSU campus. During the 1960s, you could be arrested and thrown in jail for smoking pot.

In 1971, I received a call from the popular Wichita rock & roll guitar player, Clif Major. Clif and two of his rock & roll pals, Tom Coleman and Charlie Castleberry, were putting together a bluegrass band and they needed a guitar player. I found it hard to believe that one of Wichita's best guitar players was asking me to play guitar for HIM! Clif had learned to play the banjo and dobro. Tommy Coleman learned the fiddle and mandolin, and Charlie Castleberry put down the electric bass guitar he was playing in rock bands and bought a bass fiddle. We called ourselves Prairie Grass.

Our first performance was at a little bar across the street from the Wichita State University campus called Kirby's Beer Store. By the early 1970s, Clif Major had already become a local legend as a rock & roll guitar player. His credibility around town was such that he pretty much assumed the leadership role in Prairie Grass. So, one night, Clif took us to Kirby's. It was a small bar that had never had live music. Clif talked the bar owner, Jim Kirby into letting the band play for tips. Since there was no stage, we moved the foosball table out of the way and set up there. Kirby's became a home for Prairie Grass, and when Jim Kirby opened Kirby's #2 on East Kellogg, we became the first featured band there as well. Kirby's #2 was the first bar in Wichita to become known as a place to hear bluegrass music. Even the jukebox was stocked with lots of bluegrass records.

Another bar that became somewhat of a regular gig for Prairie Grass was a place on West Douglas called So's Your Mother. My favorite memory from So's Your Mother was the night a drunk patron started requesting that we "play some Johnny Cash." The only Johnny Cash song we knew was "Get Rhythm." So, we did "Get Rhythm" and the drunk walked up and handed us a five-dollar bill. Before long, we heard him holler again, "Play some Johnny Cash!" So, we did "Get Rhythm" again and he brought us another five-dollar bill. The place was not very crowded, so I guess we sold out to the drunken Johnny Cash fan. We did "Get Rhythm" several times that night.

Where The Grass Grows Tall

Prairie Grass
L-R: Charlie Castleberry, Clif Major, Tom Coleman, Orin Friesen

The best place Prairie Grass played was a new bar in downtown Wichita called The Foundry. It was located on East Douglas, just a few doors down from the Old Mill Tasty Shop. The walls of The Foundry were covered with wooden gears and other machine parts that had been mockups for metal parts from a real foundry. The acoustics of the room were not great, but it had lots of atmosphere. We had a good time though we never made much money. I recall one night we made $35, which we split between the four of us. When the Foundry first opened, Prairie Grass alternated weekends with another young, bluegrass band, the World's Largest Prairie Dog. Band members included Greg Smith, Bill Hawks, Fred James, Ron Lynam, and Rick Howell. On the weekends when they were not at the Foundry, the band often played at a bar called the Yellow Submarine.

For his day job, Clif Major worked in the record department at large store at Kellogg and Greenwich Road in east Wichita called David's. One day, three guys from Garden Plain, Kansas came in the store. Chris Fisher and brothers, Rick and Gary Palsmeier told Clif that they were starting a bluegrass band. Chris played guitar, Rick played fiddle, and Gary was on mandolin. They called themselves Grand River Township, after the township where they lived west of Wichita. With the addition of Ed Holick on banjo and Dan Aitken on guitar, Grand River Township was soon a five-piece band. The group became part of the mix at The Foundry, as well as rotating with Prairie Grass and the World's Largest Prairie Dog at other Wichita bars.

Grand River Township
L-R: Gary Palsmeier, Dan Aitken, Ed Holick, Chris Fisher, Rick Palsmeier

Around that same time Kansas got its first real bluegrass festival, which began just south of Wichita in Haysville. The first Haysville Bluegrass Festival took place in May of 1971 at Riggs Park. The hosts of the festival were Jack & Mike Theobald & the Bluegrass Country Boys. The early festival lineups were rounded out by bands from Oklahoma. One of the Oklahoma bands that played the festival the second year was a group of teenagers that called themselves the Bluegrass Revue. Bobby Clark, mandolin player in the band recalled the time. "David Bonham sang lead and played the guitar. Billy Perry was on the banjo and his little brother, Mike, played bass. We returned to Haysville two years later, in 1974. By then, David Bonham had left the group. My buddy, Vince Gill, had replaced him." Gill moved to Louisville, Kentucky in 1975 to join the Bluegrass Alliance. But before he left, he made one more trip to Haysville with his friend, Bobby Clark, who was now playing with his older brother, Mike, in Uptown Bluegrass. Vince Gill sat in with the band that weekend playing dobro.

* * *

Prairie Grass at Winfield 1972
L-R: Clif Major, Charlie Castleberry,
Tom Coleman, Orin Friesen

In September of 1972, a new festival was started at the fairgrounds in Winfield. It was called the National Guitar Flat-Picking Championship Festival and was built around a guitar flat-picking contest. The event featured three of the nation's best-known flat-pickers, Doc Watson, Norman Blake, and Dan Crary. Most of the rest of the booked entertainers were bluegrass bands, like Lester Flatt & the Nashville Grass, featuring 14-year-old mandolin prodigy, Marty Stuart, Jim & Jesse & the Virginia Boys, the Country Gazette from the state of California, led by three-time national fiddle champion, Byron Berline, who was from Caldwell, Kansas, and a young, upstart, progressive bluegrass band from Kentucky, the New Grass Revival. That first year there was only one stage but there were still a few open slots in the schedule. Clif Major, who we considered the leader of our band, Prairie Grass, went and spoke to someone from the festival. So, we got to play on stage for the crowd at the grandstand.

Following the success of its first year, the National Guitar Flat-Picking Championship Festival began to move away from being a standard bluegrass festival to an event that featured all sorts of other types of acoustic music, including folk, blues, Celtic, cowboy, and other genres that defy categorization. Additional stages were added so that now there are four official stages, plus several unofficial stages in the campgrounds. The festival was also rebranded as the Walnut Valley Festival. Most people around the world refer to the festival as "Winfield." Folks that live in Winfield call it "Bluegrass."

Though the event was no longer technically a "bluegrass" festival, it continued to attract bluegrass musicians, due a lot to its prestigious contests and campground jamming. It also came along at the time when bluegrass was really starting to gain popularity among young people. The Nitty Gritty Dirt Band had released their landmark, three-record set, *Will the Circle Be Unbroken* album in 1972, the same year the Winfield festival began.

By the time the 2nd annual festival rolled around in 1973, Prairie Grass had disbanded. Sometime early in the festival, Mike Theobald asked me if I would be interested in joining the Bluegrass Country Boys. They needed someone to sing harmony. Since they were lacking a mandolin player, the mandolin would be my

Jack & Mike Theobald and Bluegrass Country 1975
L-R: Fred Morton, Mike Theobald,
Orin Friesen, Jack Theobald, Dan Kocks

instrument. I never did become a "real" mandolin player. I mostly just did the "chop" rhythm. Fortunately, I was not the mandolin player for long. Dan Kocks decided to move on, so I took over his position as bass player. I had never played bass at all, let alone a bass fiddle. I did not even own a bass, so I borrowed a Japanese electric bass guitar from my friend, Larry Heck. Traditionalists frowned on using an electric bass in bluegrass, but big name, "traditional" bluegrass bands like the Osborne Brothers and Jim & Jesse & the Virginia Boys were using electric basses, so I figured it was OK.

In 1974, shortly after I began playing bass, Bluegrass Country performed as the backup band for fiddler, Robert Byrd, the well-known U.S. Senator from Virginia. Senator Byrd was in Wichita to campaign for Congressman Bill Roy, who was running for Senate against Bob Dole. I remained with Bluegrass Country for 18 years. Perhaps the highlight of those years was when we went to Maggie Valley, North Carolina to perform on the TV show, *Fire on the Mountain*. The show was hosted by David Holt and aired on TNN (The Nashville Network.) It was the only nationally televised bluegrass show at that time. Several different bands were taped during the time we were in Maggie Valley. We were last. Though no one realized it at the time, we were the last group taped, ever. After that season, TNN cancelled the show.

* * *

My only venture into booking concerts was on April 27, 1978. I had been contacted by Wichita realtor, John Todd, who was a huge fan of traditional bluegrass. Todd talked me into teaming up with him to do a bluegrass show at the Wichita East High School. We hired Bill Monroe & the Blue Grass Boys, Jim & Jesse & the Virginia Boys, and James Monroe & the Midnight Ramblers. Todd put up the money. Though the concert may not have been profitable, it was an artistic success. Bill Monroe, the "Father of Blue Grass," had not performed in Wichita in years and the crowd was ready for him. Throughout the show, members of the audience shouted out requests and Monroe obliged. He was really enjoying himself. Monroe later performed in Wichita a couple of more times, the last being at the *KFDI Listener Appreciation Show* in 1986.

*Bill Monroe & Friends at
Wichita East High School*

The Kansas Bluegrass Association and its festival, the Haysville Bluegrass Festival, had begun in 1971 and interest in bluegrass music began to grow in Wichita and the surrounding area. Groups like Grand River Township, the World's Largest Prairie Dog, and my group, Prairie Grass, were considered sort of "hippie" bluegrass bands. Most of the members of those bands came out of rock & roll and were more influenced by the Nitty Gritty Dirt Band and John Hartford rather than Bill Monroe and Flatt & Scruggs. However, with the success of the Theobalds' concerts in Belle Plaine and the Haysville Bluegrass Festival, a few more traditional, bluegrass bands began to emerge in the 1970s. The first of those was the Bluegrass Jayhawkers, who came on the scene in 1972. Led by husband and wife, Nelson and Mary Jane Funk, this group, though based out of Marion, began to perform regularly at Wichita events. Nelson Funk played guitar and taught himself to build guitars. Mary Jane played the banjo. Fiddler Russ Morton often fronted the band and became one of the movers and shakers in the Kansas Bluegrass Association. The Funks had a son, Steve, who was on his way to becoming and accomplished mandolin picker, but tragically drowned in an accident at a bluegrass festival.

Wichita vacuum cleaner dealer, Carl Duncan, became a big fan of bluegrass and he and his wife, Jean, got involved with the KBA. In 1976, Carl and his son, Johnny, formed the Flatland Express and became regular fixtures at the Old Cowtown Museum on Sunday afternoons. The only other band new to the Wichita bluegrass scene in the '70s was Fresh Water. Put together in 1977 by husband and wife, Bill and Judy Sample, the group also included David Rice and Clif Major.

Bluegrass took hold in a big way in Kansas in the 1980s. New bands appeared on the scene every year. During the '80s, there were almost twenty new bluegrass bands in Wichita alone. At the time, Clif Major had his guitar store next door to the La Posada Mexican restaurant at 610 South Oliver. Beginning in 1980, Clif, along with Mike "Si" Seiwert and Ron Malcom began playing bluegrass three nights a week at La Posada as the Flint Hillbillies. When Malcom left, guitar player, Jimmy Pryor, and bass player, Charlie Castleberry joined the group. Jimmy Pryor also joined his father, Don, in a band called Bluegrass on Tap, with Jim Brasher, Larry Moody and Nathan Baker. By 1982, Baker was a part of the Chisholm Creek Boys, which also included Don Fell, Miles Newberry, Troy Majors, and Troy's daughter, Sarah. Then Mike Seiwert and Jimmy Pryor of the Flint Hillbillies, and Jim Brasher from the Chisholm Creek Boys teamed up with Tim Gleeson to form Fresh Cut. Potlatch was formed from former members of '70s bands, the World's Largest Prairie Dog and Grand River Township. Karen Boggs, Linda Cunningham and Pam Batson, with Dude Stewart on bass, became Dusty Rose. The trio of Joe Emery, Kelly Werts, and Paul Elwood formed as the Sons of Rayon, a group known for Werts' "Velcro tap dancing." When Emery left the group, Karen Boggs from Dusty Rose became the third "son." The bluegrass scene in Wichita was evolving at a pace that would make heads spin. Other Wichita bluegrass bands in the early '80s included Flinthill Special, Bluestem Revue, Not Quite Bluegrass, and Sweet Basil.

* * *

Southwind at Winfield 1982
L-R: Jeanette Driscoll, Joni Richardson, Chris Fisher (hidden),
Brian Driscoll, Clif Major

In 1982, the Wichita music scene spawned another band that had significant ties to bluegrass music. Formed around the trio vocals of Jeanette and Brian Driscoll and Joni Richardson, Southwind was an exciting, acoustic group that featured the hot, guitar and mandolin playing of Brian Driscoll. Chris Fisher, who had been one of the original members of Grand River Township, joined the group as a second guitar player. The upright bass player in the group was Jim Keefer, who was later replaced by Clif Major, who also played banjo. Southwind was the most-successful bluegrass-style band from Wichita and they continued to perform around town throughout the early 1980s.

On August 14, 1981, the members of Southwind were part of special group that I put together to open for Ricky Skaggs & Kentucky Thunder at the Cotillion Ballroom. Besides Southwind, the group, which was billed as the Kansas Bluegrass All-Stars, also included Winfield bones playing sensation, Barry Patton, former banjo player from Grand River Township, Ed Holick, who was now playing fiddle, and three members of Bluegrass Country; Mike Theobald on banjo, Greg Hissem on dobro, and me on bass and mandolin. We opened the show with Holick playing a hot version of the Bill Monroe classic, "Uncle Pen." Three years later, Ricky Skaggs would have a number one hit with that song, but he was not yet performing it in 1981.

* * *

One Saturday night in 1984, three brothers from Conway Springs, Tim, Brad and Bill Bennett showed up at Jack & Mike Theobald's show at the American Legion in Belle Plaine. That night the brothers made their debut performance. The Bennett Brothers had been singing together since they were kids, but once they discovered bluegrass music in the early 1980s, they decided to start a band. They recruited banjo picker, Mark Johnson and dobro player, Vern Whitesell to form the Bennett Brothers Band. Known for their tight harmonies, the Bennetts were soon playing bluegrass festivals and concerts throughout the midwest. Whereas most bluegrass bands in Wichita only lasted a few years at most, the Bennett Brothers performed together for over 25 years. Eventually Bill Bennett handed off his bass fiddle to his 12-year-old son, Marc, who became the sixth member of the band. In 2013, Marc Bennett was elected Sedgwick County District Attorney.

* * *

Bennett Brothers Band
L-R: Brad Bennett, Bill Bennett, Tim Bennett, Mark Johnson, Vern Whitesell

Not to be confused with the World's Largest Prairie Dog from the 1970s, the Prairie Dogs were formed in 1986. Jim Brasher and Jimmy Pryor came from Fresh Cut, and were joined by Ted Farha, Richard Crowson, and Allen Hale. When Pryor once again moved on, he was replaced by Fred Austin. Crowson had relocated to Wichita from Memphis to become the political cartoonist for the *Wichita Eagle*. By 1988, he had teamed with Karen Boggs to form Bazaar Crossing and, a year later, Lone Run. Boggs and Crowson married in 1991 and continue to make music together as Richard and Karen Crowson, including their long-running, monthly engagement at Watermark Books.

In the spring of 1987, I had the opportunity to produce my own music festival as a part of KFDI's involvement with the annual Wichita River Festival. Billed as the Kansas Heritage Days Old Time Music Festival, the event featured over 100 musicians in twenty-some folk and bluegrass acts during the two-day event. A three-dollar River Festival button was the only admission charge to the festival, which took place at the Old Cowtown Museum, so some years thousands of people attended. In the first three years of the event, performers were all from Wichita or the surrounding area. Quite a few of the musicians were part of local organizations like

Kansas Heritage Days Old Time Music Festival 1992
L-R (onstage): David Grier, Charlie Castleberry, John McEuen, Gary Palsmeier, Jeff Pritchard

the Great Plains Dulcimer Alliance, the Flint Hills Dulcimer Club, and the Kansas Bluegrass Association. Eventually I decided to bring in some nationally known musicians to headline the event. The Chicago bluegrass band, Special Consensus was the first, and they headlined the 1990 festival. The next year I brought in the Dillards, the bluegrass band that had become famous as the "Darling Boys" on the *Andy Griffith Show*. In 1992, the headliner was John McEuen of the Nitty Gritty Dirt Band. The 1993 event, which turned out to be the final year for the Kansas Heritage Days Old Time Music Festival, took on a more "western" flavor by headlining two Kansas bands, Bluestem and Kelly Werts & the Home on the Range Band. Though Wichita's version of a bluegrass festival had come to an end, Park City, just to the north of Wichita, started their Park City Bluegrass Festival around the same time of year in 1994.

The second half of the 1980s brought more bluegrass bands. Among them were Wind River, Tall Grass, Echo Canyon, Salt Creek, True Blue, and Cause for Concern. Perhaps the most successful of the new bands from that era was Prairie Wind, led by Jim Bullard. Other members included Johnny Duncan, Marvin Mueller, Dave Brown, and Paul Lisa. That group lasted into the 1990s, even though lead singer, Jim Bullard left in 1991 to form Hot Pursuit, with Kevin Hendrix, Mark Johnson, Mac McHugh, and Matt Dudte. Cause for Concern was one of the first of many musical ventures for Dennis Hardin. The group's bass player, Darren Wilcox, eventually became a member of the Chicago-based, Special Consensus. At a jam session in Chicago, he met Ken White of the Nashville group, New Tradition. Wilcox recalled the meeting. "We were jamming in the middle of the night. The other players had all gone to bed, so it was just Ken and me. At one point, Ken told me that he was thinking about moving to Wichita, Kansas. I said, 'I'm from Wichita!' So, we both ended up back in Wichita and kept on playing music together." That connection led Wilcox and White to join a new band that Robin Macy was putting together, which was initially called the Big Twang Theory, but was soon shortened to Big Twang. The group's critically acclaimed album, *Pastures of Plenty*, was released in 2000.

Robin Macy had moved from her home in Dallas to take a job as a math teacher for Wichita Collegiate High School. Prior to her move to Kansas, Macy had performed at the Walnut Valley Festival in Wichita with two of her previous bands; first Danger in the Air and then, more importantly, the Dixie Chicks. To form the latter group,

Dixie Chicks
L-R: Emily Erwin, Robin Macy, Martie Erwin, Laura Lynch

Macy enlisted two, talented sisters who also attended the festival in Winfield, fellow Texans, Martie and Emily Irwin. Laura Lynch rounded out the band. The first two Dixie Chicks albums, *Thank Heavens for Dale Evans* (1990) and *Little Ol' Cowgirl* (1992), showed a group that was equally at home with bluegrass and western music, with a few other genres of music thrown in for good measure. However, by 1993 a difference in musical direction led Macy to exit the band. Prior to the formation of Big Twang, she had worked with Mike and Vickie Theobald in Blue Plate Special, as well as in the Domestic Science Club, a trio she formed with Sara Hickman and Patty Lege. A lifestyle change led Macy to retire from teaching and purchase the Bartlett Arboretum in Belle Plaine, Kansas, where she continues to play music as well as presenting outdoor concerts by both regional and nationally known performers. Macy is currently involved with another female trio that does a lot of swing and western swing, the Cherokee Maidens.

* * *

In 1992, my bass-playing friend from Prairie Grass, Charlie Castleberry, became part of a bluegrass gospel group called Psalm Country. The band's sound was built around the vocals of Desiree Widiger and Laurie Ribordy. Widiger, who played fiddle and mandolin in the band, was born and raised in Indiana, and first began playing the violin at the age of 10. During the late 1970s, she toured the U.S. and

Psalm Country
L-R: Charlie Castleberry, Desiree Widiger, Rob Loren, Laurie Ribordy

Canada in a Campus Life/Youth for Christ band. She loved singing in the choir at church, and in 1980 and '81, she was part of the 450-member Messiah Festival choir in Lindsborg, Kansas.

Laurie Ribordy began playing the guitar when she was seven. Like Widiger, Ribordy also loved to sing in choirs. In the early 1980s, she was a member of Friends University's famed Singing Quakers. For a time, she had her own, all-female Country band called Echo Canyon. Rounding out Psalm Country was popular Wichita fiddle and mandolin player, Rob Loren

* * *

I left Jack & Mike Theobald & Bluegrass Country in the early 1990s but the band continued to perform. Around 1995, the group changed its name to the Blue Fire Band. Jack and Mike Theobald continued to lead the band but Mike's wife, Vickie, had joined on mandolin. Charlie Castleberry became the new bass player. After Jack Theobald retired, Mike and Vickie kept the band going but changed the name to Kansas Heart. The group still does occasional performances. At the time of this

Kansas Heart at the Walnut Valley Festival
L-R: Mike Theobald, Marc Bennett, Vivkie Theobald, Chris Biggs, Bob Atchison

writing, Mike Theobald works for KWLS radio in Wichita, where he and "Ranger" Stan Greer have teamed up for a Sunday afternoon bluegrass show called *Mike & the Ranger*.

A few more bluegrass bands were formed in the early 1990s, including Fresh Water, Hillary's Sister, and the Knapic Family. The Kansas Bluegrass Association continues to promote bluegrass music. Each year in February, since 1990, the KBA has hosted an indoor bluegrass festival at the Marriott Hotel in east Wichita.

CHAPTER NINETEEN

MEN WITH BIG HATS

I rode from here to Wichita without a woman's smile
The campfire where I cooked my beans was the only light for miles
Now the man with the big hat is buying.

From "Man with the Big Hat" by Jerry Jeff Walker.

(Steve Fromholz)

The term "country music" originally referred to music performed by people that lived in the country. When rural musicians and singers were first recorded, the genre was often referred to as "hillbilly music." As the music became more popular, the term "hillbilly" was found to be offensive to some, so the name of the music was changed to "country." However, another style of music was beginning to emerge from places other than the Southeast, such as Texas, Oklahoma, and California. The new style of music was driven by the popular "B" western movies and was fueled by the singing cowboy stars of those movies, Gene Autry, Tex Ritter, Rex Allen, and Roy Rogers. In 1934, Rogers teamed up with Bob Nolan, Tim Spencer, and Hugh Farr, to form the Sons of the Pioneers, a group that would go on to become the most famous western singing group in history. The last of the original Sons of the Pioneers, Roy Rogers, died in 1998, but the group continues to this day, led by Roy Rogers Jr, who his dad called "Dusty." Various combinations of the Sons of the Pioneers have performed in Wichita and the surrounding area over the years, but Wichita has an even closer connection to this famous group. Oklahoma-born, Ken Carson spent some of his childhood years living in Wichita with his family. He took an early interest in music and taught himself to play the harmonica, the Jew's harp, and the guitar. He was a member of the Sons of the Pioneers from 1943 to 1947, after which he became a staff member at NBC and then CBS, where he became a regular on the Garry Moore Show.

The Sons of the Pioneers deserve much of the credit for the genre known as western music. It was they who combined the lush, three and four-part harmonies, with the jazzy sounds of Hugh and Karl Farr's fiddle and guitar to create the "western" sound that lives on today. Add to that, the superb songwriting of Bob

Nolan and Tim Spencer, with songs like "Tumbling Tumbleweeds" and "Cool Water," and appearances in almost a hundred movies, and you have a singing group whose accomplishments will likely never be equaled.

Though the music created by the Sons of the Pioneers, and other similar groups that followed, was far from being hillbilly music, it was still close to country music. Radio stations that played "country" music also enjoyed playing "western" music, so the two terms were combined to become country & western music. Even the "western" part of C&W had its variations. Traditional cowboy music, which had always been a part of folk music, was included. So were the cowboy songs of Hollywood which were written by professional songwriters. These songs were more complicated than the typical hillbilly or cowboy song, and their chord structure was closer to that of jazz music.

What we now call "western swing" was also considered to be part of the music known as "western." Like the Hollywood western music, western swing also started in the early 1930s, but this style came out of Texas. One of the first bands to play this style was the Light Crust Doughboys, a group formed to promote Light Crust Flour of Burris Mills. Out of this group came two major pioneers of western swing music, Milton Brown and Bob Wills. Both were innovators, especially Brown. But after Brown's early death in an auto accident, the spotlight shifted to Bob Wills & the Texas Playboys. These days it is hard to think of western swing music with conjuring up the name, Bob Wills.

Throughout the 1940s and '50s, fans in Wichita tended to prefer the sounds of western music to that of the country music that was mostly coming out of Nashville. Wichita was filled with workers from the various aircraft plants. These were hard working people who like to let off a little steam on the weekends and they loved to dance. Most of the danceable music in country & western came from the western part, especially western swing. Whenever Bob Wills & the Texas Playboys or Hank Thompson & the Brazos Valley Boys came to town, they always drew large crowds of folks who wanted to dance.

Bands on the local radio stations in Wichita during the 1940s and '50s also tended to prefer the more western sound. Those groups included the Ark Valley Boys on KFH, and the KFBI Ranch Boys. That trend continued into the late 1950s and early 1960s, even though live bands on the radio had pretty much become a thing of the past and the stations were doing most of their programming from records. Mack Sanders signed on KSIR in 1958, as a full-time country & western station, and Mike Lynch and Mike Oatman turned KFDI into a full-time country & western station in 1964. Both KSIR and KFDI included a generous portion of western (especially western swing) in their C&W programming.

However, by then western music was becoming a dying art. The western movies with the singing cowboys were long gone. Cowboy songs had become a thing of the past, even though many of the country music performers in Nashville had adopted the western style of clothing, rather than the suit & tie fashion that had been popular on the *Grand Ole Opry*, or the bib-overall and gingham dress fashion that had preceded that. Fancy, sequined suits made by Hollywood tailor, Nudie Cohn, for the cowboy stars, were now showing up on the stage of the *Opry* on a regular basis. Nashville had adopted the look but not the sound. By the 1970s, the term "western" had been dropped and the music simply became "country music." But western music was not gone forever.

* * *

In 1969, a new western swing band was formed in the unlikely place of Paw Paw, West Virginia. Put together by Ray Benson and Reuben Gosfield, who went by the name "Lucky Oceans," the band was called Asleep at the Wheel. In 1970, they moved to Oakland, California, and released their first album, *Comin' Right at Ya*, in 1973. Shortly after the release of their debut album, Asleep at the Wheel made its first appearance in Wichita at the *Daryl Starbird Rod & Custom Car Show*, which was

Asleep at the Wheel at Cotillion Ballroom 1979

held at Century II Auditorium. As the group was still basically unknown, only a handful of people showed up for the band's performances. Those who were there included KFDI's "Ol' Mike" Oatman and me. Due to the success of the album and the authenticity of the music, Willie Nelson convinced the band to relocate to Austin, Texas. Though Asleep at the Wheel has undergone continuous personnel changes, Ray Benson continues to lead the band, which still plays western swing music, and still occasionally performs in Wichita, especially at the Cotillion Ballroom.

* * *

In 1976, Rex Allen Jr., son of the movie star singing cowboy, Rex Allen, had a hit with a song called "Can You Hear Those Pioneers?" The song, an obvious tribute to the cowboy singers of the past, included cameo vocals from both Rex Sr. and the Sons of the Pioneers. Two years later, incredibly in Nashville, a group was formed to bring back the sounds of the classic western groups like the Sons of the Pioneers. Riders in the Sky was put together by two performers from Michigan, Doug Green and Fred LaBour. When they started their group, they became "Ranger Doug" and "Too Slim." Fiddler, Paul Chrisman joined them a year later and he became known as "Woody Paul, the King of the Cowboy Fiddlers." I became a fan of the Riders in the Sky when I heard their first album, Three on the Trail, which was recorded in 1979.

Johnny Western and Riders in the Sky
L-R: Woody Paul, Joey Miskulin, Johnny Western, Ranger Doug, Too Slim

Riders in the Sky were new, but I was already familiar with Ranger Doug. I have long been interested in the history of country music and Douglas B. Green was my favorite writer/historian. He had also been a member of Bill Monroe's Bluegrass Boys and Jimmy Martin's Sunny Mountain Boys in the late 1960s. I discovered in a magazine that Riders in the Sky were to be playing in Nebraska and in Oklahoma with an open date in between. It looked to me like they would be driving right through Wichita on December 6, 1981, so I called Ranger Doug and booked them for an evening show at a bar called Foundry 21 on South Seneca. That same day the Riders stopped by and performed live on KFDI and did an afternoon show in Shepler's, "The World's Largest Western Store." I think they spent all the money Shepler's paid them right there in the store. After 43 years, Riders in the Sky are still performing and occasionally show up in Wichita.

One Wichitan who became an instant fan of the Riders in the Sky was hat maker, Jack Kellogg of Wichita Hat Works. Like many other fans of the Riders, Kellogg, who is better known as "Hatman Jack," fell in love not only with the band's music but also their on-stage antics. He felt the inclination to gather some of his like-minded friends and put together his own cowboy band. Dubbed the Rhythm Rangers,

Rhythm Rangers
L-R: "Hatman Jack" Kellogg, Alan "Whitey Trash" Satterly,
Henry "Hank" Nelson, "Big Tom" Dyer, Eric "E.C. Wakeen" Cale

the group included Henry "Hank" Nelson, "Big Tom" Dyer, Alan "Whitey Trash" Satterly, and Eric Cale. Cale, who is currently the director of the Wichita-Sedgwick County Historical Museum, was billed as "E.C. Wakeen and his bass, Twister." Kellogg, who played accordion in the Rhythm Rangers mentioned that the band played a variety of styles. "We did country, western, honky-tonk, Faron Young, Webb Pierce...lots of truckin' songs." The group's fondness for truck driving songs came from the recitations that often occurred in such songs. "We called 'em 'recitates,'" laughed Kellogg. "We also referred to them as the 'likin's in the middle.' We loved the on-stage schtick. We even did a Ramones song and made it sound country."

The Rhythm Rangers played at the B-1 Club on South Pattie, the Dog House on North Broadway, and at the Coyote Club where they once opened for Asleep at the Wheel. In the early 1980s, the band attempted to make their mark on the world as their "Rhythm Rides the West Tour" took them from Wichita to the west coast. Later members of the band included Rob "Bert" Bottorf, Jeff Dyson, who went by the moniker, "Jim Bob Duke Buck," and Wichita Symphony cellist, Susan Mayo, who the rest of the band called "Symphony Sue."

* * *

Another significant event in the re-popularity of cowboy and western music took place in 1990. That is the year Michael Martin Murphey released his album, *Cowboy Songs*. Murphey, who is best-known for his 1975 million-selling hit, "Wildfire," also had pop hits in the '70s with songs like "Geronimo's Cadillac" and "Carolina in the Pines." Soon his songs were crossing over to the country music charts. Though he still had his fans from his success on the pop charts, Murphey became a major star in country music, with hits like "What's Forever For" and "A Long Line of Love." Between 1976 and 1991, he placed almost 30 hits on the country charts.

Around 1973, Michael Murphey, who had not yet begun to use his middle name, performed at the Orpheum Theater in Wichita. He was the opening act for Austin, Texas singer, Jerry Jeff Walker. After Murphey's set, Walker came on stage inebriated. He was so drunk he could hardly perform and had to leave the stage after attempting only a few songs. Murphey came back out and finished Walker's set. Walker and Murphey both deserve credit for creating the music scene in Austin, Texas, especially through Murphey's performances at the Armadillo World Headquarters. One night, a member of the audience was so moved by what he saw happening, he moved from Nashville to Austin and changed his sound. His name was Willie Nelson.

In 1975, with new songs like "Wildfire" and "Carolina in the Pines" on the pop charts, Murphey headlined a show in Wichita at Century II Auditorium. The opening act was the Oak Ridge Boys. One year, Murphey was headlining the concert on the plaza at Century II, as part of the Wichita River Festival. Halfway through the concert, the show was cancelled due to a tornado warning. It was the only time since the song was a hit that he did not get to do his signature song, "Wildfire."

KFDI's John "Boy" Speer and Michael Martin Murphey

(Photo courtesy of KFDI Collection)

Though he had a western feel in his music since the beginning, his album, *Cowboy Songs*, solidified Michael Martin Murphey's position as America's #1 cowboy singer. He had fans around the world, yet he most often performed in the part of the U.S. that exemplified his music and his lifestyle, the American West. He has performed in Wichita many times, at places like Century II, the Kansas Coliseum, the Crest Theater, and the Orpheum Theater. He continues to do so.

When I was growing up on a farm in Nebraska, my favorite musical group was the Sons of the Pioneers. I fell in love with their beautiful, harmony singing on songs like "Tumbling Tumbleweeds" and "Cool Water." Spurred by the success of Riders in the Sky, Rex Allen Jr., and Michael Martin Murphey, I decided that I would like to sing cowboy music. For 30 years I had been playing bluegrass music, so most of the musicians I knew around Wichita were from that genre. I contacted three of

Home Rangers
*L-R: Orin Friesen, Stan Greer,
David Hawkins, Richard Crowson*

my friends from bluegrass, Stan Greer, David Hawkins, and Richard Crowson, and we formed the Home Rangers, basing our name on the Kansas state song, "Home on the Range."

We took pride in being the first cowboy band from Wichita, but the Home Rangers were still probably just as much "bluegrass" as we were "cowboy." We still used typical bluegrass instruments like banjo, mandolin, and dobro. In 1998 I heard that Stu Stuart was moving to Wichita from Nashville. I had first met Stu when he was playing in the Iowa bluegrass band, Pathfinder. More recently I knew him as the fiddle player for the Nashville alt-country band, Hank Flamingo. Though the band was ready to make it big in country music, country music was not quite ready for them. After one album on a major label, Hank Flamingo dis-banded and the members of the group went their separate ways. Stu Stuart was originally from Augusta, Kansas, so he decided to move back to Wichita where he still had family.

Because of Hank Flamingo, I had thought of Stu Stuart as a good fiddle player. Since he was moving to Wichita, I figured he would make a good addition to the Home Rangers. When he got to town, I called Stu and asked him to join the band. It did not take long to figure out that Stu was more than a fiddle player. It turned out that he was even a better guitar player, as well as a powerful singer.

Stu had not been playing with the Home Rangers long when I received a call from a man named Thomas Etheredge. He told me he lived on a cattle ranch near Wichita and was hosting some people from France for a barbeque. He was trying to find some cowboy music. He called the Old Cowtown Museum, and someone there directed him to the Home Rangers. After a successful and fun night at his ranch, where Stu, Richard Crowson, and I played some cowboy songs, Etheredge got the idea to start a chuckwagon supper venue. The concept of a cowboy chuckwagon supper and show was popular throughout many of the western states. The first of such was the Flying W Chuckwagon, located on the edge of the Garden of the Gods at Colorado Springs, which began in 1953. The Flying W was on the ranch of the Wilson family, who had relocated from Butler County, Kansas to Colorado. Mr. and Mrs. Wilson's daughter and son-in-law, Marion and Russ Wolfe, had also moved with them. Wolfe was originally from El Dorado and it was he who came up with the concept of a chuckwagon supper as a venue for tourists. He continued to run it until 2012, when the Flying W burned to the ground in the Waldo Canyon fire. After extensive rebuilding, the Flying W reopened in 2020, with Jesse Friesen from the Prairie Rose Rangers joining the Flying W Wranglers.

The Prairie Rose Chuckwagon Supper opened in May of 1999 on Mother's Day weekend. Etheredge had built a wooden stage and a little, corrugated metal cook shack in a bend of the Whitewater Creek. This was in a wooded corner of a 77-acre cow pasture in Butler County near Benton, just 15 minutes from Wichita. Originally, the barbeque meal was brought in by a caterer. Customers were shuttled to the area on horse-drawn wagons. The meal was served at picnic tables beneath lights that were strung through the walnut trees. It was a pretty site. After the meal, the crowd was entertained by the cowboy music and comedy of the Home Rangers.

The initial response to the chuckwagon suppers was such that Etheredge decided to do them several times a week. Stu Stuart did not have a lot going on, so he was thrilled to have an opportunity to play music on a regular basis. I had just been laid off from my full-time employment at KFDI because of an ownership change, so I was also ready to be involved with the chuckwagon suppers. Unfortunately, the other three members all had day jobs and could not commit to being cowboy singers on a regular basis. That left Stu and me.

During the time he was in Nashville, besides playing with Hank Flamingo, Stu Stuart had a cowboy band called J38 Land & Cattle Company. J38 had a chuckwagon that they would haul on a car trailer. They also had a setup where they could fix barbecue on-site. That way they could "take their show on the road," so to speak. Stu had been the lead singer in J38, so when he moved to Wichita, the group disbanded. Stu and I really wanted to continue to do the Prairie Rose Chuckwagon Suppers, so Stu placed a call to one of his pals in J38. Jim Farrell was a part-time studio engineer in Nashville. He was also a great tenor singer, rhythm guitar player, and songwriter who loved cowboy music. In other words, he was perfect for the job.

Due to family obligations, Farrell was hesitant to move to Kansas, but he decided to take the job. So, for the entire first season of the Prairie Rose, which went until October of 1999, he commuted from Nashville every week. Jim is a big cowboy and he drove a tiny car. By the end of that first season, he had literally driven that car into the ground. His car eventually found its final resting place in a hedge row on Thomas Etheredge's ranch.

Once Jim Farrell joined Stu Stuart and me, the permanent lineup for the cowboy band at the Prairie Rose Chuckwagon Supper was set. The Flying W in Colorado Springs had their Flying W Wranglers, Durango, Colorado had the Bar D Wranglers, Jackson Hole Wyoming had the Bar J Wranglers, and so on. Stu, Jim, and I became the Prairie Rose Wranglers. We finished the season at the outdoor stage, and by the time May of 2000 came around, the chuckwagon suppers moved indoors to the newly constructed Opera House. Between 1999 and 2007, the Wranglers played between 150 and 200 shows a year. In 2005 alone we did 232 shows. Not only did we get to perform at the Prairie Rose, we did numerous concerts away from home. In 2003 and 2004, we played at New York City's famous Carnegie Hall. Around

*Johnny Western and the Prairie Rose Wranglers on the Great Wall of China 2006
L-R: Jim Farrell, Johnny Western, Orin Friesen, Stu Stuart*

that same time, we began performing on a series of Caribbean cruises. In 2006, the Wranglers hosted an Asian trip billed as "The Great American Cowboy China Tour." The next year we did a series of concerts in Nashville, prior to the Prairie Rose being sold in July of 2007.

The Prairie Rose Wranglers, which by that time included a fourth member, drummer Steve Crawford, depended on the Prairie Rose for our livelihood, so we immediately contacted Wichita's Old Cowtown Museum. The directors of Cowtown felt that the Wranglers would promote interest in their destination, a living history museum portraying the way Wichita was during the cattle drive era. It seemed like the perfect fit. For a very short time, the band just dropped the "Rose" and became the Prairie Wranglers. We soon felt that a new name was in order. Most of their fans just referred to us as the Wranglers, so we changed our name to the Diamond W Wranglers, with the "W" standing for Wichita.

When the Wranglers lost our jobs at the Prairie Rose, we figured that the chuckwagon suppers there were history. However, the venue was purchased by horse ranchers, Greg and JW Johnson, who decided to continue as a chuckwagon

Roy Rogers Jr and the Prairie Rose Wranglers
L-R: Orin Friesen, Jim Farrell, Roy Rogers Jr, Stu Stuart, Steve Crawford

Prairie Rose Rangers
L-R: Orin Friesen, Kim Coslett, Jolynn MacIntyre, Jesse Friesen, Kris Johnson

supper venue. They held auditions for local singers and musicians and put together their own band they called the Prairie Rose Rangers. In mid-2008, I returned to the Prairie Rose in my old capacity as operations manager. I joined the Prairie Rose Rangers in January of 2009.

* * *

The success of cowboy music in and around Wichita is largely due to the promotional efforts of another cowboy singer, Johnny Western. Western began his career at the age of 13, singing on radio station KDHL in Northfield, Minnesota. A year later he got his own show on the station. While still in high school, Western did his first recordings and released his first record. Western recalled how that happened. "I had a friend named Bud Auge. Bud was a songwriter, and I was looking for songs to record. He was working on a song he called 'The Violet and a Rose Waltz.' He asked me to help him with some of the lyrics. Then we went into the recording studio with John Fields, who wrote down all the music and recorded the instruments while I sang." Released as a 45rpm single, "The Violet and a Rose Waltz" received some radio airplay, especially on WCOW in Minneapolis. "The WCOW DJs loved the

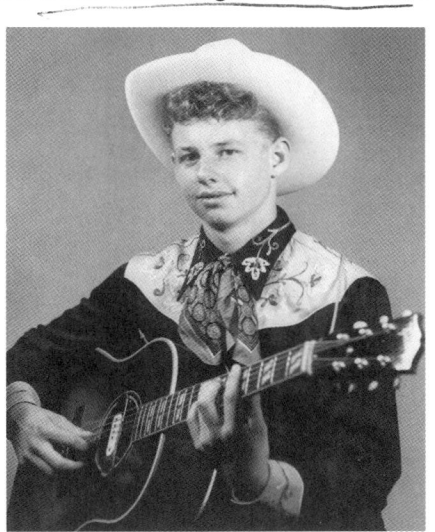

Johnny Western age 15

(Photo courtesy of Johnny Western)

song and played it a lot. One day, when Little Jimmy Dickens was in Minneapolis for a concert, he heard my record on WCOW and fell in love with it." Dickens had a friend in Nashville who was a 26-year-old songwriter from Tampa, Florida. His name was Mel Tillis. Tillis had written several successful songs for Webb Pierce but was wanting to make records on his own. "Little Jimmy Dickens brought my record of 'The Violet and a Rose Waltz' to Tillis who agreed to cut the song if he could rewrite the last verse. He also changed the name of the song to 'The Violet and a Rose' and added his name to the songwriting credits." It would be the first of nearly 80 chart records that Tillis released during his storied career. The same song would later become a hit for both Little Jimmy Dickens and Wanda Jackson. Among the many other recorded versions of the song are duet versions by Porter Wagoner and Skeeter Davis in 1962, and Dolly Parton and Pam Tillis as recently as 2008. "The Violet and a Rose" would generate a significant amount of songwriting royalties. The composer credits for "The Violet and a Rose" include Bud Auge, John Fields and Mel Tillis, but not Johnny Western. "I was just a 16-year-old kid at the time. I was just happy to be making a record. I didn't care anything about getting credit for a song I helped write."

After graduating high school in 1952, Western, then 17, almost immediately hit the road with the famous Sons of the Pioneers. "We toured throughout Iowa, the Dakotas, and Montana." Following an exciting summer, Western went back to Minnesota and was hired for his own TV show on KMMT-TV in Austin, Minnesota. On the weekends, he honed his cowboy skills by entering the calf roping competition in the local rodeos. Due to having his own TV show and hanging out at rodeos, Western became friends with the likes of Roy Rogers, Dale Evans, Gene Autry, Rex Allen, and Tex Ritter, who all encouraged him to follow his dreams. One of those dreams was to be a cowboy star in the movies. So, on January 2, 1955, Johnny Western, his wife, and baby daughter, piled in their car and headed for Hollywood.

Not long after arriving in California, Western worked at a rodeo with TV's *Range Rider & Dick West*, who were actors, Jock Mahoney and Dick Jones. Mahoney and Jones were both members of a social group called the Hollywood Christian Group. Jones asked Western if he would entertain at the group's next get-together. "I didn't realize that I was going to be singing to my heroes, Gene Autry, Roy Rogers, Dale Evans, and the Sons of the Pioneers." As a result of that night, when Gene Autry's longtime guitar player, Johnny Bond, decided to leave the band, Autry remembered Johnny Western and hired him for his show. He did his first concert with Autry in June of 1956 at Colorado State Fair's rodeo. From there, the entourage

Gene Autry and Johnny Western
(Photo courtesy of Johnny Western)

headed for Toronto, Canada for a series of shows. "It was amazing! We played to over a million people." Western remained a part of the band until Autry decided to retire from the road the following year.

After Gene Autry disbanded his road show, Johnny Western was out of a job but not forgotten. Autry's agent, Mitchell Hamilburg, signed Western with the thought of getting him into the acting business. "That was why I went to Hollywood in the first place. I wanted to be a cowboy star on the screen like Roy and Gene and Rex." With a successful agent like Hamilburg in his corner, Western was soon acting in movies and TV shows. During his first two years as an actor, he appeared in five feature films and 32 episodes of TV westerns, including *Gunsmoke, Lawman, The Tales of Wells Fargo, The Legend of Wyatt Earp, Bat Masterson, and Have Gun, Will Travel*. Following his appearance as a young gunslinger in a first-season episode of *Have Gun, Will Travel*, which starred Richard Boone as Paladin, Western wrote "The Ballad of Paladin" as a thank you to Boone and producer, Sam Rolfe. "I recorded the song, gave both of them a copy and left it at that. A couple of days later I got a phone call from Sam Rolfe, asking me to come to Richard Boone's office." *Have Gun, Will Travel* did not have a theme song, like many of the successful TV westerns. Both Boone and Rolfe liked Western's song and offered to buy it for a lump sum. That would have meant that Boone and Rolfe would be listed as the composers, but not Johnny Western. Western's agent advised him against the deal, and it was finally agreed that Western would be given a small, upfront payment, but have his name listed as one of the songwriters, along with Boone and Rolfe. That became one of the most important financial decision's in Western's life. "Ballad of Paladin" would go on to become the most successful TV western theme song of all time, both in popularity and financially.

The second part of the equation was that Johnny Western's voice was the one heard singing "The Ballad of Paladin" each week on the TV show. There were 255 episodes of *Have Gun, Will Travel*, during its six- season run on CBS which began in 1957; all but the early episodes of season one featuring Johnny Western singing the song he wrote. That almost did not happen. The TV show's musical producer was Mitch Miller, who wanted Jerry Vale to sing the song. However, Richard Boone put his foot down and insisted that if anybody was going to sing the theme song, it was going to be the guy who wrote it, Johnny Western.

Singing a song every week on one of TV's most popular shows re-started Western's career as a singer. Columbia signed him to a record deal, and he recorded the album *Have Gun, Will Travel*, backed by his heroes, the Sons of the Pioneers.

Gordon Terry, Jo Western, Johnny Western
(Photo courtesy of KFDI Collection)

Around that same time, Johnny Western began a musical relationship with another of his musical heroes, Johnny Cash. The two had first met a year earlier in Toronto when Western was still playing in Gene Autry's band. They were re-introduced by fiddler, Gordon Terry, who had become a regular part of the Johnny Cash stage show. Cash asked Western to play guitar on some of his recordings, and then to do a series of California concerts with him and his band, the Tennessee Two, Luther Perkins and Marshall Grant. "I did my first show with Johnny Cash and the Tennessee Two in Fresno on November 1, 1958." A national tour soon followed with a country music package show put together by promoter, Hap Peebles. That tour featured a stop at the Forum in Peebles' hometown, Wichita. It would be the first of many concert appearances in Wichita for Western. In 1962 alone, he played on the Johnny Cash Show at both the Hollywood Bowl and Carnegie Hall. His association with Cash resulted in countless shows together for 40 years. Along the way, Western continued to act in movies and television, put together his own touring band, and played guitar on recording sessions for Cash, Willie Nelson, and others. He also continued to make records of his own. In 1966, Waylon Jennings introduced him to Jo Sturdivant, who would soon become his wife. In that same year, he recorded a song written by Mel Tillis called, "Ruby, Don't Take Your Love to Town," which would become a hit for Kenny Rogers & the First Edition three years later.

By 1986, it seemed like Johnny Western had done it all, but then he got a call from Mike Oatman at KFDI in Wichita, offering him a job. "Oatman offered me an on-the-air position and I could choose from any of the markets in which Great Empire

Johnny Western and Johnny Cash
(Photo courtesy of Johnny Western)

Broadcasting had stations…. Shreveport, Omaha, Denver, Springfield, Missouri. I accepted the offer but only if it could be on Great Empire's flagship station, KFDI in Wichita." Oatman also agreed to a flexible arrangement where Western could take off time to perform, on the road, with Johnny Cash and others. His time as a KFDI "Ranch Hand" lasted almost 25 years, until he retired and moved back to Arizona. His last day on the air at KFDI was April 10, 2010. During his tenure in Wichita, Johnny Western became one of the best-known and most-beloved radio personalities in the history of Wichita radio. His importance to the promotion of country (and western) music during that time cannot be overstated.

KFDI Cowboy Poetry Gathering 1994
L-R: Keith Alberding, Marvin Pine, Stan Rood, Johnny Western,
Jim Rood, Bill Barwick

KFDI Cowboy Poetry Gathering 1996
L-R: Mike Oatman, Waddie Mitchell, Johnny Western,
Red Steagall, Larry McWhorter

CHAPTER TWENTY

HILLBILLY ROCK

It's the hillbilly rock, beat it with a drum
Playin' them guitars like shootin' from a gun
Keepin' up the rhythm, steady as a clock
Doin' a little thing called the hillbilly rock

From "Hillbilly Rock" by Marty Stuart

(Paul Kennerley)

In the early days of country music, records were often recorded in New York City, though other cities, such as Dallas, also served as recording centers. By the 1950s, Nashville had established itself as the "Home of Country Music" or "Music City USA." Nashville had the *Grand Ole Opry* and a plethora of recording studios. Most of the major record companies had established offices in Music City and performers and songwriters alike flocked to the city. But the West Coast also had its share of the "business." California country singers like Buck Owens, Merle Haggard, Wynn Stewart, Tex Ritter, Gene Autry, and Tennessee Ernie Ford, had established their careers without relying on Nashville.

The Bakersfield sound of Owens and Haggard had a profound effect on other musicians, not only in country music, but also in rock & roll. The Beatles were among the first to embrace the Bakersfield sound. In 1965, the Fab Four, with Ringo Starr singing lead, recorded "Act Naturally," which had been a big hit for Buck Owens in 1963. They had already dipped into country music territory earlier by recording Carl Perkins' songs "Matchbox," "Honey Don't" and "Everybody's Tryin' to Be My Baby." John Lennon and Paul McCartney even wrote several country-flavored songs like "What Goes On," "I Don't Want to Spoil the Party" and "I've Just Seen a Face." Other "British Invasion" rock & roll bands dabbled in country music, including the Rolling Stones. However, it was the Southern California folk rock band, the Byrds that really grabbed on to country music and claimed part-ownership of the genre for themselves.

The original Byrds, Roger McGuinn, David Crosby, Gene Clark, Chris Hillman, and Michael Clarke, established their own sound by combining the folk songs of Bob Dylan with the guitar sounds of the Beatles. McGuinn's jangly, electric 12-string guitar added to the new sound and folk rock came into being. It wasn't long before Chris Hillman, who had come to rock & roll by the way of bluegrass bands, began inserting country sounds into the Byrds' repertoire. His song, "Time Between," from 1967, has that Bakersfield sound. By 1968, Crosby and Clark were gone from the Byrds and a young man from Alabama had been added to the group. Gram Parsons brought with him a love of country music; a love he shared with Hillman. The result was the landmark album, *Sweetheart of the Rodeo*. Though the album originally did not sell well, it established country rock as a new genre of music. Soon Hillman and Parsons left the Byrds and started the Flying Burrito Brothers, who were even more "country." Around the same time, another rock & roll band, Buffalo Springfield had been dabbling in country sounds with the use of banjo and steel guitar on some of their recordings. Key members of that band were Stephen Stills, Neil Young, Richie Furay, Dewey Martin and Bruce Palmer, who was later replaced by Jim Messina. For some of their later recordings, Buffalo Springfield brought in pedal steel guitarist, Rusty Young. After the group folded, Furay, Messina and Young got together and formed their own country rock band, Poco. Their unique sound was later picked up and made even more successful by the Eagles, whose members had included former Poco bass player/singers, Randy Meisner and Timothy B. Schmidt. It should be noted that even the Eagles have a Wichita connection. The group had come together in 1971, combining the talents of Glenn Frey, Don Henley, Randy Meisner, and Bernie Leadon. When Leadon left the band in 1975, he was replaced by Joe Walsh from the rock band, the James Gang. Walsh was born Joseph Fidler in Wichita on November 20, 1947. His early days were spent living in a house just south of Wichita State University. For a time, Joe's father worked at Ted Combs Radio & TV, next door to Nail's Texaco at 13th & Hillside. It is the same radio and TV repair shop where I worked when I attended WSU. When Joe was around five, his parents split up and his musically inclined mother moved the family to New York City and eventually to Ohio, where she remarried. Joe was adopted by his stepfather whose last name was Walsh. To this day Joe Walsh retains an affinity for the city of his birth, Wichita.

The Byrds, Flying Burrito Brothers, Poco, and the Eagles made such an impact that other rock & roll musicians around the U.S. began to take notice and started putting together their own mixture of country and rock. However, the mixing of country and rock & roll sounds did not really take off in Wichita until southern rock came around in the early 1970s. This new form of music was exemplified by groups like the Allman Brothers, Lynyrd Skynyrd, the Marshal Tucker Band, and the Charlie Daniels Band. Around that same time, KFDI-FM began a format that included a lot of this new music. John Speer, who became the program director for KFDI-FM, recalled their sound. "We called it progressive country. It was a mixture of country, country rock, southern rock, Austin, Texas music, and even songs from hard-core rock bands. It wasn't unusual for us to go from Led Zeppelin's 'Stairway to Heaven' to Jerry Jeff Walker, with Merle Haggard in between." With this alternative country music now being heard on the radio in Wichita, musicians began to take notice.

By the early 1970s, Wichita bluegrass bands like Prairie Grass and the World's Largest Prairie Dog were covering material of the California country rock bands in places like Kirby's and the Foundry. Around that same time, Wichita's first country rock band was formed by Chuck Comly, Kip Ehrke, John Dondlinger, Doug Webb. Bruce Batson, and Bat Shunatona. Sundance, though based out of Wichita, toured throughout Kansas, as well as in Nebraska and Colorado. Later personnel changes brought Harry Dobbin and Mike Ehrke into Sundance.

By 1975, Sundance had disbanded and several of its members, Doug Webb, Mike Ehrke, John Dondlinger, and Harry Dobbin got together with Jamey Ratzlaff to form Sawdust Charley. Though they considered themselves to be a country rock band, the band played mostly songs written by the band members themselves. The band's tight sound and original material caught the attention of KFDI-FM's program director, John Speer, who began playing Sawdust Charley's songs on the air and using the group for radio station sponsored shows and dances. Due to their tremendous popularity in Wichita, the band decided to broaden their market. By 1978, Sawdust Charley was based out of Los Angeles and performed at a variety of venues on the west coast before disbanding a year later.

When Oklahoma Sunshine hit the scene in 1976, they referred to their music as progressive country. The group enjoyed playing everything from Waylon Jennings to the Rolling Stones and the Beatles. One of the original members of Oklahoma Sunshine, Chuck Haukos, recalled the beginnings. "I had been in a country band called Dick Orange and the Western Wranglers, who played regularly at the Wagon Wheel. When we started Oklahoma Sunshine, the first week it was Don Neal, Donnie Brooker, and me. The second week it was the three of us plus Vince Baker." Brooker was the drummer, but the other three band members were guitar players. Haukos recalled, "Don Neal and I could both also play bass, so we traded between guitar and bass every other set." Though Oklahoma Sunshine was a Wichita band, they started out by becoming the house band at the Montigo Club in Winfield. Haukos left after a year and went on to form the band, Wichita, with Kenny Mac Robertson, Mike West, Rita Sheeder, and Chuck's brother, Mike Haukos. For a time, Wichita became the featured band at a club called Kit Shickers. Later, the Haukos brothers were part of another country band called Prairie Dust. Meanwhile, Oklahoma Sunshine continued despite the typical personnel changes. Fiddler, Chuck Turner came on board, followed by Jeff Pickering on steel guitar and banjo, and Dave Reed on bass, giving the band more of a "country" feel.

Vince Baker recalled one special night with Oklahoma Sunshine. "One night we were playing at the Tennessee Gin Mill and Ace Freely from the rock band, KISS, showed up. KISS was in town for two nights at the Kansas Coliseum. Ace came up on stage and borrowed a guitar and played "Kansas City" with us. After we wrapped up the night at the Gin Mill, we all went to a party with Ace Freely and the other members of KISS at the downtown Holiday Inn."

Around the time that Oklahoma Sunshine formed, the Cyrus Noble Whiskey Band came together. Members included Lynn Piller on guitar and steel guitar, Bill Shumate on guitar, Mike Foster on bass, Don Clarey on drums, Barry Clark on rhythm guitar and harmonica, and lead singer, Russ Oropresa. When the Cyrus Noble Whiskey Band called it quits in 1980, Oropresa became part of a new country rock band called Tobacco Jones. This band started in 1981 and lasted for a couple of years.

Sweetwater Band at Herman Hill Park in April, 1979
(Photo courtesy of Doug Adams)

The Tennessee Gin Mill had opened in 1978, and the first house band was the Sweetwater Band, a group that featured a mixture of California country rock and southern rock. Bandleader, Doug Adams recalled their sound. "Paula Travis was our main singer and she loved Linda Ronstadt, so we did all of Linda's songs, plus Fleetwood Mac and Heart. We also did southern rock, like Lynyrd Skynyrd and the Marshall Tucker Band, as well as stuff by Pure Prairie League and the Amazing Rhythm Aces." With Doug Adams on guitar and vocals, Jerry Hinson on guitar and vocals, Mike Maxey on bass, Pat Keitel on drums, and Paula Travis on piano and vocals, the Sweetwater Band had the instrumental configuration of many country, southern rock, and rock & roll bands at the time. Adams came up with an idea to make the band sound more "country." "We didn't have a fiddle or a steel guitar, so I figured out how to make my guitar sound like a steel by using an Echo-Plex with my volume pedal and running it through an organ Leslie speaker. I had never seen anybody do that, and it worked pretty well." The Sweetwater Band lasted until 1982. By that time, Doug Adams had started a sound company called Pro Audio Systems, and began running sound for local bands, such as The Clocks, Oklahoma Sunshine, and many others. He also worked with John McBride of MD Systems. In 1989, McBride presented Adams the opportunity to be the sound engineer for a national touring act. "John McBride gave me the choice. I could either go out with the famous rock band, Steppenwolf, or some new country singer out of Oklahoma,

Sweetwater Band 2021
L-R: *Doug Adams, Mike Maxey, Paula Travis, Tony Amend,*
Pat Keitel, Jerry Hinson
(Photo courtesy of Doug Adams)

named Garth Brooks. For me it was a no-brainer. I chose John Kay and Steppenwolf." It seemed like a wise choice for Adams. Steppenwolf was known for huge hits like "Born to Be Wild" and "Magic Carpet Ride." Most people had never even heard of Garth Brooks. Still, Adams has no regrets. "John Kay is a wonderful person and I love all the time I've spent on the road with Steppenwolf." Adams still occasionally works with Steppenwolf, while running a successful sound company in Wichita. He's also writing a book about his experiences in the music business. Occasionally, the original members of the Sweetwater Band get together to perform on-stage. Progressive country remained a force in Wichita throughout the 1980s, exemplified by bands like Prairie Fire, and a group led by Paul Riggs called Saddle Tramp.

Fritz Davis had been playing music around Wichita for years. He was born into a musical family and made his first recording at the age of three. He got a guitar when he was fourteen and his musical career took off from there. Even an early career as a teacher did not deter his musical endeavors. Beginning in 1969, he worked as a duo with harmonica player Bill Garrison, who was sometimes known as "Wichita

Wilbur." In 1976, Davis teamed with Steve Koch to form the Texas Airforce. Fritz had a family history of country music involvement. His uncle Don Davis had once played with California band leader, Spade Cooley.

Classic country and folk music had been the mainstay of Fritz Davis music, but when progressive country came along, he shifted his music in that direction. He recalled the time in 1979, "We put together a band called Raincrow. We got Cliff Schilling, who was part Choctaw, to come up from Oklahoma. He played bass and banjo, and his wife, Joy, was one of our vocalists. Our piano player, Jim Mangan came from Dodge City, and Reece Pulling, our drummer, was from Australia. I played guitar and was one of the singers. Later we added Brian Driscoll on guitar, Lynn Piller on steel, and Ricky Meyer on sax."

Raincrow disbanded in 1981 but Fritz Davis was quick to assemble another band. "I started Fritz Davis & Good Medicine. We used to play at Rotten Rodney's One Horse Saloon at 13th and West Street." That group was short lived, and Davis was soon back in a more successful band, Catfish Charlie. "We had Pat Augustine on bass, Robby Kendal on drums, and Cal Bateman on guitar. I played guitar and everybody sang, except Robby. We did lots of J.J. Cale; that kind of stuff." Catfish Charlie lasted a couple of years and during that time had a somewhat regular gig at a place called Cowboys, which was located on St. Francis Street.

Following the demise of Catfish Charlie in 1983, Davis got together with friends to form several other musical combinations, including Fritz Davis & the Knight Flyers and Fritz Davis & Daybreak. Davis also worked as a solo performer, and beginning in 1984, he became an Artist in Residence for the Kansas Arts Commission. Then in 1988, he began an association with KFDI radio. As an outreach program, KFDI sponsored Davis to go to area schools to perform twenty-minute programs of folk music. When guitarist James Garver left the KFDI Ranch House Swing Band to join the band of up and coming country music singer, Garth Brooks, Davis was his replacement.

These days, Fritz Davis lives in Red River, New Mexico, where he is editor of the town's newspaper, the Red River Miner. He continues to perform at a coffee shop in Red River and has released several solo albums.

☆ ☆ SOUVENIR EDITION ☆ ☆

Hymns and Songs
OF THE
PIONEER QUARTET
KFBI

PRICE 50 CENTS

GOOD NEWS IN SONG

CHAPTER TWENTY-ONE

THE GOSPEL OF WICHITA

And the Wichita gospel radio played all the country songs you've ever known
And the signal'd come in loud and strong way down into Oklahoma all night long.

From "Wichita" by Fred Eaglesmith

Southern gospel music, sometimes referred to as white southern gospel, has always been somewhat aligned with country music. Both styles of music had their origins in the rural South. Whereas secular country music was spread by dances and honky-tonk bars, southern gospel was the music of churches and revival meetings. Radio stations, too, delivered the Gospel message by featuring programs of southern gospel music, especially on Sunday mornings. In the 1940s, KFBI had its Pioneer Quartet, which was led by the station's farm director, Lester Weatherwax. During the 1960s, Mack Sanders and his KFRM had the Plainsmen. (see Chapter 3) During the 1970s, a new version of Wichita's first radio band, the Ark Valley Boys, was put together by the Baggett brothers as a gospel quartet. (see Chapter 2) Even as I write this, KWLS country music DJ, "Gentle Ben" Ingram performs with his southern gospel quartet known as the Boys of the Fort. Ingram first put his group together when he was living in Fort Scott, Kansas, thus the name.

* * *

When I was growing up on the farm in Nebraska, I got a lot of my interest in music from my dad. He loved to sing and did so every chance he could. There was no radio on Dad's tractor, so he would entertain himself by singing. We could sometimes hear him from half a mile away, singing at the top of his voice over the sound of his 720 John Deere. He loved songs like "Ain't Gonna Rain No More" and "Hey Good Lookin'." But Dad's favorite music was southern gospel. He did not grow up anywhere near what I would call southern gospel territory, but he loved that music, especially the male quartets. His favorites were the Statesmen, J.D. Sumner & the Stamps Quartet, and especially the Blackwood Brothers. Most of the record albums we owned were by those quartets, along with gospel albums by Red Foley and Tennessee Ernie Ford. I was too young to remember much about it, but my dad once took me to a concert in a church to see the Blackwood Brothers. Many years later, after my dad had left the farm and purchased a service station, he once filled the Blackwood Brothers' tour bus with fuel and refused to let them pay.

Growing up in a house where most of the records were southern gospel music, I guess it's only natural that I would also enjoy southern gospel. I would often tune my old Zenith radio to XERF, which was located on the Mexican border, and listen to the gospel quartet sounds of the Chuck Wagon Gang. Early in my broadcasting career, I worked as a studio engineer at KARD-TV, Channel 3, in Wichita. Some of my duties involved working on the *Elmer Childress Show*, a live, southern gospel show hosted by Elmer Childress, his wife June, and their daughters, Pam, Debbie and Shari. Childress often had gospel groups drop by the TV studios to perform live. One of my best memories from that time was mixing the sound for a quartet who were all sharply dressed in matching, double-breasted suits. That was my introduction to the Oak Ridge Boys.

Childress would sometimes have other guests on his show that did not perform gospel music. The most memorable time for me was when Elmer's guest was motorcycle daredevil, Evel Knievel. Following his interview with Childress,

Elmer Childress Family on KARD-TV
L-R: Debbie, Pam, June, Shari, Elmer
(Photo courtesy of Elmer Childress)

Elmer Childress Family on KARD-TV
L-R: Debbie, Elmer, Pam, Shari (front), June
(Photo courtesy of Elmer Childress)

Knievel came into the control room and motioned to me. As I came to him, he grinned and unscrewed the top of his fancy walking cane. He then pulled out a flask of whiskey. At that point I realized how Knievel was able to get the courage to jump his motorcycle over a dozen buses.

Elmer Childress had already had a successful career in southern gospel music before he came to Wichita. "I joined my first quartet when I was 13," recalled Childress. "I sang bass. I guess my voice changed early. With most of the quartets I worked, I didn't even sing. I just played piano." In 1948, Childress played piano for the short-lived, Home State Quartet, a group based out of Little Rock, Arkansas. Later that same year, the Home State Quartet disbanded and several of the members, including Childress moved to Illinois to become members of the newly reorganized All American Quartet. Southern gospel quartets usually worked with just one accompanist, a piano player. Good pianists were highly in demand, and Elmer Childress was good. The next year found Childress in Fresno, California, playing the piano for the well-known Gospelaires Quartet, led by Don Smith, who had previously sung in the Blackwood Brothers Quartet, among others. His stay on the west coast did not last long as Childress was lured back to Illinois to rejoin the All-American Quartet. That job was also short-lived, because in 1952, he was hired to be the pianist for America's best-known southern gospel group, the Stamps Quartet. Formed in 1920 by Frank Stamps, the Stamps Quartet, based out of Dallas, was responsible for establishing the southern gospel quartet tradition of having "four guys and a piano." His next move was to Indiana, where he worked with the Melody Masters Quartet and the Southland Quartet. One more move took him back to California and the Rangers Quartet, a group that formed in Texas in 1935 as the Texas Rangers. Just like the country music groups of the 1930s and '40s, the Rangers moved around the Country, to promote themselves on various radio stations to find new audiences. They moved to Kentucky, North Carolina, and several other southern states before moving to Topeka, Kansas and WIBW. By the time Elmer Childress joined the group, they were based out of Hollywood. In 1956, not long after Childress joined the Rangers, the group decided to move to Wichita. By that time, he was not only playing the piano but had taken over the spot as baritone vocalist. The Rangers' time in Wichita didn't last long. They decided to dis-band and the various members went their separate ways. Elmer Childress decided to stay in Wichita and make a career change.

After all the moving around, he finally decided to put down roots and got a job working for KARD-TV. He became a much-loved weatherman on the Channel 3 evening news, and cordial host of his noontime gospel show, that also featured his family. "I almost didn't get that gospel show," he remembered. "Channel 3 had me doing all kinds of other things, besides the weather. I hosted a talent show, and junior auction, and was even a cowboy, hosting western movies for kids. I kept asking the station manager, Bill Moyer, for a gospel program but he kept turning me down. Finally, I got a job offer from a station in Oklahoma. When Moyer found out that I was likely going to leave, he offered to let me have my gospel show to entice me to stay." The *Elmer Childress Show* aired live, daily, on KARD-TV for over 20 years. Often Childress would bring several of his favorite gospel groups to Wichita for "all night gospel sings." He also hosted and produced a gospel music show for KFDI radio in Wichita. Childress made one final move, this time to Madison, Wisconsin where he became the weather director on WMTV. He retired from TV in 1998 but continued to record his radio show for KFDI in Wichita until 2019, making it the longest-running radio show in Wichita history. The *Elmer Childress Show* (radio version) had been on the air for 56 years.

The Gospel of Wichita

Singing Ledbetters

* * *

One of the most successful gospel groups in Wichita history is the Singing Ledbetters. The family band came together after Reverend Jack Ledbetter and his wife, Nadine, moved their family to Wichita from Arkansas. Reverend Ledbetter would organize revival meetings in town and his daughters would get up and sing. However, their brother, Glenn, wanted nothing to do with it. He enjoyed drinking and took a job as a bouncer in a nightclub. That all changed in 1963 when he attended church with his family. He remembered that morning. "I was hung over from the night before, but that day, God entered my life and I was saved by Jesus." That was a defining moment in Glenn's life. He soon organized his family into a singing, gospel group, which went on to record over 30 albums. They traveled the U.S. and hosted many gospel sings in their hometown of Wichita. In 1972, following the success of one of the Singing Ledbetters albums, Glenn talked Mike Oatman of KFDI into letting him do a Sunday morning gospel show. That program exists to this day on AM 1070, now known as KFTI.

* * *

Riverside Boys
L-R: Kent Allen, Billy Rader, Dennis Rader, Rod Ward, Don Baker,
John Baxter, Ron Baxter

A gospel group that came on the scene in 1972 called themselves the Riverside Boys, a name they borrowed from their church, South Riverside Baptist. The group was organized by Wayne "Bud" Rader, owner of Rader Vacuum Cleaners, located in the South City Shopping Center. The group featured the talents of Rader's sons, Billy on guitar, banjo and lead vocals, and Dennis on drums. The original configuration of the vocal quartet included Ron Baxter on tenor, John Baxter on baritone, and Kent Allen singing bass. Don Baker played bass guitar and saxophone while Rod Ward played the piano. When Allen left, he was replaced by Ted Seaman who was later replaced by Gary Salkill. Tim Raymond became the piano player when Rod Ward left.

Drummer Dennis Rader eventually took over the baritone singing. He recalled his time with the group. "We started the group after seeing the Oak Ridge Boys at a gospel concert at Century II. (They received) multiple standing ovations with 5,000 people in the house. The Riverside Boys played mostly churches, (but at) almost every church we played we included instrumental numbers such as 'Foggy Mountain Breakdown,' 'Yakety Sax' and 'Last Date.' For about six years we made three appearances nearly every weekend throughout the year…all around the Wichita area, down into Oklahoma, and up toward Kansas City." The talents of the Riverside Boys were soon noticed by Ol' Mike Oatman and Terry Burford of KFDI. In 1977, they were invited to open KFDI's 6th Annual Listener Appreciation Show, which also featured Sonny James, Donna Fargo, and gospel singers, R.W. Blackwood, and his wife Donna. "KFDI also helped us promote and all-night gospel sing that became an annual event which took place at Lawrence Stadium. For lots of years we aired a 30-minute, Sunday morning radio program on KFDI."

Encouraged by their regional success, the Riverside Boys relocated to Florida in January of 1978. But several issues among the band members caused the group to disband in August. What might have been discouraging for some turned out to be positive for the Rader family. They started a major tourist attraction at Panama City Beach, Florida called the Ocean Opry. The Raders put together their own Branson-style show, but also featured concerts by Nashville stars. Though the Ocean Opry no longer exists, the music of the Rader family continues. Both of Dennis Rader's sons have become successful Nashville producers and sidemen. Brent Rader has worked for Billy Dean, Jo Dee Messina, Colin Raye, and for the last several years has been the band leader for Joe Nichols. His brother, Danny, is a three-time Academy of Country Music award winner, who has played on 50 #1 hits. He has worked with Jason Aldean, LeAnn Rimes, and Gretchen Wilson. Since 2010, he has been Keith Urban's lead guitar player.

Beginning with the Burkes Brothers and Big Chief Henry's Indian String Band in the 1920s, the radio bands in the '30s and '40s, the honky-tonkers of the '50s and '60s, and even up to today, Wichita's musicians and singers have made their mark on country music. Wichita, Kansas, in the heartland of America, continues to inspire. In the title song of their 2013 album, Golden, Lady Antebellum sang, "The sunset falls in Wichita, yellow dances through the blue, wheat fields catch a glimpse of heaven, makes me think of you."

EPILOGUE

Through the stories in the pages of this book, I hope I was able to show you a little of the importance of country music in Wichita, Kansas. Though this book is a history of country music in Wichita, it is not a complete history. While interviewing people for this project, I realized that everyone has stories. One of my goals was to dig up the stories behind the music. I hope those stories will inspire others to share their own stories, even if it is just with family and friends.

As I sit here writing the final words of this book, most of Wichita, like the rest of the Country, is shut down because of the Coronavirus. The clubs and the concert halls are closed. There is no live music happening anywhere in town. Hopefully, we will be able to ride out this pandemic and get back to normal soon. As I look back, I realize how much things have changed over the years. KFDI-FM is still playing country music, but if Marvin Rainwater was still around, he wouldn't recognize it. People no longer ask me, "Whatever happened to Marvin Rainwater?" Now the question I get asked most often is, "How's Johnny Western?" I just tell them that Johnny is fine, living the good life in Arizona, with his wife, Jo. Bekki and I are holed up on our Rocking Banjo Ranch not far from Wichita. The other night we turned on Netflix and watched a movie called *The Last Thing He Wanted*, which starred Anne Hathaway and Ben Affleck. Though the film was hard to follow, we stayed with it until then end. Immediately following the final scene came the golden voice of Johnny Western singing, "Have gun will travel reads the card of a man...."

ACKNOWLEDGEMENTS

This book was inspired by the Wichita Rock Music Project Team and the book they published, *Wichita Rock & Roll 1950-1980*, which was edited by my friend, Dr. Jay Price, of Wichita State University. The idea for that book was the result of research done by one of Dr. Price's students, Joshua Rupp. Longtime Wichita musician, Harry Dobbin was art director. The rest of the consulting members of the team included Doug Webb, Mark Archibald, Ron Shauf, Ron Starkel, Jim Hill, Randy Crump, Joe Sauer, and Curtis Payne, along with Eric Cale, Director of the Wichita Sedgwick County Historical Museum. During the months that led up to that book, many Wichita musicians gathered on a regular basis at Margarita's Cantina to reminisce about local rock & roll history. Though I, personally, never played rock & roll music, I enjoyed it, was around it, and knew quite a few of the people who made it. I also have a deep love of Wichita history. Dr. Price invited me to the informal gatherings at Margarita's, and I enjoyed watching the book take shape.

My wife, Bekki, and I were privileged to attend the release party of *Wichita Rock & Roll 1950-1980*. As we wandered through the packed crowd at Margarita's, several people told me, "Orin, you need to write a book like this about country music in Wichita." The more I thought about it, the more I liked the idea. Wichita has a rich history of country music, but I had never seen much written about it. I decided to see what I could find at the library. I went to the downtown branch of the Wichita Public Library and spoke with the woman in charge of local history. I asked her if she had any books about country music in Wichita. She left for a few minutes and brought me a book. "We have to keep this under lock and key," she said, "so people don't walk off with it. It's the only book we have on the subject." It was my book, *Goat Glands to Ranch Hands: The KFDI Story*. I knew right then that I needed to write another book. I had started working on *Goat Glands* 20 years before I ever finished it. Without help from my co-author, Bud Norman, and inspiration from Pat O'Connor of Rowfant Press, I likely would never have finished that book. I owe them both a huge amount of thanks.

The Wichita rock & roll book covers a 30-year period, the heyday of live rock & roll bands in Wichita. I knew right away that I was not going to be able to put the country music of Wichita into such a tight package. Country music predated rock & roll by many years. Early rock & roll was spawned out of country music in the 1950s. Bill Haley & the Comets, Elvis Presley, Carl Perkins, Jerry Lee Lewis, and the Everly Brothers all had their roots in country music. Recorded country music went back to the 1920s, and I discovered that live country music in Wichita went back that far, as well. I knew I would not be able to justify a history of country music in Wichita without including those early performers. A more difficult decision was deciding where to stop my research. Though there are still bands playing rock & roll in Wichita, the Wichita Rock Music Project Team decided to stop after the 1980s. I used my experience as a country music DJ to guide me to an end date. Though I had been a part-time disc jockey/announcer since 1964, I did not become a full-time DJ until 1987, when I started doing the midnight to 6:00am shift on KFDI. I was a full-time KFDI "Ranch Hand" all the way through the 1990s. I still do a weekly show on KFDI, *Bluegrass from the Rocking Banjo Ranch*, but country music has changed quite a bit since I was a full-time country DJ. I decided to take the history in this book up to the ending of the 20th century. I'll leave it up to someone else to write the story of the next hundred years.

Perhaps one of the most difficult decisions I had to make was how to relate my personal experiences. I recently read the book, *Bill Monroe: The Life and Music of the Bluegrass Man* by Tom Ewing. Tom had been a member of Monroe's Blue Grass Boys and had his personal experiences to tell in the book. He chose to do so by writing about himself in third person. I thought about doing that myself for this book. However, I had several people convince me to do otherwise. They told me that enough people were aware of who I am through my 50+ years in both radio and playing in bands, that it would be more interesting if I wrote my personal experiences in first person. So that is the way it is in this book.

I was born in 1946, and grew up on a farm near York, Nebraska. I cannot recall a time when country music wasn't part of my life. Even when I got caught up in the music of the "British Invasion" of the 1960s, I never let go of my "country" connection. I appreciated it when the Beatles or the Rolling Stones would record a country song. I loved it when my favorite American rock band, the Byrds, started

Acknowledgements

putting country music into their repertoire. Even during my own "long-hair" days of the 1970s, I still preferred my cowboy boots, jeans, and western shirts that I bought from Shepler's. And though I loved to see the rock bands on TV, I always enjoyed the weekly shows by Porter Wagoner and the Wilburn Brothers. I would spend my hard-earned money on live concerts by big-name acts from both rock & roll and country. One week it might be the Grateful Dead and the next week it might be Buck Owens and the Buckaroos. Though I began playing in bands around the same time I got into radio, I have always enjoyed listening to others' music more than I did playing my own. It has been an honor to get to play music from coast to coast and even other parts of the world, such as China. I was thrilled to get to play at Carnegie Hall, two years in a row. I have had the pleasure of sharing the stage with some of the biggest names in the music business, and even got to sing on stage with one of my musical heroes, Bill Monroe. Yet I have a deep fondness and respect for those musicians and singers from right here in Wichita, Kansas who, after hard work at their day jobs, chose to spend their nights and weekends playing in smoky bars, honky-tonks, and dance halls, for the enjoyment of their hometown friends. Some of these pickers and singers went on to national stardom, but many were just known to their local fans. Still, they are all part of Wichita's history. For this book, I have tried to dig deep. I apologize if I have omitted anyone.

Writing this book was a labor of love, and it would have been an impossible task without the help and inspiration from so many others. First, I want to thank Dr. Jay Price, Chairman of the History Department of Wichita State University, for inviting me to sit in on the sessions that led to the book, *Wichita Rock & Roll 1950-1980*. I owe a huge amount of thanks to Eric Cale, Director of the Wichita-Sedgwick Country Historical Museum. Throughout this project, Eric not only encouraged me, he brought ideas and led me to people I might have missed on my own. He also read through my entire manuscript and suggested changes. I would also like to thank the other staff members of the museum for their help and support, especially curator Jami Frazier Tracy for the use of some of the photos from the museum's collection. I also want to thank Barb Myers of Rowfant Press, and her mother, who both read my manuscript, pointed out mistakes and offered suggestions. My son, Jesse Friesen continues to amaze me with his many talents. He did the setup of this book and helped with the final editing. Jesse also designed the book cover, which turned out way better than I had imagined it.

This book would not have happened without my many years in radio, especially those years spent playing country music on KBUL and KFDI. During those few short years at KBUL, I got to spend countless hours talking to a true radio legend, Mike Hoyer, a member of the Country Music Disc Jockey Hall of Fame. Another one of the DJs on KBUL was "Alan McKay," whose real name is Larry Waggoner. Larry is not only one of the best radio engineers in the U.S., he is also one of my best friends. We met in Senorita Tejeda's Spanish Class at Wichita State University in 1967 and have been friends ever since. It was Larry who recommended me for my first job in commercial radio, as a newsman on the brand new KEYN-FM. During my radio career, I have been blessed to never having worked for someone I didn't like. There were the great radio station owners; Bob Freeman, Lowell Deniston, and Frank Carney of KEYN, KBUL and KQAM, and Mike Lynch and Mike Oatman of KFDI. I even worked for Country Music Hall of Fame member, Charley Pride, for a short time, as well as for the legendary Mack Sanders. I got to work for a lot of great managers and program directors, like Gary Dick, Greg Dean, and Roger Mundy of KEYN. No one in radio deserves my thanks more than John Speer. He was not only my supervisor at KFDI, he was (and still is) one of my closest friends. He introduced me to Bekki and was my best-man at our wedding. John has been a great source of encouragement and inspiration over the years. Thanks John Boy!

Two more KFDI Ranch Hands that deserve a big thanks are Don "Little Donnie Do Dad" Walton and Johnny Western. Don helped me fill in a lot of the blanks and introduced me to many of the Wichita country musicians of the 1960s. It makes me sad to know that Don is not around to read the final version of this book. I miss those conversations we used to have about country music. Johnny Western is also a dear friend who has a vast knowledge of music stored in his head. If I could only remember a small portion of what Johnny told me over lunches during our years together at KFDI, I would have material for another book.

Social media is a great resource for connecting with people and finding stories that I might otherwise have missed. Facebook has been especially helpful, and I would like to thank many new Facebook friends for their memories and tips. They include Chris Reyer, Mike Maxton, Rex Victory, Jon Weaver, Pat Wilson, Dan Rouser, B.W. Norris, and Barb Myers.

Acknowledgements

I want to thank those musicians who took the time to be interviewed. A list of those names is provided at the end of the bibliography. In no particular order, I also want to thank the following people who have supported me along the way: Michael Martin Murphey, John McEuen, Dan Hays, Ken Spurgeon, Larry Heck, Deb Goodrich, Beccy Tanner, Beverlee Brannigan, Pat O'Connor, Skip Gorman, Krysti Carlson Goering, Keith Wondra, Jim Ratts, Ranger Stan Greer, David Hawkins, Richard Crowson, Hatman Jack Kellogg, Dan Dillon, Greg & JW Johnson, Jane Hershberger, Frank & Judy Goodrich, Roger Ringer, Greg Cahill, Dwain Terry, Lance Cowan, "Big Al" Thiessen, Mike Hylton, Stan Holmes, Mike Theobald, Riders in the Sky, Gene Elders, Red Steagall, Rob Loren, Rusty Rierson, Thomas Etheredge, Stu Stuart, Jim & Martha Farrell, Steve Crawford, my kids, Josh, Jesse, and Annie Friesen, and most of all, my wonderful wife, Bekki.

I would like to list all of you whom I've come to know through radio, music, history, ranching, church, etc., but that might take up an entire book. I have been blessed with so many friends.

A SELECTED LIST OF WICHITA CLUBS, CONCERT HALLS, DANCE HALLS, AND DIVES DURING THE 20TH CENTURY

Country music has been performed in Wichita in a variety of venues from tiny bars to large concert halls. The following list is a work in progress. A complete list may never be possible.

Name	Address or Location
Al's V Bar 7	518 W Harry
Alaskan Ice Palace	700 S Hydraulic

Home of the KFH Barn Dance on Saturday nights. Usually had roller skating or roller dancing.

Arcadia Theater	201 S Water

The Arcadia was built in 1918 and could seat 1500.

B-1 Club	South Pattie
BEC Playhouse	217 W Douglas
Biggies	West St & 47th St South
Bloody Bucket	2400 Block of South Meridian
Blue Moon Ballroom	3401 S Oliver – near Boeing

Built in 1940. Destroyed by fire in January of 1960

Bonanza	3537 N Broadway
Caprice Ballroom	Goddard
Carriage Inn	S Hillside
Chateau Beer Garden	600 block of N Emporia
Club Rodeo	10001 E Kellogg Drive
Cotillion Ballroom	11120 W Kellogg
Cowboy	Originally 5327 E Kellogg

Later moved to 2nd & Mosley in Old Town

Name	Address or Location
Cowboy Inn "Wichita's Largest Western Club"	329 S West St.

Many of the great touring performers such as Hank Williams played at the Cowboy Inn. Burned down in 1955.

Name	Address or Location
Cowboy Inn	642 N St. Paul
Coyote Club (Formerly Rock Castle)	3813 N Broadway
Crest Theater	4825 E Douglas
Cypress Club	S. Broadway. Later Harry & Seneca.
Dave's Cave	on Orient Blvd
Dew Drop Inn	on Water St, just north of Kellogg
Dog House	2113 N Broadway
Double D Lounge	1534 Ida
Draw One Lounge	121 N Seneca
Eagles Lodge	69th St North
81 Club	
EJ's Red Lion	East Kellogg
Elk's Lodge	
Emperor Club	1100 block of S Seneca
Forty Niner Club	on N Arkansas
Forum	231 S Water, where Century II now sits

Built in 1911. Torn down in 1965.

Name	Address or Location
Foundry	600 block of E Douglas
Foundry 21	S Seneca
4 Ls	551 W Douglas
Fox Canyon	near Kellogg and Market
Frankie's Lounge	4801 W Douglas (owned by Frankie Schultz)
Frontier Ballroom	13000 W Kellogg
Golden Knight	1916 E Pawnee
Hangar Club	located in a bowling alley on E. Harry

Name	Address or Location
Hap's Club	
Hi-Ho Club	47th St South & Broadway
Became the Western Swinger	
Hillcrest Lounge	7464 S Broadway
Hobble-De-Hoy	3813 N Broadway (1972)
Was formerly known as the Rock Castle	
Cowboys	St Francis
Honky Tonk	on W Douglas
Jesse's Supper Club	425 E 51st St North
Jody's Hitching Post	2305 S Broadway
John & Ada's	3615 W Douglas
Johnny & Bonnie's Ballroom	West of Seneca on Douglas
Joyland Park	2801 S Hillside
Little Missouri	near Broadway & Harry
Kansas Coliseum	1279 E 85th St North, Valley Center
Kirby's Beer Store	3227 E 17th St North
Kirby's #2	E Kellogg
Kit Shickers	47th St South & Broadway
Kraut Club	Haysville
Long Branch Club	31st & Seneca
Lucky 7	102 E 29th St North
Lucky's Club	31st & Meridian
Mambo Club	2459 N Hillside
Maples Club	W Maple 2 blocks west of West St
Mary Carter Club	W Maple
Masonic Home	Seneca & Martinson
McGraw's	S Rock Rd, between Harry & Pawnee
Miller Theater	100 Block of N Broadway
Mint Club	Seneca & 31st St South

Name	Address or Location
Moose Lodge	9801 E Kellogg

    formerly the Trig Ballroom

Mop Hall

New Shadowland Dance Pavilion

    . . . . 2459 N Hillside

Oakies . . . . 500 block of E Douglas

Orpheum Theater. . . . . 200 N Broadway. Built in 1922.

Penny's Lounge. . . . . on N Arkansas

Pirates Cave. . . . . N Broadway between 29th & 37th

Podnuh's . . . . S St. Francis

Rock Castle . . . . 3813 N Broadway

    Built in 1935. Later became the Hobble-De-Hoy, and then the Coyote Club.

Rotten Rodney's One Horse Saloon

    . . . . 13th & West St

Saddleboogie Saloon . . . . 212 E 47th St South

Sam's Place . . . . W Kellogg

Sands Klub . . . . 1523 W MacArthur

Shadowland Dance Pavilion . . on S Lawrence (now Broadway)

So's Your Mother. . . . . W Douglas

South Forty Dance Hall . . . . . . 5700 S Broadway, Haysville

    owned by Bill Selby who had owned the Brookside Club

Sportsman Club

Stardust (original)

    destroyed by fire

Stardust . . . . Broadway & 47th St South (east of Broadway)

    Western Swinger was west of Broadway

Swingland . . . . 3103 N Broadway

Tennessee Beer Mill . . . . George Washington Blvd & Harry

Tennessee Gin Mill . . . . George Washington Blvd & Harry

Selected List of Wichita Clubs, etc.

The Eye . . . . 2nd & Hydraulic

The Hut . . . . on K-42
    Later became an American Legion Hall

Thelma's No. 1 . . . . 2nd & Hydraulic

Tiger Club . . . . on 31st St South, across from an American Legion Hall

Tiki Club . . . . S Broadway

Trig Ballroom . . . . 9801 E Kellogg
    became the Moose Lodge

U and I. . . . . Harry & Meridian

Viking . . . . on W Maple

Wagon Wheel . . . . 47th & West St

Water Hole. . . . . 21st & Broadway, south of the Rock Castle

Western Cavalier . . . . Meridian & Orient Boulevard

Western Swinger (originally the Hi Ho Club)
    . . . . Broadway & 47th St South
    Later became Saddleboogie Saloon.

Various VFWs and American Legion Halls

BIBLIOGRAPHY

Billboard Magazine – July 6, 1963

Council Grove Republican – Nov. 9, 1959

Country Music Hall of Fame & Museum

Country Music News – April 18, 1968

Country Music Records: A Discography, 1921-1942 – Tony Russell & Bob Pinson – Oxford University Press, 2004

Country: The Music and the Musicians – The Country Music Foundation 1988

Cowboy Songs and Other Frontier Ballads – John A. Lomax – The MacMillan Company, 1918

Cowboys and Kansas: Stories from the Tallgrass Prairie – Dr. Jim Hoy – University of Oklahoma Press 1995

Definitive Country: The Ultimate Encyclopedia of Country Music and Its Performers – Barry McCloud Berkley Publishing Group, 1995

Fret Board Journal

Goat Glands to Ranch Hands: The KFDI Story – Orin Friesen with Bud Norman – Rowfant Press, 2013

Hatch Show Print: The Story of a Great American Poster Shop – James Sherrarden, Elek Horvath, Paul Kingsbury – Chronicle Books, 2001

He Was Singin' This Song – Jim Bob Tinsley – University of Central Florida Press, 1981

Hillbilly-Music.com – Dave Sichak

History of Wichita and Sedgwick County – O.H. Bentley – G.F. Cooper & Co., Chicago, IL 1910.

Jimmie Rodgers: The Life and Times of America's Blue Yodeler – Nolan Porterfield – University Press of Mississippi, 2007

Johnny Western: Heroes & Cowboys – Dale Vinicur – Bear Family Records 1993

Kansas Bluegrass Association newsletters – Various issues

KFBI News – July 6, 1936

KFDI Country Music News – Various issues, 1977-1979

KFDI Ranch Hand Roundup newspapers – Various issues

Looking Ahead with Radio – KFBI Radio 1951

Mid-America Folklore – Pat O'Connor -- Spring 1993

Ralph Peer and the Making of Popular Roots Music – Barry Mazor – Chicago Review Press, 2015

San Antonio Rose: The Life and Music of Bob Wills – Charles R. Townsend – University of Illinois Press, 1976

Southern Gospel History – sghistory.com

The Active Age – Ted Blankenship -- January 2019

The Black Experience and the Blues in 1950s Wichita -- P.J. O'Connor – Mid America Folklore 1993

The Harmony Illustrated Encyclopedia of Country Music – Fred Dellar, Alan Cackett, Roy Thompson Harmony Books 1986

The Illustrated History of Country Music – Patrick Carr – Random House/Times Books 1995

The Mountain Broadcast Vol. 3 – November 1942

The Music Reporter – June 16, 1958

The Origin of the Electric Guitar – Eric Cale – Wichita-Sedgwick County Historical Museum, 2019

The Steel Guitar in Early Country Music –Anthony Lis

Top Country Singles 1944-1993 – Joel Whitburn – Record Research Inc., 1994

Wichita Beacon newspaper – Various issues

Wichita Century: A Pictorial History of Wichita, Kansas 1870-1970 --- R.M. "Dick" Long – Wichita Historical Museum Association, Inc., 1969

Wichita Eagle newspaper – Various issues

Wichita Jazz and Vice Between the World Wars – Joshua L. Yearout – Rowfant Press, 2010

Wichita Rock & Roll 1950-1980 – Wichita Rock Music Project Team, 2017

INTERVIEWS

(all interviews by author, except where noted)

Doug Adams	March 17, 2020
Denzil Alcorn	2018
Vince Baker	February 12, 2021
Frank Baughman	2018
Cheryl Bellew	April 18, 2019
Ray Benson	January 24, 2020
Sam Bidwell	April 12 & 18, 2019
Ron Binkley	January 10, 2018
Doris Buss	October 8, 2019
Polly Campbell	January 10, 2018
Elmer Childress	March 20, 2020
Bobby Clark	January 4, 2021
Monty Coble	February 12, 2021
Richard Crowson	April 12, 2020
Charlie Daniels	September 27, 2019
Rodney Dillard	March 20, 2019
Doc Embree	by Dick Hill
Bucky Fowler	2018
Jerry Hardman	August 28, 2019
Chuck Haukos	March 18, 2020
Terry Henry	February 11, 2018
Stan Holmes	October 10, 2019
Rob Loren	2019
Geri Mapes Isaacs	2019
Martina McBride	May 16, 2020
Jesse McReynolds	September 6, 1991 & February 19, 2021
Jim McReynolds	January 15, 1985
B.W. Norris	2018

Jay Petersen & Jane Kopiska . . 1985
Kenny Pruitt . . . . February 5, 2018
Dennis Rader . . . . March 20, 2019
Daryl Schiff . . . . May 11, 2020
John Speer . . . . February 25, 2020
Shoji Tabuchi . . . . March 19, 2019
Dwain Terry . . . . numerous interviews in 2019 & 2020
Phil Uhlik . . . . January 10, 2018
Rex Victory . . . . August 29, 2019
Don Walton . . . . January 25 & February 5, 2018
Johnny Western . . . . January 23, 2020
Darren Wilcox . . . . June 21, 2020

Index

A

Ackerman, Dr. Lyle 111
Acuff, Roy & the Smoky Mountain Boys 84, 111, 145
Adams, Carl & the Longbranch Boys 87
Adams, Doug 199, 200
Aircap Records 115
Airport Hilton 136, 141
Aitken, Dan 163, 164
Alabama (the band) 149
All American Quartet 205
Albright, Sonny 55, 56
Alcorn, Denzil & the Citations 115-118, 120
Aldean, Jason 209
Allen, Clay 116
Allen, Kent 208
Allen, Rex 177, 180, 190
Allen Jr, Rex 180, 183
Allman Brothers 197
Allsup, Tommy 65-67
Aloha Motel 69
Amazing Rhythm Aces 199
American Federation of Musicians 33
Anderson, Gene & His Honky-Tonkers 88
Andrews Sisters 36
Andrus, Gary 77
Andy Griffith Show 173
ARC Records 49
Arcadia Theater, New York City 16
Arcadia Theater, Wichita 43
Ark Valley Boys 19, 23-35, 40-41, 43-44, 65, 77, 147, 179, 203
Armadillo World Headquarters 183
Arnold, Dale 94
Arthur Godfrey's Talent Scouts 84
Ashworth, Ernie 98
Asleep at the Wheel 67, 124, 179, 180, 182
Aspinwall, Hugh 54
Atchison, Bob 176
Auge, Bud 189-190
Augustine, Pat 201
Aurandt, Paul 47
Austin, Fred 156-157, 160, 172
Autry, Gene 24, 75, 177, 190-191, 195
Axton, Hoyt 122

B

B-1 Club 182
Baggett, Curt 44, 147, 203
Baggett, Ron 44, 147, 203
Baker, Don 208
Baker, Monty 95, 146
Baker, Nathan 169
Baker, Vince 117-118, 121, 198
Balman, Leona 109
Bamboo Club 117
Bar 16 Ranch 76-77
Bar D Wranglers 186
Bar J Wranglers 186
Barker, Ray 88
Barnes, Bob & the Country Boys 93-94
Barnes Brothers 91, 93
Barnes, Sid 91, 93
Barnett, Elmo 92-93
Bass, Dwayne 94
Bateman, Cal 201
Bat Masterson 191
Batson, Bruce 197
Batson, Pam 169
Baughman, Colette 43
Baughman, Frank 41-44, 133
Baughman, Rex 43
Baxter, John 208
Baxter, Ron 208
Bayers, Eddie 122
Bazaar Crossing 172
Beatles, The 87, 149, 195-196, 198
Beauchamp, George 13-15
BEC Playhouse 43
Bedient, Howard 125
Beech, Walter 3, 16
Belew, Carl 89
Bellew, Cheryl 123-125, 127
Bennett, Bill 171
Bennett, Brad 171
Bennett Brothers 171
Bennett, Marc 171, 176
Bennett, Tim 171
Benson, Ray 179-180
Berline, Byron 165
Bidwell, Sam 101, 118-124, 147

Big Chief Henry's String Band 10-11, 209
Big D Jamboree 116
Big D Jubilee 81
Big Dog Studios 156
Biggies 123
Biggs, Chris 176
Big Twang 173-174
Bill & Elmer 48
Binkely, Ron 109
Bits & Pieces 157
Blackwood Brothers 203, 205
Blackwood, Donna 209
Blackwood, R.W. 209
Blake, Norman 165
Bluebird Corner 86
Blue Fire Band 175
Bluegrass from the Rocking Banjo Ranch 161
Bluegrass Hall of Fame 57
Bluegrass Jayhawkers 168
Bluegrass on Tap 169
Bluegrass Revue 164
Bluegrass Ramblers 111
Blue Plate Special 174
Blue Sky Boys 55
Bluestem 173
Bluestem Revue 169
Bobby Wiley Rhythmaires Show 77
Boeing 71, 78, 89, 129
Boggs, Bill 27-28, 31-32, 37, 39, 48, 77
Boggs, Karen 169, 172
Bolen, Arnold 95, 117
Bolen, Ronnie 95
Bonanza 88, 116
Bond, Johnny 190
Bone, Merlin 126
Boone County Jamboree 60
Boone, Richard 191
Bottorf, Rob "Bert" 182
Boulanger, Tom 153, 155
Bowles, Jason 44
Bowles, Jim 43
Boyd, Bill & His Buckshots 88
Bozeman, John (see Mack Sanders) 57
Bradshaw, Terry 113
Brasher, Jim 169, 172
Brewer, Charles 11

Brewer, Gage 11-17, 26
Brewer, Loti 16
Brewer, Mary 11
Brewer, Teresa 84
Brinkley, John R. 22, 47
Brooker, Bob 93, 96, 118
Brooker Brothers Band 96
Brooker, Donnie 198
Brooks, Garth 122, 126, 138, 156, 200
Brother, Frederick 13
Brown, Clarence "C.Q." 25, 27-28, 31-32, 34-39
Brown, Dave 173
Brown, Dennis 119
Brown, Jim Ed 123
Brown, Ken 80, 81
Brown, Milton & his Musical Brownies 7, 59, 178
Broz, Richard 156-157
Bruce, Ed 147
Brumley, Albert E. 100
Brumley Jr., Albert 100
Brunk's Comedians 7
Bryce, Sherry 61
Buffalo Springfield 196
Bullard, Jim 173
Burford, Terry 112, 209
Burkes Brothers 9, 11, 209
Burkes, Charlie 9
Burkes, Dorothy 9
Burkes, Weldon 7-9
Burkes, William Theodore "Billy" 7-9
Burnette, Smiley "Frog Millhouse" 36, 38, 75
Burns, George 31
Buschow, Doris 13
Buss, Doris 19, 31-32, 34, 37-39
Buss, Leonard 31
Byrd, Senator Robert 167
Byrds, The 152-153, 195-197

C

Cabaret Oldtown 156
Cactus Jack 156
Cady, Del 126
Cale, Eric "E.C. Wakeen" 2, 16, 181-182

Index

Cale, J.J. 201
Call, Jack Wesley "Cactus Jack" 63
Camaro Records 117
Campbell, Glen 103
Campbell, Les 49, 53
Campbell, Polly 48, 52-54
Cantrell, Dale 79-81
Capitol Records 36, 57, 62, 67, 71-72
Capps, Jimmy 122
Caprice Ballroom 99
Cargill, Henson 43
Carnegie Hall 186, 192
Carney, Frank 143
Carr, Patrick 29
Carriage Inn 97
Carter, Jody 144
Casey, Al 79-80
Cash, Johnny & the Tennessee Two 62-63, 133, 162, 192-193
Cash, Tommy 133
Castleberry, Charlie 162-163, 165, 169, 172, 174-175
Catalino, Vic 70
Cates Sisters 63
Catfish Charlie 201
Cause for Concern 173
Caywood, Rick 157
Century II Auditorium 133, 147, 180, 183, 208
Cerday, Clay 94
Cessna, Clyde 3
Channel 13 Barn Dance 116
Chaparell Playboys 88
Charlie Daniels Band 70, 197
Chavez, Paul 153, 155-156
Cher'O-Key Records 89
Cherokee Maidens 174
Chet-Mark Records 89
Childers, Claude 28, 30-32
Childress, Debbie 204-205
Childress, Elmer 204-206
Childress, June 204-205
Childress, Pam 204-205
Childress, Shari 204-205
Chisholm Creek Boys 169
Chisholm, Jesse 3

Chisholm Trail Gun Club 120
Chow Time 23, 41
Chrisman, "Woody" Paul 180
Christinsan, Roy 25
Chuck Wagon Gang 204
Citations 116, 118
Clarey, Don 198
Clark, Barry 198
Clark, Bobby 164
Clark, Gene 196
Clark, Hap & the Log Cabin Boys 101, 120
Clark, Jessica 4
Clark, Petula 85
Clark, Roy 57, 60, 63, 71, 124
Clarke, Michael 196
Classic Country One Man Band 127
Clevenger, Kenny 118
Cline, Patsy 63, 138
Clocks, The 199
Clothier, Earl 81
Coble, Monty 151-152
Cockeyed Cowboy Club 149
Coconut Grove, Los Angeles 16
Cohn, Nudie 179
Coleman Employees Club 96
Coleman Jr., Sheldon 156
Coleman, Tom 162-163, 165
Collie, Biff 147
Collins, Dugg 99
Colorado State Fair 190
Columbia Records 78, 192
Comanche Meat Company 44
Comanche Roundup 42-43
Commander Cody & His Lost Planet Airmen 144
Cook, Ted 48
Cooley, Spade 201
Cooper, Wilma Lee & Stoney 63
Copas, Cowboy 63
Copeland, Mike 146
Coral Records 84
Corky's Corral Gang 31-32, 34, 36-37, 39, 78, 80
Cornbelt Jamboree 50
Cornelius, Gary 118, 126
Coslett, Kim 188

Cotillion Ballroom 108, 135, 137, 147, 170, 179
Country Gazette 165
Country Music Association 62, 118
Country Music Disc Jockey Hall of Fame 99, 144
Country Music Awards Show 150
Country Music News 88, 119
Country Radio Hall of Fame 61
Country Rhythm Boys 41, 81
Country Rip Riders 149
Cousin Clarence (see Brown, Clarence)
Cowboy Inn 41-43, 57, 65-67, 96, 101
Cowboy Joe 152
Cowboys 201
Coyote Club 182
Crane, Terry & the Blue Diamonds 100
Crary, Dan 165
Crawdaddies 148
Crawford, Steve 187-188
Crest Theater 43, 183
Crockett, Dave 25
Crosby, Bob 40
Crosby, David 196
Crownover, Gene 40, 42, 67
Crowson, Richard 172, 184-185
Cunes, Russell 25
Cunningham, Linda 169
Cypress Club 97
Cyrus Noble Whiskey Band 198

D

D-Bar-H Gang 38-39
Dagle, Kathy 43
Dakota 156
Dallas Spirit 16
Daniels, Charlie & the Jaguars 63, 69-71, 124, 141, 148, 197
Daryl Starbird Rod & Custom Car Show 179
David's 163
Davis, Art 66
Davis, Bill 37, 42-43
Davis, Buddy 70
Davis, Don 201
Davis, Fritz 153, 200-201
Davis, Jimmie 61, 75
Davis, Shelly 143, 146
Davis, Skeeter 190
Dawson, Dave 25
Day, Doris 30
Day, Joel 151-152
Dean, Billy 209
Dean, Eddie "Denny" 25, 28
Dean, Jimmy 57, 63
Deaton, Billy 112
DeBus, Cal 39
DeGrant, Ronnie 76
Delmore Brothers 49, 55, 72
Dennis, Denny 30
Denniston, Lowell 143
Derby Barn Dance 81
Detour 153, 155
Diamond W Wranglers 187
Dickens, "Little Jimmy" 41, 50, 77, 189-190
DiGregorio, Joey "Taz" 70
Dillard, Rodney 111
Dillards, The 111, 161, 173
Dillon, Dean 130
Dinner Bell Gang 48, 53-54
Dinning, Ginger 35-36
Dinning, Jean 35-36
Dinning, Lou 35-36
Dinning, Mark 36
Dinning Sisters 35-36
Dixie Chicks 173-174
Dixie Records 106
DJ Cookin' 140
Dobbin, Harry 197
Dobro 14, 145, 159
Dog House 182
Dole, Bob 157, 167
Domestic Science Club 174
Dondlinger, John 197
Donnie Huffman Band (see Huffman, Donnie) 157
Doors, The 57
Dopyera, Rudy 14
Dopyera, John 13-14
Dopyera, Rudy 14
Double D Lounge 88
Double Take 152

Douthit, Perry 52
Drake, Pete 117
Draw One Lounge 88
Driscoll, Brian 170, 201
Driscoll, Jeanette 170
Drumm, Pauline (see Campbell, Polly) 52-53
Dry, Bill & the Rhythm Riders 95
Dudte, Matt 173
Duncan, Carl 169
Duncan, Johnny 169, 173
Dunnegan, Tina & Thunder Road 140
Durrett, Gary 154
Dusty Rose (see Midnight Rose) 149, 169
Dusty's Jamboree 27, 38
Dycus, Marion Frank 122, 129-130
Dyer, "Big Tom" 181-182
Dylan, Bob 21, 196
Dyson, Jeff "Jim Bob Duke Buck" 182

E

Eagles, The 196-197
Eagles Lodge 134
E.B. McCullough Upholstering Company 18
Echo Canyon 173, 175
Edgar, W.C. 125
Edison, Thomas 21
Edminster, Leichester "Corky" 25-28, 31-32, 34-37, 39, 80
EJ's Red Lion 124
Ehart, Mark 30
Ehart, Phil 30
Ehrke, Kip 197
Ehrke, Mike 197
81 Club 116
El Tivoli Country Club 7, 8
Elder, Eric 154
Electro guitars 14-15
Elliott, "Wild" Bill 119, 128
Ellis County Fair 151
Elmer Childress Show 204, 206
Elmo B & the Other Three (see Barnett, Elmo) 92-93
Elwood, Paul 169
Embree, Esther 50-52
Embree, Guy W. "Doc" 50-52

Emery, Joe 169
Emmons, Buddy 145
Emperor Club 88, 96
Engels, Matt 157
Ericson, Sue 121
Esquire Jumptette 69
Etheredge, Thomas 185-186
Evans, Dale 170, 190
Evans, John 152
Everly Brothers 129
Eye, The 97, 108

F

Fail, Lucky & Mod Country 93
Fain, John 97
Falke, Steve 151
Fargo, Donna 209
Farha, Ted 172
Farmers & Bankers Life Insurance Company 18, 47
Farrell, Jim 186-188
Federal Bureau of Investigation 104
Federal Radio Commission 22
Fehleisen Wichita Band and Orchestra 4
Fell, Don 169
Fender, Leo 75
Ferguson, Tex & his Drifting Pioneers 33-34, 40
Fey, Jim 154
Fibber McGee & Molly 31
Fields, John 189-190
5th Dimension 78
Finnegan, Mike 78
Fire on the Mountain 167
Firewater Band 152
Fisher, Chris 163-164
Flatland Band 147-148
Flatland Express 169
Flatt & Scruggs 161, 168
Flatt, Lester & the Nashville Grass 159, 165
Fleetwood Mac 199
Fleming, Darrell 119
Flint Hillbillies 169
Flinthill Special 169
Flint Hills Dulcimer Club 173

Floren, Myron 19
Flying Ark 31
Flying Burrito Brothers 196-197
Flying W Chuckwagon 185-186
Flying W Wranglers 185-186
Foley, Red 41, 72, 84, 203
Fontana, D.J. 117
Ford, "Tennessee Ernie" 29, 72, 195, 203
Forrester, Howdy 11
Fortner, Snazzy 28, 30, 32, 34
Forum, The 4, 29, 43, 62, 192
Foster, Mike 198
Four Guys 117
4 Star Records 34
Foundry, The 163, 197
Foundry 21 181
Foust, Butch 94-95
Foust, Joe 94
Fowler, Brent 134-135
Fowler Brothers 43, 133-141
Fowler, Bucky 43, 133-141
Fowler, Don 42-43, 133-134
Fowler, Kandace 138-139
Fowler, Karla 138-139
Fowler, Kelcy 138-139
Fowler, Kristine 138-139
Fowler, Scott 43, 133-135, 138
Fox Canyon 123
Fox Theater – Newton 139
Frankie's Lounge 91, 93, 107
Franks, Tillman 112, 115
Freely, Ace 198
Freeman, Bob 143
Fresh Cut 169, 172
Fresh Water 169, 176
Frey, Glenn 196
Friends University 175
Friesen, Jesse 185, 188
Friesen, Orin 2, 126, 143, 160-166, 184, 187-188
Frisby, June 17-19, 31, 109
Fritz Davis & Daybreak 201
Fritz Davis & Good Medicine 201
Fritz Davis & the Knight Flyers 201
Frizzell, Lefty 122
Frontier Ballroom 43, 88

Frontier Days Rodeo, Wichita 58
Full House Band 156
Funk, Mary Jane 168
Funk, Nelson 168-169
Funk, Steve 169
Furay, Richie 196

G

Gage Brewer's Country Band 15
Gage Brewer's Hawaiian Entertainers 12-13
Gage Brewer's Hawaiians 13
Gage Brewer's Radio Orchestra 13, 15
Galen, Roy 48
Galen-Williams Hillbilly Band 48
Garden of the Gods 185
Garrish, Sonny 122
Garrison, Bill "Wichita Wilbur" 200
Garver, James 156, 201
Gasaway, Gene 40, 67, 91, 93
Geddes, David 131
Gemini Records 117
Gibson, Don 96
Gibson, Esther (see Embree, Esther) 52
Gibson, Hoot 60
Gill, Vince 164
Gilley, Mickey 126, 149
Gilley's 149
Gleeson, Tim 169
Golden Chance Steak Saloon 120
Golden Jubilees 115
Golden Knight 88
Golden Nugget 60, 151
Golden West Singers 30
Gonzales, Don 129
Gooch, Merlin 91
Gordon, Larry 95
Gosfield, Reuben "Lucky Oceans" 179
Gospelaires Quartet 205
Graber, Kurt 139, 151
Grand Master Fiddler Championship 148
Grand Ole Opry 57, 67, 98, 116-117, 123, 129, 145, 150, 179, 195
Grand River Township 163-164, 168-170
Grant, Marshall 192
Graves, Dan 151

Index 235

Gray, Elmer 48-49
Great American Broadcasting 61
Great American Cowboy China Tour 187
Great Empire Broadcasting 105-106, 154, 192-193
Great Plains Dulcimer Alliance 173
Greiffenstein, William 4
Green, Douglas B. Green (see also Green, "Ranger" Doug) 181
Green, "Ranger" Doug 180-181
Green, Tom 70-71
Greer, Stan 160, 176, 184
Groom, Dewey 116
Guellette, Nacrissa Adaline 10
Guitorgan Guitar Synth 77
Gunsmoke 191

H

Hadacol Caravan 58
Hager, Sarah Susan 10
Haggard, Merle 123, 133-134, 140, 195, 197
Hahn, Jerry & Quintet & Brotherhood 76-78
Hajacos, Rob 122
Hale, Allen 172
Hall, Clarence 10-11
Hall, Harold 10-11
Hall, Henry (see Big Chief Henry's String Band) 10-11
Hall, Jimmy 65-67, 95
Hall, Nellie 10
Hall, Susan 11
Hall, Thomas Jefferson 10
Hamilburg, Mitchell 191
Hamilton, Colburn 88
Hamilton, Diane 76
Hangar Club 97-98
Hank Flamingo 184-186
Hardin, Dennis 173
Hardman, Jerry & Saddleboogie Band, Nite Life 124-127
Harris, Berry 67
Harris, Robin 105, 107-109, 112
Hart, Sammy 78-81, 85
Hartford, John 161-162, 168
Hartley, Bob 156

Harvey, Norman & the Westerners 119
Harvey, Paul (see Aurandt, Paul) 47
Harwell, Orvil 11
Haukos, Chuck 198
Haukos, Mike 198
Have Gun, Will Travel 191-192, 211
Hawkins, David 184
Hawkins, Hawkshaw 41, 62-63
Hawkins, Vic "Puny" 25, 28
Hawks, Bill 163
Haysville Bluegrass Festival 164, 168
Hazen, Jack 58
Heart 199
Heartland 157
Heck, Larry 167
Hee Haw 60
Helmer, Grant & the Swing Aires 94-95
Helms, Billy 81
Helms, Johnny 126
Henderson, Scott 124
Hendricks, Carl 105, 108-109
Hendrix, Kevin 173
Henley, Don 196
Henry, Terry & the Rockin' Rowdy Country Band 150-151
Hensley, Dottie 95, 112
Hensley, Gene 95, 112
Herring, Robert Worley "Deputy Dusty" 22-23, 27, 38-39
Hickman, Sara 174
High Country Show Band 81
Hightower, Gary 146
Hi-Ho Club 69-72, 107, 123
Hill Billy Paradise 119-120, 128
Hill, Tommy 117, 129
Hillary's Sister 176
Hillman, Chris 196
Hilton, Gary 126
Hinson, Jerry 199-200
Hipps, Emitt 43, 101, 159
Hissem, Greg 160, 170
Holick, Ed 163-164, 170
Holly, Buddy & the Crickets 66, 115
Hollywood Bowl 192
Hollywood Christian Group 190
Holmes, Stan 145-147, 159

Holt, David 167
Home on the Range Band 173
Home Rangers 184-185
Home State Quartet 205
Honeymoon Ranch Boys 43-44, 133
Honn, Dorothy 29
Hoopii, Sol 12
Hoover, J. Edgar 104
Hopkins, Dean 44
Horn, Upton 42
Horrigan, Beulah 29
Horton, Johnny 115
Hot Pursuit 173
Houser, "Uncle Dick" 155
Houston, David 112, 115
Howard, Harlan 1, 90
Howell, Rick 163
Hoxie, Jack 25
Hoy, Dr. Jim 5
Hoyer, Mike 144
Hudspeth, "Arkie" Jay 44
Huffman, Donnie 157
Hughes, Adam 138
Hughes, Randy 63
Hut, The 94
Hymn Time 54

I

Ice Capades 40
Ingram, "Gentle" Ben 203
In Kahootz 157
International Entertainment Buyers Association 63
Irsik, Jon 151-152
Irwin, Emily 174
Irwin, Martie 174
Irwin, William Portwood 16
Isaacs, Bud 29-30
Isaacs, Geri Mapes 29-30

J

J38 Land & Cattle Company 186
Jackson, Harold "Shot" 145
Jackson, Junior 42-43
Jackson, Wanda 63, 190

James, Chuck 80-81
James, Dub 80-81
James, Fred 163
James Gang 196
James, Sonny 209
James, Tommy Lee 133
Jarman, Jack 159
Jenkins, Buster 147, 159
Jenkins Music 18
Jennings, John 65
Jennings, Waylon 66, 124, 192, 198
Jesse's Supper Club 149
Jewel Records 69
Jim & Jesse & the Virginia Boys 55-57, 161, 165, 167
Johnny & Bonnie's Ballroom 93
Johnson, Greg 187
Johnson, JW 187
Johnson, Jimmy & the Country Playboys 88, 91
Johnson, Kris 188
Johnson, Mark 171, 173
Johnson, Robert 10
Johnson, Ted 48, 51, 54
Jones, George 63, 98, 130
Jones, Dick 190
Jones, Grandpa 50
Jordan, Bill & Longbranch Jamboree 117, 121
Journal Broadcast Group 106
Joyland 43, 105, 112, 130, 133, 137, 150, 152, 156, 160
June Frisby Academy (see Frisby, June) 17-18, 31, 109

K

Kaipo, Joe 7-9
KAKE Radio 35, 129
KAKE-TV 22, 27, 38-39, 58
KANS 31, 34-36, 39-40, 47, 63, 78-81
Kansas (the band) 30
Kansas Arts Commission 201
Kansas Battle of the Bands 150
Kansas Bluegrass All-Stars 170
Kansas Bluegrass Association 168-169, 173, 176

Kansas Coliseum 123-124, 134, 136, 183, 198
Kansas Gas & Electric 144
Kansas Heart 175-176
Kansas Heritage Days Old-Time Music
    Festival 172-173
Kansas State Fair 28, 31, 107
Kansas Supreme Court 33
KARD-TV 42-43, 204-206
Kay, John 200
KBUL 58, 144-147
KCMK-FM 63
KDHL 189
KDKA 21
KEDD 76-77, 82
Keefer, Jim 170
Keitel, Pat 139, 199-200
Kellogg, Jack "Hatman Jack" 181-182
Kelly, Claude 133
Kelly, Pat 151
Kendal, Robby 201
Kenny & the Imperials 131
Kentucky Barn Dance 57
Kerby, Tom 79-81
KETA 116
Keyes, Mike 160
KEYN 58, 143-144
KFBI 5, 9, 35, 47-58, 65, 81, 89, 104, 179
KFDI 22-23, 44, 47-49, 53-56, 67, 81, 99,
    104-109, 112, 117, 121, 124-126, 129-
    167, 172, 179-183, 186, 192-194, 197,
    201, 203, 206-211
KFDI Listener Appreciation Show 167
KFEQ 33
KFH 13, 19, 22-35, 40-42, 47, 54, 58, 65, 80,
    135, 179
KFKB 22, 47
KFRM 58-61, 117, 121, 203
KFUM 13
KFXF 13
KGBZ 9
KHEY 103-104
KHI-TV 60
KICT 59, 61
Kilgore, David 151
Kimble, Doug 123
King Records 60

Kinsey, Jack 10
Kirby, Dave 140
Kirby, Jim 162
Kirby, Pete "Bashful Brother Oswald" 145
Kirby, Wade 140
Kirby's Beer Store 162, 197
Kirby's #2 162
KIRL 81, 104
Kit Shickers 123, 198
KJRG 89
KLEO 81, 143
KMA 50, 52, 144
KMMJ 51
KMUW 160-161
Knapic Family 176
Knievel, Evel 204-205
Knight, Jimmy 76
Koch, Steve 201
Kocks, Dan 159-160, 166-167
Koefer, Bobby 69, 81
KOFO 154-155
KOOO 58
KPEG 129
Krenzer, Betty 78
Krenzer, Mathew 78
Krenzer, Ralph (see also Hart, Sammy) 78-81
KRLD-TV 116
KSGL 58
KSIR 58, 62, 106, 143, 179
KTVH 58, 77, 87
KWCH 77, 121
KWKH 115
KWLS 176, 203
KXEL 56, 59
KZSN 135, 138

L

LaBour, Fred "Too Slim" 180
Lady Antebellum 209
Lamplighters Club 42
Lanham, Roy 30
La Posada Mexican Restaurant 169
Laswell, Vern & the Silver Star Playboys 107
Lawman 191
Lawrence Welk Show 19

Leadon, Bernie 196
Lear, Bill 3
Leather & Lace 149
Ledbetter, Glenn 207
Ledbetter, Reverend Jack 207
LeDoux, Chris 125
Led Zeppelin 197
Lee, Brenda 41
Lege, Patty 174
Lee, Johnny 126, 149
LeGarde Twins 62
Legend of Wyatt Earp, The 191
Lennon, John 195
Leslie, Hugh 125
Lester Flatt, Earl Scruggs & the Foggy Mountain Boys 159
Lewis, Curly 81, 91, 93
Lewis, Jerry Lee 129
Liberty Records 66-67
Light Crust Doughboys 178
Lisa, Paul 173
Little Missouri 97
Lodestone 156
Lomax, John A. 4
Lone Run 172
Lonesome Frank & the Kitchen Band 130
Long, Wyatt 99
Longbranch Club 117, 121
Longbranch Jamboree 117, 121-122
Lonzo & Oscar 129
Loren, Connie 140
Loren, Rob 138-141, 147, 175
Lotus 135-136
Loudermilk, John D. 85
Louisiana Hayride 115-116
Love, Cindy 150
Love, David 150
Love, Mike 150-151
Lovelady, Dana 107-108
Lovell, Don 136
Lovell, Gene 93
Lovell, Marge 93
Lucky's Club 97
Lynam, Ron 163
Lynch, Cindy 154
Lynch, F.F. "Mike" 104, 106, 154-155, 179

Lynch, Frank 80-81, 104
Lynch, Laura 174
Lynn, Loretta 131
Lynyrd Skynyrd 197, 199

M

Macy Jr., Ed 153, 155-156
Macy, Robin 173-174
Madison, Cheryl (see Wayne, Cheryl) 152
Mahoney, Jock 190
MacIntyre, Jolynn 188
Mainord, Jack 61
Major, Clif 145, 162-163, 165, 169, 170
Majors, Sarah 169
Majors, Troy 169
Malcom, Ron 169
Mambo Club 17
Mancini, Henry 40
Mandrell, Barbara 115
Mangan, Jim 201
Mann, Manfred (Earth Band) 78
Mapes, Geri (see Isaacs, Geri Mapes) 29-30
Maples Club 93, 97
Marlboro Country Music Talent Roundup 123
Marlboro Country Showdown 134
Marriott Hotel 176
Marshall Tucker Band 199
Martin, Dewey 196
Martin, Jason 152
Martin, Jimmy & the Sunny Mountain Boys 159
Mary Carter Club 98, 100
Mary Carter Paint Store 98
Mathewson, William "Buffalo Bill" 3
Mattea, Kathy 126, 150
Mattingly, Roger 146
Maynard, Ron 91, 99
Maxey, Mike 199-200
Mayo, Susan "Symphony Sue" 182
McAuliffe, Leon 65, 93
McBride, John 135-137, 199
McBride, Martina 133, 135-137, 152
McCall, Darrell 63, 147
McCartney, Paul 195
McCarty, Owen & His Troubadors 88

McCaskey, Royal 80
McClish, Doris (see Buss, Doris) 31
McConnell Air Force Base 156
McCormick, George & his Clinch Mountain Boys 63
McCune, Anita "Hoppy" 77
McEuen, John 172-173
McGuinn, Roger 196
McGuire Sisters 138
McHugh, Mac 173
McJimsey, Pat 153, 155-156
McKay, Alan (see Waggoner, Larry) 143-144,
McKinney, William "Red" 28, 32, 34, 37
McKinzie, Mac 76, 79-81
McLean, Bill "Cap'n Bill" 38
McNally, Mary Anne 35
McReynolds, Jesse 55-57
McReynolds, Jim 55-57
M.D. Systems 135-136, 199
Mead, James R. 3, 9
Meek, Jim & the Country Showmen 140
Meisner, Randy 196
Melody Masters Quartet 206
Melody Playboys 87
Mercury Records 41, 72, 113
Messina, Jim 196
Messina, Jo Dee 87, 209
Meyer, Ricky 156, 201
Michigan Barn Dance 34
Midnight Rose 149
Midwestern Hayride 60
Midwestern Jamboree 115
Mike & the Ranger 176
Miller, Charles Nelson "Chuck" 72-73
Miller, Mitch 191
Miller Theater 13, 59
Mills, Ronnie 150
Milsap, Ronnie 134, 149
Ministar Guitar 7
Mint Club 87, 125
Mixed Company 149
Mollendick, Jacob 16
Monroe, Bill & his Blue Grass Boys 159, 161, 167-168, 171
Monroe Brothers 55
Monroe, James & the Midnight Ramblers 167

Montana, Patsy 53
Montigo Club 198
Moody, Larry 169
Moody, "Skidrow Joe" 120
Moore, Jess 99
Moose Club 71, 118
Moose Lodge 137, 146
Mop Hall 43
Morgan, George 63, 89, 98, 129
Morse, Ella Mae 72
Morton, Fred 160, 166
Morton, Russ 169
Moss, Irene 28, 30
Moss, Jody 28, 30
Moss, Lucy 28, 30
Moss Sisters 28, 30
Moten, Bennie & His Victor Recording Orchestra 13
Moyer, Bill 206
Mr. D's 143
Mueller, Marvin 173
Mullendore, June Frisby (see Frisby, June) 19
Mullican, Moon 62-63, 72
Murphey, Michael Martin 111, 140, 182-183
Murrell, Carl 121

N

Nail's Texaco 96
Nashville News 145-147
National-Dobro Corporation 14
National Guitar Flat-Picking Championship Festival 165
National Semi-Pro Baseball Congress 62
National String Instrument Corporation 14
Neal, Don 147, 198
Nelson, Henry "Hank" 181-182
Nelson, Ken 62
Nelson, Willie 67, 124, 130, 150, 180, 183, 192
Newberry, Miles 169
Newell, Fred 122
New Grass Revival 165
Newman, Jimmy 85
Newton, Ira 79-80, 117
Newton, Roger 121

New Tradition 173
Nichols, Joe 209
Nichols, Lee 42
Nichols, Tim 87
Nilsson, Harry 85
Nite Shift 123-125, 149
Nitty Gritty Dirt Band 166, 168, 173
Nomar Theater 78
Norris, B.W. 73
Norman Lee Orchestra 40
Northwest Western Swing Music Society 141
Not Quite Bluegrass 169
Nydegger, Vern 48

O

Oak Ridge Boys 183, 204, 208
Oatman, Andy 103, 153, 155
Oatman, Jane 106
Oatman, Michael Clifton "Ol' Mike" 43, 99, 103-106, 144, 153, 179-180, 192-194, 207, 209
Oatman, Michelle 155
O'Connor, Mark 123, 147
Ocean Opry 113, 209
Oklahoma Sunshine 118, 198-199
Oklahoma Swingbillies 65
Old Cowtown Museum 169, 172, 185, 187
Old Mill Tasty Shop 163
Orange, Dick & the Western Wranglers 198
Oropresa, Russ 198
Orpheum Theater 13, 182-183
Osaka Okies 111
Osborn, Joe 122
Osborn, Donna 119
Osborn, Marvin & the Rhythm Gamblers 88, 96-97, 119, 156
Osborne Brothers 159, 167
Owens, Buck 119, 123, 129, 195
Oxford, Brad 147
Oxford, Vernon 89-90, 147
Ozark Jubilee 41, 84

P

Painted Post Rangers 60
Paladin 191

Palmer, Bruce 196
Palsmeier, Gary 163-164, 172
Palsmeier, Rick 151-152, 163-164
Parker, Billy & Western Swing Band 93-94
Parker, Wanda 93-94, 96
Parsons, Gene 153
Parsons, Gram 196
Parton, Dolly 129-130, 190
Pathfinder 184
Paula Records 69
Paxton, Larry 122
Pearl, Minnie 58, 129
Peavler, Curly 25
Peebles, Harry "Hap" 62-63, 129, 131, 192
Peer, Ralph 8
Peer International Corporation 24
Penetrators, The 136
Penny, Herbert Clayton "Hank" 59-60
Percy, Marvin Karlton (see also Rainwater, Marvin) 83
Perkins, Carl 62, 195
Perkins, Luther 192
Petty, Norman 66
Pickering, Jeff 123-124, 198
Pickford, Mary 81, 89, 104
Pierce, Webb 58, 129, 182
Pier-San Broadcasting Company 58, 61
Pierson, Jeannie 58
Piller, Lynn 154, 198, 201
Pioneer Quartet 203
Piper, Scott 153-155
Pirates Cave 97, 116
Pizza Hut 143
Plainsmen 60-62, 203
Plantation Boys 60
Pleasant Valley Playboys 115-116
Poco 196-197
Podnuh's 134
Pokorny, Bill 97
Pollard, DeWayne 58
Poncan Theater 139
Popeye & His Pals 39
Posey, Hiram 117-118
Potlatch 169
Povenmire, Richard 159
Powder River Band 89

Index

Powell, Bill 95, 117
Powell, Don 107-108, 112
Powell, Jerry 109, 117, 123
Powell, Jimmy 109
Prairie Dogs 172
Prairie Dust 198
Prairie Fire 200
Prairie Grass 162-163, 165-166, 168, 174, 197
Prairie Party 58
Prairie Rose Chuckwagon Supper 185-186
Prairie Rose Rangers 185, 188-189
Prairie Rose Wranglers 186-188
Prairie Wind 173
Presley, Elvis 61, 119, 124
Presnell, Darla 156-157
Presnell, Tracy 153, 155
Price, Ray & the Cherokee Cowboys 71, 89, 93, 129, 131, 140
Pride, Charley 124, 136, 140
Pritchard, Jeff 122, 147-148, 151
Pritchard, Mary 147
Pro Audio Systems 199
Pruitt, Kenny & the Oakies 95, 146
Pruitt, Rosa 95
Pryor, Jimmy 169, 172
Psalm Country 174-175
Pulling, Reece 201
Pure Prairie League 199

Q

Quillen, Dave 154

R

Rader, Billy 208
Rader, Brent 209
Rader, Danny 209
Rader, Dennis 113, 208
Rader Vacuum Cleaners 208
Rader, Wayne "Bud" 113, 208
Radio Aces 9
Radio Cowboys 59
Raincrow 201
Raines, Randy 123
Rainwater, Marvin (see Percy, Marvin Karlton) 41, 81, 83-86, 118, 211
Ramsey, Donny 150-152
Ranch House Swing Band 153-156, 201
Range Roundup 52
Range Rider & Dick West 190
Rangers 9
Rangers Quartet 206
Rapid Fire 156
Rapp, Barney 30
Ratzlaff, Jamey 197
Raven, Eddy 157
Ray & the Countrymen 93
Ray, Phil 150
Raye, Colin 209
Raymer, Don 150
Raymond, Tim 208
Raymor Records 35, 38
RCA Records 10, 90, 130, 138
Rector, Rusty 81
Reed, Dave 198
Reed, Vernon 30, 32
Reeves, Del 63, 144
Reeves, Jim 129
Renollet, Brad 134
Restless Heart 150
Revere, Paul & the Raiders 85, 133
Rhythm 'N Heart 156
Rhythm Rangers 181-182
Ribordy, Laurie 174-175
Rice, David 169
Rice, Sleepy 48-51
Richards, Beau 125-126
Richardson, Doyle 43-44
Richardson, J.P. "The Big Bopper" 66
Richardson, Joni 170
Rickenbacher, Adolph 14
Rickenbacker International 14
Rico, Tony & the Moonlighters 80, 148
Riddle, June 91
Riddle, Tommy 91
Riders in the Sky 180-181, 183
Rierson, Rusty 157
Rigby Gray Hotel Corporation 22
Riggs Park 164
Riggs, Paul 123, 200
Rimes, LeAnn 209
Ritter, Tex 3, 42, 62, 177, 190, 195

Ritz Ballroom 13
River City All-Stars 126, 150
Riverside Boys 113, 208, 209
Ro-Pat-In 14
Robbins, Hargus "Pig" 122
Robbins, Marty 89
Robertson, Kenny Mac 198
Rock Castle 87, 97
Rockabilly Hall of Fame 49
Rockin' Rebels 131
Rodeo, The 124
Rodgers, Jimmie 7-10
Rogers, Buddy 81, 89, 104
Rogers, Kenny & the First Edition 192
Rogers, Roy 75, 177, 190
Rogers, Roy Jr "Dusty" 177, 188
Rolfe, Sam 191
Rolling Stones 87, 195, 198
Ronstadt, Linda 199
Rotten Rodney's One Horse Saloon 201
Rowland, Doug & the Fireglows 147-148
Roy, Bill 167
Royal, Billy Joe 85
Rozell, Bernie 76-77
Russell, Ben 151
Russell, Jimmy 123-151

S

Saddleboogie Saloon 126, 151
Saddle Tramp 200
Salkill, Gary 208
Salt Creek 173
Sample, Bill 169
Sample, Judy 169
Sam's Place 119, 123
Sanders, Mack 57-63, 106, 117, 143, 153, 179, 203
Sanford, Tony 123
Sands Club 94, 97
Satterly, Alan "Whitey Trash" 181-182
Sawdust Charley 197
Sawyer Brown 150
Sawyer, Ray 98
Scheer, Gary 134
Schiff, Daryl 135, 136

Schiff, Jeanne 135
Schiff, Martina (see McBride, Martina) 135-136, 152
Schiff, Marty 136
Schiff, Steve 136
Schiffters 136-137
Schilling, Cliff 201
Schilling, Joy 201
Schmidt, Kim 151
Schmidt, Timothy B. 196
Schnipet, Jack 25
Schultz, Paul 125
Scott, Ted & the Western Drifters 88-89, 119-121
Screen Actors Guild 36
Seaman, Ted 208
Sears, Roebuck & Company 21
Sedan, Neal 42-43
Sedgwick County District Attorney 171
Seiwert, Mike "Si" 169
Selby, Bill 123, 151
Sessions, Ronnie 122
Shadowland Dance Club 13-16
Shamrock Club, Washington D.C. 84
Sheeder, Rita 198
Shepard, Jean 62-63
Shepherd, Bob 124
Shepler's 181
Shook, Jerry 117
Shores, Ray 71
Show Biz 120
Sho-Bud Guitars 145
Shumate, Bill 198
Shunatona, Bat 197
Simmons, Jay 61
Simmons, Leon "Lee" 61
Singing Ledbetters 207
Singing Quakers 175
Sisco, Ted 9
Sisk, Jerry 79, 81, 121-122
Skaggs, Ricky & Kentucky Thunder 123, 134, 170-171
Slack, Freddie 72
Slate Creek 150
Slaughter, Eldora 9
Slaughter, John 9

Index

Sledge, Loyd 89, 118
Sledge, Millie 89
Slim Chance 149
Smith, Bob 76
Smith, Bobby 39
Smith, Carl 63, 85, 117
Smith, Don 205
Smith, Greg 163
Smith, Guy 63
Smith, Jan 98
Smith, Jerry 56, 117
Smokehouse Trio 31
Snow, Hank 77
So's Your Mother 162
Sonnier, Jo-el 147
Sons of Rayon 169
Sons of the Pioneers 27, 30, 56, 177-178, 180, 183, 190, 192
South City Shopping Center 208
South Forty Dance Hall 126, 149
South Riverside Baptist 208
South Sea Island Studios 75
Southern Exposure 156-157
Southernaires 66
Southern Charm 139
Southern Club 66
Southland Playboys 87
Southland Quartet 206
Southwestern College 160
Southwind 170
Sovine, Red 129
Spark-O-Life Feed Company 48
Spark-O-Life Gang 48, 53-55
Spear, Johnny 31
Special Consensus 173
Speer, John "Boy" 137, 154, 183, 197
Speir, H.C. 10
Spicher, Buddy 122
Spoonhour, Dan 94-95
Sportsman Club 101
Sproules, Tommy 44
Stamps, Frank 206
Stamps Quartet 60, 203, 206
Stancer, Kim 138
Stanford, Everette "Hank" 49-50
Stanley Brothers 159, 161
Stanley, Charles A. 21
Star, Randy 55-56
Starberry 140
Starday Records 41, 117
Stardust 72, 95
Starr, Kenny & the Country Showmen 130-131
Starr, Ringo 195
Starrett, Charles 75
Statesmen 61, 203
Stearman, Lloyd 3, 16
Steel Diamond 156
Stephens, Coleman 160
Steppenwolf 199-200
Stevens, Brad 153
Stevens, Doug 143
Stevens, Greg 100, 105, 108-109, 122
Stewart, Dude 139, 169
Stewart, Wynn & West Coast Playboys 107, 122, 195
Stills, Stephen 196
Stonemans 43
Strait, George 123, 130
Strawboss 152
Stuart, Marty 124, 152-153, 165, 195
Stuart, Stu 184-188
Sturdivant, Jo 192
Suggs, Tommie 58
Sullivan, Dwight 94-95
Sumner, J.D. 203
Sundance 197
Swallow Airplane Manufacturing Company 16
Sweet Basil 169
Sweetheart of the Rodeo 161, 196
Sweetwater Band 199-200
Swingland 97, 101

T

T-Bone Steakhouse 112
Tabuchi, Shoji 87, 107, 111-114
Tales of Wells Fargo, The 191
Tall Grass 173
Taylor, Archie 32
Taylor, Carmol 147

Taylor, Chris 161
Ted Combs Radio & TV 196
Tennessee Gin Mill 198-199
Terry, Dwain (Western Swing, Western Continentals) 88-101, 120
Terry, Gordon 192
Texas Airforce 201
Texas Quality Network 49
Texas Rangers 206
The Cowboy 152
Thelma's No. 1 88
Theobald, Jack & the Bluegrass Country Boys 159-161, 164, 166, 175
Theobald, Mike 159-161, 164, 166, 170, 174-176
Theobald, Vickie 174-176
Thompson, Hank & the Brazos Valley Boys 67, 77, 99-100, 122, 124, 140-141, 148
Tiki Club 97
Tillis, Mel 61, 93, 189-190, 192
Tipton, Webb 79-80
Tivara, Helen 48
Tivara, Margaret 48
TNN (The Nashville Network) 123, 167
Tobacco Jones 198
Todd, John 167
Traveling Strings 120
Travis, Merle 100
Travis, Paula 199-200
Travolta, John 149
Trebbe, Kenneth (see Starr, Kenny) 130
Treefrog 154
Trig Ballroom 43
Trinkle, Wes 109
True Blue 173
True Value/GMC Truck Country Showdown 150, 152
Tubb, Ernest 50, 78, 81, 88
Tubb, Justin 84
Turner, Chuck 198
Turner, Zack 87
Twitty, Conway 43, 116-117, 131
Tyler, T. Texas 50

U

Uhilk, Phil 108-109
Uhlik Music 108-109
Under the Gun 156
Uptown Bluegrass 164
Urban Cowboy 126, 149
Urban, Keith 209

V

Vale, Jerry 191
Valens, Ritchie 66
Van, Gary & his Western Starlighters 62
VanDyke, Leroy 41, 62, 72-73
Vantage Records 89
Varnum, Ralph 54
Vetter, Jim 76
Vickers, William (see Catalino, Vic) 70
Victory Trio 27-29, 31, 35
Victory, Bud 27-29, 32, 35, 37, 39
Victory, Oby 27-29, 32, 35, 37, 39
Victory, Ray "Tex" 27-29
Victory, Rex 23-30, 32, 34-37, 39
Vincent, Guy 92-93
Vocalion Records 49

W

WAAP 21-22, 47
Waggoner, Larry 143-144, 146
Wagon Wheel Club 93, 97-98, 101, 118, 123, 134, 198
Wagoner, Porter 41, 129-130, 190
Walker, Billy 41, 63, 112
Walker, Clint 76
Walker, Jerry Jeff 177, 182, 197
Wall, Gary 123
Waller, Fats 72
Walnut Valley Festival 148, 166, 173, 176
Walnut Valley Folk Festival 160
Walsh, Joe aka. Joseph Fidler 196
Walton, Don "Little Donnie Do Dad" 106-108
WAPI 59
Ward, Ron 208
Watermark Books 172

Watson, Doc 165
Watson, Gene 147
Wayne, Cheryl 152
Wayne, John 61
WBAP 7
WCOW 189
WCRW 22
WEAH 21-22
Weatherwax, Lester 203
Webb, Doug 197
Webb, Jimmy 103
Welborn, Howard 61
Welch, Gillian 159
Welch, Troy 120
Weller, Freddy 133
Wells, Deacon 42-43
Wells, Kitty 124
Werts, Kelly 169, 173
West, Dottie 63
West, Mike 198
West, Shelley 124
Westerfield, Nadine 48, 52
Western, Johnny 124, 180, 187, 189-194, 211
Western Sunsets 87
Western Swinger 72, 95, 107, 111-112, 123, 125-126
Western Swinger Band 107, 112
Westgate Fun Center & Dance Palace 150
WEY 21-22
Whales Tale 73
Wheeling Jamboree 84
Whiskey River Band 151-152, 157
White, Clarence 152-153
White, Ken 173
Whitesell, Vern 171
Whitewater Creek 185
Whitley, Keith 130
WHO 144
WIBW 206
Wichita (the band) 152
Wichita Country Club 40
Wichita Eagle 23, 172
Wichita Jazz Festival 40
Wichita Linemen 100, 105, 108-109, 111, 117, 122, 134, 137, 145, 148, 153
Wichita River Festival 136, 172, 183

Wichita-Sedgwick County Historical Museum 2, 12, 14-18, 57-58, 182
Wichita State University 78, 103, 160, 162, 196
Wichita Symphony 182
Wichita West High School 115
Widdup, Harold 99-100
Widiger, Desiree 174-175
Wilcox, Darren 173
Wiley, Bobby & the Rhythmaires 27, 75-77, 81
Wiley, Grace 75
Wiley, Milo 75, 79
Williams, Darlene 25, 28
Williams, Doyle 49
Williams, Hank 58, 77, 113, 115
Williams, Leona 133
Williams, Tex 67
Williams, Zeke & his Rambling Cowboys 48-50
Willing, Foy & the Riders of the Purple Sage 56-57
Willis Brothers 129
Wills, Bob & the Texas Playboys 7, 40, 59, 65-67, 69-70, 93, 178
Wills, Chill 37
Wills, Johnnie Lee & His Boys 66, 93
Wilson, Gretchen 209
Wilson, Mr. & Mrs. Don 185
Wimberley, Bill 40-41
Wind River 173
Windsor, Dave 125
Winger, Debra 149
Wintergarden Club 13
Wise, Tommy 98
Wiseman, Mac 63
WLS National Barn Dance 36
WLW 59
WMMN's Sagebrush Roundup 50
WNVA 56
Wolfe, Marion 185
Wolfe, Russ 185
Wooden, Steve 48, 50, 53, 58
World's Largest Prairie Dog 163, 168-169, 172, 197
Worrel, Joe 156-157

Wright, Keith 120
WSB 59
WWL 59
WWVA 84
Wycoff, Joe & the Melody Playboys 87, 95, 99
Wynette, Tammy 115

X

XERF 204

Y

Yellow Submarine 163
Yesterday's Playboys 99-100
Yockey, Chuck 101
You Can Be a Star 123
Young, Billy Joe & his Confidentials 69
Young, Faron 63, 85, 112, 182
Young, Jesse 120
Young, Neil 196
Young, Red 107
Young, Rusty 196
Yount, Jay 160